Brown Sugar
and a Bone in the Throat
JEAN'S LIFE

By D. Jean Mathie Scott
with Elsie K Neufeld

Cover photo montage descriptions:

1) *Relaxing in Rocanville.*
2) *Another day, another smile, 1995.*
3) *Family photo, 1929.*
4) *Six years old in Brandon.*
5) *Portrait taken in 1990.*
6) *Showing off in front of the Edna's house, McAuley.*
7) *Secretarial work, Vancouver Labour Council, 1946.*
8) *In Chicago, promoting the Memorial Society, 1966.*

Publisher is: Scott, D. Jean
Publisher prefix is: ISBN 0-9739406-
ISBN 0-9739406-0-3

Book design: Daryl Rose • RoseCreative.com
Printed by: Abbotsford Printing Ltd.
Editor/ghostwriter: Elsie K Neufeld (eskn@uniserve.com)

The author gratefully acknowledges the financial assistance of
the University College of the Fraser Valley in producing this book.

"I came to explore the wreck.
The words are purposes
The words are maps
I came to see the damage that was done
And the treasures that prevail."

-Adrienne Rich

THANKS GO TO:

Elsie K. Neufeld, without whom this book wouldn't be. Your intelligent insight into what I was trying to say brought this book to life.

Spencer, his wife Sonia, my grandchildren Greg and Melanie, and my sister Pat, for their encouragement and intense interest. Without your ongoing support, this book couldn't have been possible. Thank you very much.

Daryl Rose, your superb artistry resulted in a cover that so beautifully reflects my life-story; and for your assistance in formatting the text and photos.

Anne Russell, for your assistance with formatting the book, and for your friendship. You are a treasure!

Pat Carfra, niece, dear friend and soul-mate, and your huggable husband Jim.

Phil and Sharon Blaker, for 'taking care' of me. You two are precious.

Art Anderson, for your ongoing interest in my life story & wise counsel: "Don't try to write the whole story at once; write one chapter at a time." I am honoured by your endorsement.

Mary Woo Sims. Your fine work for human rights is an inspiration; and I am so proud to know you. I am humbled that someone of your esteemed background would endorse this book.

Dr. H.A. Bassford. Your friendliness and genuine warmth towards me is so appreciated. I am humbled by your words and grateful for your endorsement.

Marjorie Scott, my sister-in-law, for asking, no less than weekly, "What's doing with the book?" Your interest helped keep me going.

My sister-in-law Mary Stewart, for your kindness and interest in my life.

My caring nieces, Mary Fraser and Susan Mathie Wilbert; you are so good to me.

Michael Hare, the minister, and the congregation of Carman United Church. Your support means more than words can say.

Pat DeCorby & Cookie, for your ongoing support, interest and friendship, and your permission to use Edna's letters. Pat, I followed your advice, to "do something with them!"

The many women's groups that I have served with zeal and ardour; I am grateful for the education I received from you. You are significant to my story.

UCFV, for your financial assistance – especially Brad Whittaker, for your efforts in arranging funding; and Yvon Dandurand, for reading the manuscript. Your generosity is overwhelming.

TABLE OF CONTENTS

FOREWORD

How do you compress 93 years into one book? It isn't possible, of course, though, hopefully, this book provides enough glimpses into the life of Jean Scott for readers to envisage its vastness and complexity. It has been my great privilege to work with Jean to achieve just that; and what a ride it's been!

Jean and I first met some years ago at a fund-raiser for the Ann Davis Transition House in Chilliwack, BC. Her enthusiasm as MC was impressive and I was further impressed when she sat down at the piano and belted, yes, belted out the song, "Bread & Roses", her clear soprano voice soaring above the other two hundred or so. The topic was "life-stories" and the value and necessity of everyone telling hers. Jean was swept up in what I had to say and immediately offered to organize a subsequent gathering for me to speak at; that meeting took place at the public library, with some fifty people in attendance. Jean surfaced again, a year later, at Chilliwack Elder College where I taught "Women & Writing". Her enthusiasm had waned, visibly so; she explained that she was exhausted from caring for her very ill husband. And then our paths didn't cross again for several years, though I heard, through a mutual acquaintance, that her husband had died, that she had breast cancer, and finally, that she had moved to Langley, British Columbia.

In February 2005, Jean Scott left a message on my answering machine, saying that she had moved back to Chilliwack, had decided to complete her memoirs and "might you help me with that?" We met in her home for further discussion, and the rest, you could say, is history; but it's so much more: the outcome of that discussion is this book.

Jean had already written extensively about her earlier life, and wanted to continue being the primary writer – with my guidance. She was eager to get at it, and after several more meetings, and much consideration, I proposed a "map" and our journey began. While Jean wrote new stories, I pored through her files, piecing together stories she'd written over the years, by hand, on two typewriters, (one manual, another electric), and on two computers. She also provided letters, (copies and originals), newspaper clippings, a book on her hometown and photos. I cut, pasted, transcribed, edited and backfilled with information gleaned from our weekly meetings; and encouraged Jean to keep writing. Which she did, excitedly so; each week she conveyed another handful of printed stories.

Within weeks, I was immersed in the life that is Jean's, and soon felt like I knew Jean's family and friends almost as if they were my own; at one meeting I jokingly wondered aloud who I was, where my life ended and hers began – I had plunged that deeply into the details of her life! The work was exciting, enlivening, exhausting and occasionally, for both of us, verged on overwhelming.

Jean's life bears witness to the tenacity of the human spirit, that part of each of us which, when challenged, either rises to the occasion or recoils and collapses. Jean has faced, survived and learned from the obstacles she encountered in life, be they poverty, heartache, single parenthood, unemployment, underemployment, discrimination, divorce, cancer, sexual harassment, the physical ravages of middle and old age, losses galore; and joys! Time and again, she picked up the pieces, broke into song and moved on. Jean is tough, but not at the expense of tenderness. She is passionate and compassionate; she is stubborn and open-minded, an eager life-long learner. She is smart, curious and multi-talented; and few fight as fervently for justice as she continues to do at 93; and, I suspect, will do not only to her last breath, but in her last breath.

So, read on; and enjoy the ride! I have no doubt that you, the reader, will be as astonished and inspired by Jean's life-story as I was and that, like a song, it will catch in your throat and sing you into a new awareness, breathless, but hopeful; for though life is a carousel – going up, going down, around and around – Life is good!

Elsie K Neufeld
October, 2005

Brown Sugar
and a Bone in the Throat
JEAN'S LIFE

By D. Jean Mathie Scott

with Elsie K Neufeld

CHAPTER ONE
Before My Time

Brandon, Manitoba was the destination for many British immigrants in the early 1800's and with the steady influx, the small settlement quickly grew into a flourishing town.

In the year 1881, two young couples made the momentous decision to cross the Atlantic and start anew in Canada: William and Jeannette Isabella Mathie, of Paisley, Scotland; and Arthur Charles and Annie Alice Spencer Wells of England.

In Canada, William Mathie, a carriage painter, had to take whatever work was available; the still "raw" settlement of Brandon, where the couple began their new life, did not use carriages. With usual Scottish brawn and solid business ken, he did reasonably well. Here, the couple was to produce a fine family of three daughters and four sons. The birth of the youngest son is pertinent to my own story.

An early fall morning in 1882. Jeannette Isabella Mathie is resting. Another boy. He is a lovely baby, with clean features and finer bone structure than his siblings. His father, William Mathie, takes the day off to be of help to the midwife and

Brandon, Manitoba, 1886.

3

daughter Gladys. The older sons are busy with chores on the family farm. Jeannette and William choose the baby's name: Gordon Alexander. Both names are richly Scottish, have a good feeling on the tongue; and both have a ring that spells fine, male boyhood.

Gordon came into that family loved and admired for his good looks and genuinely pleasant personality. Gordon Alexander Mathie was my father.

The second couple, Arthur Charles and Annie Alice Spencer Wells, had a rough time after leaving their London home. They crossed the Atlantic on the last sailing, yes, sailing vessel (thereafter ships were powered by steam), a terrible ordeal, especially for the pregnant Annie Alice. High seas forced the ship into an iceberg just off the coast of Newfoundland. An inebriated captain tried to ram the ship through and the trauma of the near shipwreck haunted Annie Alice all her life, especially in her dying hours. Worse, she gave birth to a stillborn infant whom they buried at sea. They named the baby Florence Henrietta.

Having lost all their possessions, the couple wrote to relatives in England and asked for help. "You've made your bed. Now lie in it," was the response. Although not known for certain, it seems that the couple had married against the wishes of parents and that they were cousins. They had taken a bold decision in coming to Canada; and now Arthur, or "The Major" as he was referred to since his Army days, wanted to try "the west".

The brave young couple headed westward, to a small settlement on the outskirts of Brandon. It was here that they had another daughter, whom they named Rosalie Annie Spencer-Wells. This child survived and became my mother.

It was the Major who chose the name Rosalie; already he had a fondness for this land, especially the profuse, fragrant prairie rose. Indeed, he was a lover of flowers and all plants, often bringing potted plants into the house, setting them in pans of water, not caring how it looked. "Capillary moisture they need, my dear," he would say, and then, to the annoyance of his wife, fill another tub right in the middle of the dining room.

Rosalie's second name, Annie, was after her Mother. Too young to retain memories of living on a friend's farm outside of Brandon, in what was then called Roseland, Rosalie did recall being transported alongside her mother on an ox cart into the then tiny shack-and-tent town that was Brandon.

In Brandon, the Wells family occupied the upper floor of a commercial building. Here, a life-long friendship developed between Grandma and her neighbour Mrs. Curtis, then also between their daughters: Rosalie and Irene.

Rosalie was a sensitive child. She recalled watching Mr.

Annie Alice Spencer Wells.

Curtis, a carpenter, at work in his shop. "I was about four," she related, "and I stood at the window one storey above where he worked…and I'll never forget the sadness and awe I sensed as I watched him hammering and sawing, building a little coffin for a young girl…."

When times improved, both families moved to houses situated near the old Brandon gaol. Irene Curtis and young Rosalie played together on the graves of the people who had been hanged in that very spot. Irene said, "We never realised that we were dancing on their graves; we had such a good time and nobody told us not to play there."

Rosalie was shy and found it a bit hard to be sent to school, but she was a good student according to her own opinion, and enjoyed learning – except when the teacher read "Black Beauty" and Rosalie covered her ears, put her head on her desk and sobbed.

Why Rosalie and her only sibling Percy didn't get more schooling, especially considering their parents' excellent

Rosalie and Percy Spencer Wells, 1900.

education in England, remains in question. Rosalie completed Grade IV and it's possible that Percy did the same. He had a miserable experience when the teacher suggested he needed eyeglasses; and Rosalie felt sad for him when their father disagreed, insisting, "There's nothing wrong with his eyes." Brother and sister were fond of each other, a feeling that was evident throughout their lives, whether family relations were strained or not. Percy always referred to himself humorously as "your little brother".

When Rosalie was in her early teens, her Mother had another son, Roy, who died in infancy from nephritis. Rosalie nursed him throughout his brief life and in 1966, during a trip to Brandon, she (Mother) showed me the house where they lived at that time, her sadness at Roy's brief life still evident.

Rosalie loved her father and all her life referred to his special qualities. She quoted him time and again: "If a thing's worth doing, it's worth doing well." Once, when Mother and Grandma had discussed someone in a critical tone, Grandpa overheard them and said, angrily, "If you can't say anything nice, don't say anything at all!" Mother never forgot that and often repeated it to me.

Rosalie and her mother were deeply fond of each other, too. Times were hard for them in their earlier years in Brandon and perhaps they grew together through the difficulties they faced. One afternoon, when they saw someone coming toward their house, and there was no tea in the cupboard, nor much of anything to serve, Rosalie's mother, (Grandma) said, "Let's just pretend there's no one home."

ROSALIE THE SEAMSTRESS

When Rosalie was about 15 she was hired by Nation & Shewan's, a flourishing store in downtown Brandon. Perhaps her mother's talent as a seamstress, as well as the better pay of a profession as dressmaker, took my then young mother from clerk to the upstairs where she learned that painstaking and demanding craft where "every dress was lined and boned." What an ordeal! But all her life, Mother loved fabric for its texture, weave, and colour; and nowadays she would have been a designer of note.

Mother related with humour how, one day, at the height of noon-hour traffic, her voluminous skirt and one of her several petticoats then worn by every woman (hers was scarlet!) caught in the spokes of her bicycle wheel. Since it could be disentangled only by dismounting and walking slowly backwards, she did so, in full view of the public. Customs being very different then, that was highly embarrassing.

Another incident that reveals her life-long modest attitude took place on a streetcar one day after work. Rosalie sat alone, near a respectable banker and his colleague when she noticed the banker nudge his friend and then point at a female passenger. "Damn fine ankles," he said. Rosalie was mortified. Not only at the woman who had allowed her dress to shift upwards, but at the banker for using such language!

ROSALIE AND GORDON

The Major, his wife Annie and their daughter Rosalie, who'd been taught by nuns at the local convent, all played the piano skilfully. Rosalie's father also played the tubular flageolet and sang a good tenor, as did her brother Percy; but it was the piano at the Mathie residence that got the most practice.

Of the Mathie brothers, Gordon, my father, had the best voice: strong, with a good range, and excellent pitch. Of the Mathie sisters, it was Marie, the youngest, who always sang with angelic sweetness in a splendid soprano. Mother referred to the Mathie gatherings as if those were the very best kind of social events, with everyone around the piano singing lustily.

It was most likely that Gordon and Rosalie's courtship began after one such evening, when Gordon escorted Rosalie along the several blocks between their homes. Their relationship grew and deepened, though some people, according to Aunt Belle, Father's sister, were more than a little surprised when Gordon and Rosalie became engaged. Not that they didn't approve; it was just that Gordon was considered "quite a catch" and Rosalie was just a bit quieter than the kind of girl he'd been observed giving the odd wink. "Your mother wasn't, perhaps, classed as the prettiest girl," Aunt Belle told me, "but she always had a certain animation that gave her looks something special." If Rosalie Annie Spencer Wells wasn't a smashing beauty, she managed to snare the best looking Mathie son, even brothers Frank, Will and Lew said so.

With only family members and a few close friends present, Gordon and Rosalie were married in St. Matthews pro-cathedral on June 19, 1907. Mother's wedding attire was modest: a brown, tailored suit with matching accessories. With her colouring, her lovely eyes (she'd inherited her Father's "snapping brown eyes"), dark brown hair, her demure and naturally dignified manner, she must have been truly a charming bride. Gordon was quite ill for a few days just prior to the ceremony, but he recovered in time.

But back to the joining of these two good families. With relatives of means and esteemed reputations, Gordon chose to take Rosalie on a honeymoon to Hartney, Manitoba, to meet Walpole Murdoch, Gordon's maternal uncle, who, according to his peers, was the best editor and publisher "in the western region". It couldn't have been easy for Rosalie, but if she found the visit not to her liking she didn't protest; it didn't even occur to her that she should question her new husband. In later years, when one of her daughters asked, "why didn't you give Dad your opinion when you felt it was better than what he was planning?" Mother replied, "I did once." "And what was the result?" "He sulked, and I didn't offer my opinion again."

Gordon the Grocer

Gordon Alexander Mathie had left school in Grade V and then started work as a delivery boy for Symington's Grocery, the city's best and biggest grocery store. Within a year he was promoted to clerk and six years later he was operating a rented store in Brandon's downtown, somewhere near Tenth Street and Rosser Avenue. Gordon had charm and made friends easily; he was a delightful seller of goods, but cared little for the mundane duties of bookkeeping – and, unfortunately, never would. When business was good, the books took care of themselves, for there was profit enough to keep his store well stocked, with money left over for household and family needs.

By the time Gordon Alexander Mathie's first child was born (Irene, born on May 4, 1908), his life was a success from any point of view. True, he and Rosalie still occupied a rather third-class home, but the neat little grocery store provided a good living.

Several years later, a thriving grocery business came up for sale at 251-3rd Street, a fine location for the years 1910-1920, since no other grocery was within many blocks in the

Rosser Avenue, Brandon, where Dad's work as clerk began.

city. Its purchase price was manageable, there was living space at the back of the store for the now three member family, and it occupied a part of the city populated by middle income families – among tree-lined streets and near the corner of Lorne Avenue with its elegant St. Augustine's Cathedral. With Rose, as Gordon liked to call his wife, having clerical experience, and Grandma Spencer Wells living nearby to help out, it was truly a family-run enterprise.

The structure, with the store and little store-room occupying the front section, had plenty of room; the attached living quarters included a fair-sized living room and dining room, a kitchen, a back porch and stoop, and one bedroom at the rear of the store-room with one north-facing window.

It was in the light from that window that I entered this world.

CHAPTER TWO

Brandon: From Birth to Eight Years Old

"Jean, Jean, ma bonny, bonny Jean, Come to my arms once again, Although your feet are flat, still you're none the wore o' that; You're my bonny, blue-eyed Scotch lassie Jean."

It was just a little Scottish ditty with an up-beat rhythm – a happy song that, consciously or sub-consciously, assured me of love and support. I don't remember Dad singing it, but Mother often sang it, as though it pleased her to do so; and I know it pleased me. I truly believe that Mother wanted to convey that while we shared our lives. That was evident often, and would certainly have been a constant but for the series of unexpected, unwanted happenings that afflicted the family of Gordon and Rosalie Mathie, those two young people who met in the most pleasant of circumstances, with no reason to doubt that their falling in love, marrying and having babies would ever be otherwise.

I was their second child and I am sure I was welcome.

Just two weeks earlier, the great Titanic had gone down after it struck an iceberg off the coast of Newfoundland. News in that year travelled by telegraph and into the newspapers. It was a shock of horrendous proportion and

A panoramic view of Brandon around 1912, the year I was born.

13

friends of the family were asked not to tell my mother for fear she would suffer premature labour; but my mother and I had already bonded. Almost mystically we both knew that there would be many awesome and shocking events in the future – events where she and I would know a miscellany of experiences: with music and humour softening the mirthlessness and cruelty of illness, poverty and deep disappointments.

It was a lovely Sunday morning when my sister Irene stood at the sidewalk announcing, "I have a new baby sister" to parishioners on their way to St. Augustine's pro-cathedral. Everyone adored Irene, and because of her naturally beautiful looks and personality, nicknamed her "Dolly". Not quite four, she already showed an aptitude for musical talent.

Two strong women gave me a powerful start in life: Rosalie Annie Spencer Wells Mathie and Nurse Jane Hall, the woman who assisted the doctor in my birth. A good friend of Grandma Spencer Wells, Nurse Hall was an English midwife, a woman of strong character, outstanding generosity and compassion (a fine portent for the baby; and I have often felt angels were present too, and passed on to me her qualities).

Ad promoting life in Brandon, Cosmoplitan Magazine, 1912

From then on Jane Hall was a cherished member of our family, fondly referred to as "Nursie". And I was given the name "Jean", the Scottish version of Jane – Dorothy Jean Mathie.

Born April 21, a full-term baby, my conception must have been July 11th, and once, when Pat, my younger sister, asked where I got my energy, I jokingly said, "But didn't you know, Pat, I was conceived in a moment of sheer ecstasy!?" (Pat's reply? "Oh dear, they must've been asleep when I was." And Mother was horrified.)

It would be difficult for anyone to be born in a better place; I really do believe when and where I was born couldn't have been happier. In the year 1912 my father's grocery store on 3rd Street in Brandon was a place of wonders, happy customers and mouth-watering tastes.

The store was in the front of the modest structure. The entrance was up a couple of steps, flanked by two big windows that displayed bananas and other sale items. The shelves on two side walls held interestingly packaged staples: Keen's Mustard, Royal Baking Powder, Old Dutch Cleanser, wonderful tins of jam, jars of honey and pickles; and more. Two counters ran along each side of the store, spaced away from the shelves with just enough room for the clerk serving customers to step and reach for items. At one time, my Uncle Lew had worked in the store and Mother, with her past experience of work as a clerk, was a dandy helper, too.

A third, shorter, counter stood opposite the entrance; here, the big round of cheese took a full yard (three feet) of space, while, just above, was the 8-inch thick ball of string. A little to the left of the cheese sat a splendid and decorative cash register. Most customers paid cash for their orders. Most customers were women, and most of those women were housekeepers who walked from somewhere within the square mile area which the store served.

My father created a jovial atmosphere inside that store;

there seemed no difference to me between serving customers who came to replenish their pantries and having friends drop by. "Hello, Mrs. Massin; how are you today? And how's the family?" Dad called enthusiastically. Two stools allowed the shopper to sit and chat while her order was filled, packaged and wrapped. Dad's easy way of keeping conversation going, together with his delight in telling a joke, made shopping an experience to look forward to.

How my Dad loved a joke! Sure they were too corny for today's customer; but back then no one referred to anything as cool. "Mrs. Massin," he said when she entered the store one day, "did you hear about the accident down the street at the bakery?"

"Oh no, Mr. Mathie. What happened?"

"The girl serving raisin cookies was electrocuted, they say."

Mrs. Massin emitted a little scream. "How terrible! How did it happen?"

"She stepped on a cookie and the currant ran up her leg!"

Mrs. Massin burst into laughter and Dad joined in the fun, slapping his thighs and rubbing his palms together with glee.

That was the template which set the pattern for me then and for the rest of my life. There, in those beginnings, I learned how to greet people in good cheer, whether with words or a song.

There can be little doubt that I took my first steps waddling from our household through the store-room and into the store, where Dad's long white apron provided surer footage. Or, reaching up, I could grasp his black sateen armlets that mother had made to keep his shirt cuffs from fraying, and that saved her, as well as the woman who helped out, a bit of the rubbing on the overworked washboard.

Dad's dress was his daily habit, as carefully put together as any military or priestly garb. Standard dress for Dad meant dark trousers and a white shirt buttoned up to the chin where it met his celluloid white collar, a collar wiped clean each morning before it was hooked onto the button at the back of his shirt. I used to watch him as he tugged the long white apron over his head, wrapped it around his torso, tied the long strings at the back, then wound them around his mid-section once, brought them back to the front again and there, with his remarkably deft hands, tied them into a "storekeepers knot". The armlets – that part of his 'uniform' he slipped on last – covered his shirt sleeves from wrist to below the elbow and added a dramatic, finished look. On his feet, Dad always wore well-polished, black kid boots that, according to male customers I overheard, were an astonishing size seven. To the end, Dad's apparel gave him a sense of order and professionalism; and he was never, ever, anything else but a 'grocer'; and, to the last, he would say that with pride.

The store and our household were joined, so a walk through the storeroom to the store was an almost magical passage. Inside that little store-room stood 3-foot square boxes of teak, lined with lead foil that Mother saved and cut into strips for curling our hair. The spicy aromas of East Indian teas inside the boxes caused you to pause and sniff until your nose tickled so bad you sneezed. Some teas, like Red Rose or Blue Ribbon, were packaged, but there was no

Mathies Grocery and living quarters at 251 - 3rd Street,
where I was born. Photo taken in the 1970s.

such thing as a tea bag – an abomination to true tea drinkers who referred to them as "really nothing more than old cigarette butts!" Nearby, gunnysacks bulged with rice, other cereals and granulated sugar. Oh, for a solo walk through the store-room so I could stop by the wooden barrel of brown sugar which was so tall I had to stand on my tip-toes to dip my right hand inside and grab a fistful, much of it lost as I withdrew my hand, scrunched the remaining sweet stuff into a ball before stuffing it into my mouth. Brown sugar in the throat – it went down so easily.

Everything came in bulk, to be measured, weighed and packaged later into brown paper bags; and priced, from the smallest, five cents worth, to the largest – something like ten pounds of sugar, in brown craft paper. Waxed paper was used for sliced meats and cheese. I loved to watch Dad slice cooked ham, the fearsome blade going round and round while he rhythmically turned the handle with an obvious air of knowing what he was doing, the cut ham dropping into his left hand....

I loved the pungency of it all! And how that work and living arrangement provided my life with a deep sense of serenity and security; and of friendliness and wholesomeness, too, for in every hour, from waking till bed-time, day in and day out, safety was a certainty, with both parents close.

It was there, in Mathie's Grocery, that I quite innocently began my first job. I remember the first time Dad inducted me into the weighing of sugar, how proudly and carefully I measured it on the beautiful brass trimmed scales, tapping the brown paper bag to settle the contents – just like Dad showed me. He demonstrated how to pry open the crates of fruit and how to use the banana knife. Bananas came on their own thick stem; and the curved blade was stuck back into the stem as soon as the order was filled.

I watched in awe as Dad packaged and wrapped orders, his fine-boned hands taking the string in his right fingers,

Age two on mother's knee with Rene hiding her face.

Mother, Grandmother, Irene "Rene" and me at two years of age.

Sunday afternoon family photo. Back row: Grandma, Nurse Jane Hall "Nursie", Father. Middle Row: Uncle Percy with me on his knee, Mother beside, and Rene in front.

smoothly twirling it around a parcel and then, with a quick, difficult-to-follow twisting of fingers, the string was knotted and SNAP! Try as I might, I never was able to break the string like that, but today, when I send a gift, I wrap it just as my father did. Another, forever vivid, picture remains: there's Dad, my dad, on the sidewalk outside the store, at the corner of the building, winding the awning up, or letting it down. He did it, each time, even after hundreds of times, with an air of proprietorship, as a near sacred rite, to either commence the service for the day, keep the store cool from the sun, or just because he was closing up. In those moments, he was master of all he surveyed.

I was thrilled when I was able to help in the store – learning necessary disciplines that have lasted what I can now refer to as 'a lifetime'.

OUR HOME IN BRANDON

From the walk through store and storeroom, you entered the room that housed the piano, gramophone and the oak card table with its green baize cover and fine brass tacks. That table was an expensive item: the top could be folded, leaving a half-table surface, the two halves were hinged with nickel hardware, some of which, after several moves, were lost and, like every thing that wore or came apart, never mended.

I have the best memories of that room. Across from the door to the outside sat Mother's piano and next to it, the gramophone, occasionally playing the sweet tune, "Nights of Gladness". Sometimes the rhythm of that tune moved Dad and Mother to do a little waltz, creating a mood, at least in me, of wonder and awe. Their smiling faces while they performed this lovely impromptu dance bring pain and pleasure as I recall; pain because of the tough years later, when there was no gramophone, nor any mood to dance; and pleasure because of the moment's sweetness. I wonder; did that memory stand my parents in good stead in their final years?

On the east wall of our dining area, a large picture of the Duchess of Devonshire hung above the oak dining room table. The matching buffet was elegant, with a long oval mirror above cutlery drawers lined with purple velvet. Below the drawers, two compartments held Mother's wedding Limoges china and across the length of the buffet was a long drawer filled with linens – exquisite pieces of fancy work, some done by Grandma Wells; the small doilies kept inside the never-seen-since long cretonne roll lined with tissue paper and tied with a blue ribbon. Another item I'll never forget is the two-seater oak and leather settee. Coming home from school, I scurried along the wooden sidewalk, hoping to not trip (Mother said she couldn't remember a time when my knees weren't scabbed from falling), then entered the house and, out of breath, I perched myself on the firm arm of the settee, almost wetting myself as I waited. And waited – to use the flush toilet. Mother recalled that, too.

The kitchen was next; it contained a smaller table and a small cook stove. And off the kitchen, were two bedrooms. Until I was five, my sister Irene and I had two single beds in the smaller bedroom, while Mother and Dad had the first bedroom – roomy enough for their brass and white enamel double bed and a bureau that would be sold when we experienced real poverty. The dresser's wide mirror was held by two gently carved standards and, gracing its top, were a few of Mother's pretty things: a genuine Wedgwood hair receiver that made an unpleasant scratching sound whenever Mother removed the heart-shaped top; a brush and comb boudoir set, the mirror's frame and handles made of deer's horn; a tray for buttonhooks; and the green glass jewel case – an unusual piece, with a white bead design and pretty gold footings. Just off my parents' bedroom was a small room for the toilet and wash basin; there was no bath.

A lean-to shed was off the kitchen and its door gave way to a small platform. A clothesline hung in the yard, useful to

Rene and me when we produced impromptu shows of music, speech and vivid drama, and needed to hang sheets to separate audience and performers.

Dad always had a few exotic birds in one corner next to the lane, and on the opposite corner, in the small garage, there reposed, for a time, a splendid vehicle, a blue Reo with lots of nickel trim. Mother's one and only attempt to drive was exciting. We were at the Fair Grounds. Apparently Mother needed to change gears but panicked when the bear's cage loomed ahead. She simply threw her arms in the air, uttered "whoops!" and let Dad take over.

When the Reo later suffered a broken axle, the pattern was already at work: if it's not working it won't be fixed. The car sat unused for a while and then Dad sold it, 'as is'.

But my very first memory is of when Uncle Lew, Dad's brother, went to war. I wasn't quite yet four. The Great War was talked about all the time and we kids listened. In 1916, Uncle Lew left with his battalion for France. I wasn't allowed to go to the CPR station and it was maddening because I knew it was a big event. Getting a soap box from the storeroom, I placed it on the carpet of the living room, climbed onto it, and then rocked myself back and forth, all the while chanting, "I'm going to the war. I'm going to the war." Rene said that the farewell at the station was terribly exciting and "it was the only time I ever saw Dad cry."

FEBRUARY 6, 1917

I awoke to sounds coming from the kitchen. "Mother! Mother!" I called; and when she didn't appear I started to cry. I was surprised when Dad entered the bedroom, got me up and carried me to the kitchen where Nursie held a baby in the crook of her arm as she bathed him. Dr. Beer stood close by. I could tell that my father was pleased to have a son; he was very happy, but Mother just lay in bed in their bedroom and didn't try to get up and comfort me. I wasn't impressed with this new little being and returned to bed. They named my brother Charles Gordon; but Dad was always called "Gord" so his son was called "Don".

It is no exaggeration to say that Don's arrival made a noticeable difference in my life, and probably in sister Rene's as well; she became Grandmother's favourite. Before Don arrived, Mother seemed much closer to me. I suppose it was near the due date when she sat with me one Sunday and told me the story of the priest's helper hearing the voice of God and answering, "Speak, Lord, for thy Servant heareth". This left an impression for all my life; and I don't remember another such incident.

Irene and I moved out of our bedroom, into what had been the storeroom.

With so much of Mother's attention going to Baby Don, I felt so lost at one time that I was playing with matches in the new bedroom and, accidentally, a lighted match touched the scrim curtain. Frightened, I tried to put the fire out, but the fire brigade had to be called. I was unceremoniously hustled next door.

It was the first of two fires in our home. Another larger fire broke out in the store room. "My furs, my furs!" Mother shouted, meaning the ones Dad had given her when Don was born – a special gift for delivering a son. Dad carried Mother, who had baby Don in her arms, through a convenient hole we always kept open in the fence and, for fear of the car's gas tank exploding, several men pushed the grand Reo out of the garage and up the lane towards Lorne Avenue.

SPANISH INFLUENZA

The horrifying Spanish Influenza hit Brandon and Dad fell ill. I was sent to stay with Grandma as soon as he took ill and our store was sealed shut with a sign in the window declaring it illegal to enter. Mother and Rene could talk with Grandma and me only through the glass in the door. Mother ordered an ambulance on a Friday morning, but it couldn't pick Dad up until sometime Saturday evening – such was the demand on its services. There was no bed for Dad either; he was laid on the hospital floor where, he later told us, within minutes, the male patients on either side of him died. I will never forget seeing Dad for the first time after he recovered and was home again. I entered the living room and looked at the person sitting in the dining room armchair. Who was he? He looked so weak! Was gaunt to the point of skeletal, and his face was covered with brownish stubble, cheekbones high and sharp under his hollow eye sockets.

Dad's recovery was considered a miracle.

SCHOOL DAYS

When I was six, Mother walked me along well-treed streets to the yellow brick building that was Brandon Central School and introduced me to Miss Black. I wasn't frightened, just a bit awe-struck. I have a distinct memory of being surprised when Miss Black explained that the letters "o-n-e" were to be pronounced "won"; and another of our principal,

Me at age six and my first school, Central School 1918.

Mr. Tingley, angrily striking Carl Yeager on the head with the school bell (it bled) as we all stood in line, ready to march into our classrooms. I also remember wanting to be favoured to take the hand of a favourite teacher as we walked home after school. My shyness kept me from asking.

I passed into Grade two without any fanfare. Mother had little time for me, as I recall, and sometimes I was aware of that.

Don was only eight months old when Mother realised she was pregnant again. Sister Gladys Patricia, "Pat", arrived on July 22, 1918 in the Brandon Hospital, during a prairie thunderstorm. She was named after Dad's eldest sister and for the daughter of the then Governor General of Canada, the Princess Pat. Mother always said she chose the latter name aptly. Another cot was placed in the room where Irene and I had slept since Don's birth. Only 17 months apart, and with the same pale blonde hair, Pat and Don were often mistaken for twins.

Then, one year later, Mother was pregnant again. When the time came, I was sent to stay with Grandma.

Grandma. Each Christmas she asked me to pose, standing on a chair, while she got the measurements for a fancy pinafore; and each Christmas when I asked who she was making it for, she replied, coyly, "Oh, it's for the little girl up the street." I never once caught on. She must have found her grandchildren a new experience, since she was an orphan.

I enjoyed visits with Grandma. Whenever I was sent up to Frederick Street to visit her, we had a ritual of eating, then sitting in the dusk, creating our own concert: I sang a song and spoke a poem and Grandma regaled me with songs and poems she brought with her from her childhood in England. I still sing "Who killed cock robin?" and can hear Grandma stentoriously singing, "I, said the sparrow, with my bow and arrow; I killed cock robin." She also read to me: "John Gilpin was a citizen of credit and renown..." and she would chuckle when John lost his wig while riding furiously to his goal.

I should have known that something unusual was happening that day when I was sent to Grandma Wells for supper and an overnight stay; but I didn't. As always, we shared her bed, but the next morning I woke up alone. Grandma's landlady, Mrs. Harrison, answered the door when I knocked and asked, a bit worriedly, "Where is my Grandma?" Grandma's suite was a part of Mrs. Harrison's house, and I was always a bit afraid of Mrs. Harrison, for visits with her were lessons in behaviour. "No crumbs on the dining room table, please," and "Don't run your hands up and down on the plush cushion on the chair," – something I liked doing, to feel the rough and soft wale of the plush.

I sat at the table on the morning of April 27th, feeling lonely and forlorn. Why would Grandma leave without telling me where she was going? Now, of course, I know she'd been called on very short notice to take care of Rene, Don and Pat.

"All my babies came quickly," Mother said more than once; and Betty's birth was no different. With Nursie away in Calgary, operating her own Nursing Home, Mother turned to another reputable midwife, and Betty (Annie Elizabeth), Mother's last baby, arrived suddenly at Miss MacLean's Nursing Home. On the drive over, Mother's water broke and she urged Dad and the taxi driver to "Please hurry!" When they arrived, Father carried her into the Home.

Rene and I were allowed to visit Mother at Miss MacLean's, where everything was spotless and Mother had a comfortable looking bedroom. Betty was in a pretty basket and was almost as pink as the lining. I was in awe at the perpetual appearance of another family member. A cot was added to Mother and Father's bedroom, and now every room was filled!

My other clear memories of early 1920 are of the many visits by Grandma and Uncle Percy, and of the ongoing discussions about our shortage of space. Many times I heard Mother and Dad commenting on how "World War I changed everything for everyone." For the first time the government levied taxes – supposedly temporarily! And Mother told me that Dad complained to her on this. So, with the additional burden of new taxes and the birth of three children in thirty-three months, some difficult decisions had to be made.

Was leaving friends and family behind taken into consideration? Or did Father wish to prove something to them?

Both Mother and Father had been born in Brandon and lived there all their lives. The Mathie family had all grown up together; Uncle Will was a baggage man on the CPR, Uncle Frank, a customs officer, and Uncle Lew, a signal man with the Canadian Army in France. Dad's older sister Gladys was married to George Laing, manager of Pioneer Fruit Company, and Aunt Belle was married, at 16, to Laughlan McTavish, a CNR employee; Aunt Marie was to marry Uncle Harry Hill when he came home from being one of the rare flying aces in

CPR depot in Brandon, 1920s. The same spot I stood with my schoomates when Edward, Prince of Wales stepped off the train. He spoke to us and asked the superintendent, "Would you allow me to grant a two-day holiday for these children?"

W.W.I. I always felt that Mathies were a close-knit family and Mother's stories of becoming a part of that family with their wonderful feasts and music made me realise how she enjoyed her new relatives. But something had to be done!

Moving Plans

It was not unusual for my parents to be sitting at the card table with Grandma Wells and Uncle Percy, playing either a game called "500" or Crokinole, my Uncle Percy's expression that of a man thinking happy thoughts and Grandma talking, pleasantly, with a little laugh now and then. Mother sat in, but was often up, attending to one of the small children.

But in the early part of the year 1920 something was different. Now, when I'd come in from playing outside, the adults talked earnestly and with no notice of my comings and goings. Dad would be away from the store and, although some help was found – first a Galacian woman and then an Englishwoman to help with the constant washing, "nappies" were in need of daily attention. Mother also waited on the customers.

What I didn't yet know was that the talks around the card table were about my parents, Uncle Percy and Grandma pooling their money to buy a general store in the little town of McAuley, Manitoba, 100 miles west of Brandon. A Brandon photographer, named Davidson, owned the store and the house that was part of the deal, and had recently foreclosed on the mortgage with a Mr. Holmes. Davidson was obviously shrewd and intent on getting a profit from his investment. Why my father didn't just lease out the living quarters at the back of Mathie's Grocery and rent more suitable housing for his family nearby instead of moving us to a small town 100 miles west, is still not entirely clear. Dad said he wanted us to grow up in a country town....

It was only when school was out that Mother informed us that we'd be moving – moving away from Brandon. Why hadn't she said something sooner? She must have been too busy, her time swamped with nappies, bottles, wet sheets, dirty clothes, and oh, such a lot of hungry mouths. In any case, I was not pleased with the news. Born right in that home where I'd had eight wonderful years, with all my friends up and down the street, and that warm-hearted Curtis family just over the board fence who seemed as close as or even closer than relatives; they were like family. We often spent Sunday afternoons together, under the maple trees that Mr. Curtis had planted along the fenced property line; and Christmas with the Curtis's was a ritual. Their gifts were put under the tree in the corner of the living room and Mother always helped Rene and I select something for them. How Mother must have missed those times in later years! And little did I know, when Mother broke the news we were leaving Brandon, that we were going to have several months of upheaval before resettling.

Dad probably got a reasonable price for the grocery business when he sold it and the property at 251 3rd St to Mr. Esselmont, a retired policeman, but it is likely that taking over a General Store with a good house attached took all his cash. Grandma Wells and Uncle Percy, shareholders in the venture, had already moved to McAuley, into rooms above the store which they had created into a suite. Dad went next and lived above the store too, while we stayed behind, waiting for the previous owners, the Holmes family, to move out of the house that was part of the deal. I can't say what happened to create problems, but I did hear Mother explaining to people that we couldn't move until that house was available. So we moved out of our home and rented a temporary house.

It was a shabby house, located on a street across the road from the Brandon jail. There was no fence around it, and I was fascinated to see the prisoners out at work every day in their strange striped costumes. But the awful thing I remember about staying there was waking the first night, scratching bites on my body. I sat up, put on a light (there was electricity) and found bed bugs! How could I go to sleep again? I got up, found my little summer coat that Mother had made (with fake date-stone buttons) and huddled again in my bed, miserable...until I dropped off to sleep. Mother's difficulties were even worse; she was coping with a new baby and the two little children, Don and Pat, who also required a lot of care.

We didn't stay long in that house; Mother rented another which we occupied for only a month. We also stayed with the Curtis family and, for the last while, a kind friend of Mother's, Mrs. McDunough, who lived just below the First Street Bridge, took us in. It was so strange living with another family; and Mother seemed to be in bed more than usual.

It was while we lived with the McDunough family that the Ladies Aid of St. Andrew's Presbyterian Church came over one evening and presented Mother with a beautiful tray. It had a mahogany frame, fine brass handles, and a beautiful floral design in the cloth that was protected by good quality glass. "I don't deserve it!" Mother said, surprised they'd give her a party and such a beautiful gift. "Indeed you do," they responded, assuring her that they'd miss her greatly. No doubt their visit cheered Mother on in what must have been a most difficult time. Father was gone, leaving Mother behind to look after five small children; and no place to call home.

MY FATHER

How difficult I find writing about our father!

"Dad should never have had kids," sister Pat said in later years, with conviction and in her usual direct and simple manner.

Those are strong words.

"We scared the life out of him," I replied, a pretty poor riposte, but a true statement. I believe that when each of us five were born to him, Dad didn't know how to realise, accept and function as a parent.

"And we are here," I said to Pat, trying to soften her remark, and with the realisation that I am only here through my parents' lives becoming entwined. Though really, wasn't I in total agreement with her? Throughout my life when someone, friend or otherwise, told how much it meant to have a father they loved and respected, I was always left with a palpable feeling of something good that I never experienced.

Nor was Dad an astute businessman. If so, why did he sell the business and attempt to operate the general store in a small village where there was already keen competition from Stewarts & Miller, another general store?

"Wasn't my father an excellent salesman?" I asked Uncle Lew once. He had worked for Dad at the first store and at the store on 3rd Street, Brandon. Though I knew he liked his brother Gordon, Uncle Lew answered with emphasis, "Yes, he was such a good salesman that he could be sold anything!"

I believe too, that Mother knew all this from the day they were married, or perhaps a few days before, when Dad became ill and the wedding was almost postponed. But she

My Father, Gordon Mathie.

31

didn't demur; instead she became part of his manner of thinking and doing. And went along with his plans that, this time, meant a move to McAuley from Brandon – the place where both Father and Mother were born and had lived all their lives.

CHAPTER THREE
From Brandon to McAuley

Call it the Fates, call it destiny, call it whatever you want: I spent seven years in McAuley when I was in my most impressionable years; but it should be stated that I had nothing to do with the decision to arrive there, and was marked with that experience indelibly for the rest of my life....

When the Irish settled in McAuley in the 1890s, it was called Rutherglen, but the CPR changed the name to McAuley because, by the time they laid rails for the branch line from Kirkella through McAuley (all the way to Regina), there were forty-four families of McAuleys in the then Rutherglen.

The move to McAuley was a radical change; our family went from life in a city – where we had enjoyed indoor plumbing, electricity, horse-drawn fire engines, Woolworth's, an honest-to-goodness dime store and an established social life – to a village of settlers of Scottish and Irish families, where everyone knew everyone else and called elders by first

"Mathie & Wells", from 1920. We called it the 'the tin store' because it had fancy tin siding. Photo taken 1985.

names unless corrected by Mother or the scowl of one of the Ladies Aid, that group of women who taught you your place in the community and the absolute rules of respect for one's elders.

According to my mother, Dad purchased the business in McAuley because we'd outgrown our living quarters in the Brandon store. Now, of course, Dad's responsibilities were much heavier, not merely for the store's operation, but also because he had persuaded Uncle Percy and Grandma Wells to invest their savings into the business. Clearly, my father was optimistic and confident that this new venture was one where he could display his remarkable talent, the same talent that shot him upward within one year of being a delivery boy to a clerk in Symington's Grocery in Brandon.

The family moved from Brandon to McAuley on September 1, 1920. It was a damp, chilly morning. Mother herded us on to the CPR train. Betty wasn't well, so Mother was concerned with her while Irene and I were to see that Don and Patty, aged 3 and 2, were taken care of. In 1920, the trip to McAuley took about three hours.

The train ride was exciting. I ran my hand back and forth on the rough green plush that covered the wicker seats which I had swung around so that our group could face one another. But we were tired, had risen early to catch the 7:30 a.m. train and our few sandwiches didn't satisfy.

When we set foot on the platform of that neat little CPR station, Dad was there to meet us. The station agent, B. L. Patterson, said "Hello" to Mother, gave us a quick once-over, and then hurried toward the baggage car at the other end of the train to assist in unloading our bags.

Dad later bought an old Model-T Ford car, but on that morning we walked the distance from station to home. I'm sure we made a fine sight for the townspeople who saw us: my parents in front, Dad carrying a large suitcase and Mother the five-month old baby, well wrapped against the cool

September air. All the way home Dad seemed to be talking to Mother. She said very little, until later. Rene trudged slightly behind, complaining quietly, a bag of diapers in one hand and clutching the sealer of baby formula in the other. I lagged behind with Don and Pat.

We walked across the tracks, down past the Post Office, turned the corner at the Union bank, went on past the Presbyterian manse, crossed the road to walk by Mrs. Wright's and there, in the lane between Mrs. Wright's house and ours, sister Rene stumbled on the rough path (there was no sidewalk) and the baby formula hit the stony ground. Rene burst into tears and I got my brother and sister away from the broken glass. Mother said later it was like an omen of things to come. And that, "All the way home from the station Dad complained about Perce (her beloved brother) and that was only the beginning...."

Dad made a fire in our small kitchen stove, and then returned to the store. Thankfully, Mrs. Wright had witnessed our arrival and came right over, offering milk for the baby and assuring Mother that it was just a short walk to Big George McAuley's for fresh milk. "She could go and get it," she said, looking at me. "I have a honey pail you can use." Everything was strange and very unsettling, especially since I'd never been sent for milk, or anything, up to that time. In Brandon, milk was delivered; I'd never even been close to a cow. No one told me that I needn't be afraid of the herd near the barn and, thinking they were all bulls, I was terrified!

I paid the ten cents and returned to find Mrs. Wright sitting in our old rocker, holding Betty on her knee while Mother tried to find dishes and cutlery from the big wooden barrels that had been shipped ahead, but not opened. Only some of our furniture and household goods had arrived, in fact one barrel (goods were packed in wooden barrels in those days) packed with china, kitchen ware and silverware, was never located.

There were many discomforts in our new home. There was no running water and, "Where's the toilet?" I asked Mrs. Wright. Mother rose to the occasion when I was directed to "the backhouse", an outside structure she always referred to as the "W.C." something I learned later meant "water closet". Although I was glad to finally have my own bedroom, I didn't like the backhouse at all! The odour was unpleasant, even a good sprinkling of lime didn't erase the smell; and having had toilet paper previously spoiled me forever from the harsh orange wrapping papers and worse, Eaton's and Simpson's catalogues pages, especially when only the stiffer, coloured pages were left.

Mrs. Wright, who'd already proved herself such a good neighbour, showed us how to use coal-oil lamps. Mrs. Dobson, who lived just back of us, became Mother's friend, too; when harder times came, it was she who took Mother out for rides in the Chevy, a much needed break for Mother.

That McAuley was different from Brandon became clear to me very quickly when I was walking with Grandma to her abode and said, "Grandma, when can we go downtown?" She gave me a rueful, tiny laugh and said, "My dear, *this* is downtown!" My disappointment was deep, for when Grandma and I went "downtown" in Brandon, it was an event; she went to such a variety of stores – or so it seemed – and to the fine old library and joy of joys! We went to Mitrou's Ice Cream Parlour & Candy Store where I always received a bag of peanut brittle.

At Home In The Big House

A two-and-a-half storey, four bedroom house was part of the McAuley store deal. We called it the Big House because we had never known such spaciousness before. The house was a typical square, two storey prairie home. Downstairs were a hallway, stairs with banister, a kitchen, a pantry, parlour and dining room.

Upstairs were the bedrooms that Mother soon allotted. At the top of the stairs to the right was mine, painted green with stencilled green roses. The largest, across the hall, was for Dad and Mother and baby Betty's white enamelled metal crib; up the hall on the right was a spare room and across from that was a nice sized room done in pink with stencilled red roses; Rene requested and was given that one. Mother placed the 'dresser' (our name for it) at the end of the hall next to the door to the balcony since the baby's crib filled the space in the larger bedroom, and besides, now that we didn't have running water, two washstands with necessary accoutrements were installed, each having a full set of washbasin, large matching pitcher and china chamber pot, one set in Rene's room. For my toilet needs there was the tin pot, the article named by our good Nursie as the Tin Gin. All the pots had to be emptied into a blue and white speckled enamel pail (the commode) which we used in winter, when going outside was too cold for bared bottoms. How did we keep it clean? With Lysol and a kettle of boiling water that had to be carried from room to room daily.

Downstairs, straight ahead of the entrance hall was the kitchen. There was room by the west window in the kitchen

The Big House, part of the deal with The General Store, 1920-22.

for a small table and just behind, if you sat looking at the back door, was a good-sized pantry. Back to back of the dining room wall was the usual country sink, this one without a pump. Now that was one of the unexpected and onerous duties we had to learn within the first hour of moving in – getting water from a well, not from a tap, as we were used to! Our first choice was Mrs. Wright's pump across the lane; across the road was the harder-to-pump Mr. McNeil's.

To the left of the dining room was a door to the cellar, while the north door opened on to a shed which had a door to the outside yard facing east. Every house in those days had a shed, and this house had one that was almost as wide as the house itself. Sealers of food, vegetables, the washing machine, extra boots, a short clothesline and more filled the shed. One experience I'd rather forget was when Dad brought home a large goose and offered me fifty cents to pluck it. Fifty cents was a good sum, since all we got for Sunday School was a nickel or a dime. I began plucking, and though the fluffy down wasn't too tough to pull, the heavier feathers were. Well, I thought, I'll do this in stages; so I left the goose and went on with my life.

We had a dog, one with short wiry hair. That dog found the goose, nibbled at it, didn't like it and decided to have a nap. What he lay down on was a soft silk baby dress given to Mother for little Betty. By the time the dog was discovered, his rough coat had ruined the silk dress and he'd spoiled the goose, not to mention my reputation as a good plucker. But before that happened, I went down to the store and asked if I could have the 50 cents. "Have you finished?" Dad asked, surprised. "Just partly," I said. So he gave me 25 cents and, of course, that's all I ever got.

To the left of the stairs was a medium sized parlour, and through the double doors from the parlour was a dining room that easily housed the dining room suite. The parlour contained the gramophone, which stood near the large window with a view towards Rutherglen School, the carpet we'd brought from the Brandon living room and Mother's elegant Matthews piano. The piano was too wide for the metal gate, so the movers simply broke the 18" cement fencing – another never-repaired item.

In 1920, pianos were transported in wooden "piano boxes", and lucky the girl who fell heir to one – in this case me! There was ample yard space on both sides of the house; and etched in my memory is the corner farthest from the house, where my 'playhouse' stood under a big tree. Torrid, real-life drama went on in that make-believe domicile. Once, when Uncle Percy came by just after we'd filled a sealer jar with pee, we tried to convince him that "it's water from the slough just over the road near the willows". I knew he didn't believe us.

SCHOOLDAYS

McAuley had a pioneer with a vision who persuaded the town and farm citizens to consolidate the local one-room schools and build one big one in town, convey students in vans or cars and hire teachers for different grades.

On an early morning in September 1920 my mother

Rutherglen School. Torn down in the 1990s. I have a brick as a souvenir.

39

walked Irene and me from our new home to register us as pupils: Rene into Grade VI and I in Grade II. My first two years had been in Central School Brandon, a modest looking building compared to this new school. The two and one-half storey structure was impressive to an eight-year-old.

We were ushered around to the back door and as we stepped into the broad hallway, our eyes caught the fine staircase leading to the second floor. It was wide, with a turn halfway up, then more stairs. On the wall of the staircase hung a large picture frame, portraying veterans of World War I: six soldiers and Nurse McNalley (see *A Century of Memories*, 1993).

Miss Isbister wrote my name in the register, thanked Mother for escorting me and told me I could take the seat second from the front by the north window. Like every school, each room had fine big windows, and a neat cloakroom for our coats, hats, mitts, rubbers and galoshes, with, at times, wet moccasins drying under the steam radiator.

From day one I was happy in that room and with that teacher, except for one incident. Our group of readers stood at the front of the class; I had read my piece but was reluctant to move; the flap on my grey flannel underpants had become unbuttoned and now my pants had fallen below my hemline. I didn't want anyone to see my horrid underwear. Grandma Wells had made them and even if she was renowned for her sewing, especially buttonholes, this time she'd made the holes bigger than the buttons. "Jean, you may take your seat," Miss Isbister said again. The third time was an order. "I can't," I said, tearfully. But I couldn't hold out any longer. I half turned, tried to walk backwards towards my desk and, of course, my predicament was then obvious to all. Those snickers rubbed my pride; worse was Miss Isbister's attempt to keep from laughing aloud.

Fate was cruel, too, because to leave the room to button up

my flap, there was no other way out but to walk with as little movement as possible. Nothing helped. The flannel garment flapped around my calves; I couldn't run, though I really wanted to.

As for my Big Sister Rene, when the boys found out that Rene's middle name was Spencer, they nicknamed her 'Suspenders'. One night, when we were skating, they had a heyday calling that name out as they whizzed past her. "Shall I go home and call Dad?" I asked, upset. "Of course not," she retorted, "can't you see we're having a good time?" Rene was smart and seemed so grown up while I, according to her, was just a 'dumb cluck'. Rene was popular with her crowd, and she seemed to laugh a lot when she talked about their good times together.

A memory that lives with me is the noon hour when Rene excitedly burst into the kitchen and declared, "I've been asked to be the organist!" In a village like McAuley there could be only one place where an organist was required: in church. Even so, it was an honour, and Mother and Dad said so emphatically. I stood back and took it all in, with a hungry envy.

From Grade II, until I graduated upstairs, my playmates and I used our finest creative talents to build our own little rooms in the trees behind the school. With the odd apple box or orange crate, a broken saucer and a bottle for flowers, we vied with each other for the prettiest 'playhouse'. The verdant, pungent earth there produced violets of the bluest of blue and it begs recording that we picked the now almost extinct lady slippers sometimes by the handful! Cowslips, buttercups were held under the chin. "Do you like butter?" we'd ask. In the spring we tore sprigs of pussy willows and thick bunches of crocuses.

When our school held its annual Fair in conjunction with the community Fair, the trees were raided for thick, leafy branches to make booths and to decorate the tables in the basement where our Junior Fair displayed our entries. In those first years in Rutherglen, I won a prize for my sketch of the municipality and for running in the 100-yard dash. But the memory that makes my nose tingle is the fresh wholesome aroma of newly harvested vegetables displayed on the rented planks from McDonald's Lumber Yard that flanked the walls of the boys' basement room (the girls' basement room was the Fair's comfort station). Every class had its entries, every student had a share in something so well-planned and executed by Rutherglen!

Another sharp memory of schooldays is when Mr. Beveridge, the Inspector, made unannounced supervisory visits, often catching teachers by surprise. He would knock gently, open the door and walk up to the teacher's desk. Miss Isbister, in her always-white cotton blouse and long black skirt, never failed to blush noticeably, though Mr. Beveridge spoke quietly, asking we students a few questions.

One day, when I was in Mrs. Wishart's room, Mr. Beveridge almost had an ink bottle right in the face. There was continual pandemonium in that room, almost daily, but especially when Mr. Jim White's fine garden was ready for harvesting. Just a short walk from the school, that garden was raided mercilessly by the Rutherglen boys. If you weren't watching, you could get a hard chunk of carrot in the eye or a potato on the side of your head. John Chalmers must have run out of vegetables that afternoon because he let an ink bottle fly, missing his target but striking the door just as Mr. Beveridge opened it and stepped into the room. Sudden silence. Mrs. Wishart yelled (as she often did) at the culprit, "John, leave the room. Go upstairs!" When such a penalty was imposed the entire room sat in absolute silence, counting the number of times the victim was smacked.

ANOTHER SCHOOL MEMORY

Would a student today understand what I loved most

about school, particularly how it was in a small town where life rotated around events of such thrilling importance?

For weeks before Christmas an almost suffocating excitement grew as, day after day, we practiced our 'drills' on chalk-drawn plans and hoped our opposite number wouldn't forget her place. Then, finally, we were there, on the little stage in the IOOF Hall. I was to lead the six on my side and my friend Viv was to lead from the other side. "Rum tum tu tum," went Miss Isbister on the piano. Left, right; left, right; move onto the stage now. I can't! My dress is caught on a nail holding it in place. "Go on, go on!" whispered my teacher. What to do? Tear my cheesecloth angel dress? That's what I did, because the show must go on.

To give a rousing start for the program all of us crowded onto the platform, ready to raise the roof with our pent-up urge to sing. Even the first year students were part of the opening number; but the excitement was far too much for some; and there was crying and even worse – Gladys Baird's stomach churned and she threw up in the front row! Her mother cleaned it up.

I raced through Grades III, IV and V in two years, at first with Miss Mabel Notman, a quiet spoken teacher, followed by Miss Stewart, who used her own unique method of subduing boys' misbehaviours: she would dash down the aisle, grab the arm of the culprit and pinch! Oh, how she would pinch! But I have her to thank for teaching me to write beautiful handwriting.

SEPTEMBER 1921

We've lived in McAuley for a year now and I feel so safe and happy. My baby sister Betty is growing and Mother isn't as worried about her as she was when we first moved here. Once I came inside to find Dr. Goodman with Betty on his knee; he was examining her gums because apparently he and Mother thought she should be teething. As I stood there, he pricked her gums with his scalpel. "Lancing," I heard him say. Well, Betty teethed alright and the only other thing I'll record about her babyhood is that she wouldn't stop sucking her thumb and Mother sent me to McRory's Drugstore for "bitter aloes", a brown powder which she rubbed on Betty's thumb and which, apparently, stopped the habit.

But she must have been quite ill when we first arrived, because I recall not long after, when Old Mr. Thompson stopped by, he said, "to see the new family in town". After eating a bowl of gruel Mother had made for Betty and offered to share with him, he got up to leave. "Shall we have a word of prayer?" he asked; and Mother quietly answered, "Yes." The two of them stood together, Mother, as always, wearing an apron, her hands gently folded and head bowed; and tall Mr. Thompson with a long, "Jesus-like" beard, saying a prayer. Years later, Rene told me she'd overheard Dr. Goodwin tell Mother "I thought we were going to lose this baby, she was so ill from getting 'dirty' milk." He meant unpasteurized milk.

A year later and Betty is much better. I think Don will be allowed to go to school soon; and Mother will like that

Valentine for Edna that I made from a scrap of wallpaper. Edna and I became best friends in McAuley, and remained life-long friends.

because he and Pat seem to fight a lot.

I'm nine years old now. Edna, my good friend, is 10. We both like boys and are superstitious about some things, like when you see the new moon, look over your left shoulder and make a wish. Or, if a bird lights on the window-sill of your bedroom, that's a sign that you'll hear about a death. And don't spill salt; it'll bring bad luck.

Edna and I make 'Trade Lasts'. It means that if I tell her something nice that someone said about her, she has to tell me something as a trade. If something bad happens twice, you know something else will happen; things come in threes, good or bad. Bad, like that one cold Saturday morning when Dad had been at the store for a few hours and Mother was getting Pat, Don and Betty dressed with my help. Rene was upstairs, making the beds and, because it was such a chore to wash bedding in those days, Mother asked Rene to please step out onto the balcony and shake the sheets to freshen them a little. In winter, our storm door had a diamond-shaped glass insert, and I was peering out at the wintry scene when I heard a strange sound. I opened the door and walked onto the little frozen porch. The sound came from Rene. She lay on the frozen sod, with one of our sleighs partly under her. Her eyes were rolled high in their sockets and she didn't speak to me. I ran to Mother and said, "Rene is lying on the ground making some strange noises." "What do you mean 'on the ground'?" Mother asked. Then she seemed to sense something, put Betty down and came out to where Rene lay. She bent over her. "Go get your father. Quickly! And the Doctor," she said urgently.

I didn't stop for my coat or mittens, I just ran as fast as my legs would carry me, pushed the store door open and blurted out, "Dolly's fallen off the balcony and looks awful and Mother said come quickly and get the Doctor!" Since there was another girl in town named Dolly, the rumour soon spread that Dolly White fell off our veranda!

I never saw Dad run as he did that morning, and good old Dr. Goodman was there from his home just one block away. He wanted Rene inside but checked her first for broken bones. Then Dad, and one of the men who'd heard about the accident, lifted her carefully under Dr. Goodman's instruction and carried her up to her bedroom. She was unconscious for several hours and moaned until Dr. Goodman gave her a sedative. Mrs. Wright and Mrs. Dobson came over to look after us kids while Mother cared for Rene, washing the blood off her bloated face, and easing her in any way she could. Rene's friends were allowed to visit Rene for a few minutes the day after the accident and were shocked by her appearance. Worse, and life-long, was the pain in Rene's hip, caused by falling onto the runner of the upturned sleigh. When Rene had walked out onto the balcony that morning, she'd slipped on the ice and fallen over the railing.

Another unforgettable incident during our time in the Big House was when the Waddells came up from Brandon to visit. It was a summer evening and the little veranda was a comfortable spot to sit and chat. Lately I'd been impressed with a sight that took place every morning, and some evenings, just a block away. Old Mr. Forsyth owned a black stallion. He would stand in one spot, turning slowly as he exercised the handsome beast. Round and round it cantered, emitting a strangely beautiful whinny. This sight was new to me! The fire-engine horses in Brandon were exciting, the ice-man's horses were sturdy but quiet and the bread-man and milkman used the meekest of horses.

Perhaps the summer air had affected me. I began to strut in a circle, my arms jack-knifed, my feet lifting perkily off the ground and then, in front of Mother and Dad's guests, I emitted my version of a black stallion's whinnying. "Jean!" said Mother. "Stop that and go away!" Prancing, puffing and circling, I said, "I'm a stud! I'm a stud!"

"Stop that! Go away!" ordered Mother tersely. I wilted and

reluctantly ended what I thought was a nice variation for people from Brandon to observe!

CHURCH LIFE IN MCAULEY

I make no bones about relating the sweetness of my Sunday School years, especially my heart-stopping excitement when I was invited, at age 11, to ask my parents for permission to sing in the "senior" choir!

My fondest recollections are of life in McAuley, where daily existence revolved around the little Presbyterian Church, the town's only church. In every kind of activity, the church had a role – from christenings to communion, from parties for young or old, from weddings to funerals – and our daily lives had a pleasant pattern, with strands of church life interwoven throughout.

In that town and at that time in my life, Sunday was a very special day. On waking, you knew it was Sunday. Still fresh from Saturday night's ritual bath, you dressed in your best clothes, stood as still as you could while Grandma helped get the tats out of your hair so that an especially fine silk ribbon bow could be worn, held by a barrette. Mother or Dad found the little nickels, or a dime, and with younger sisters, we joined our friends walking to Sunday School.

Because my teachers took pains to know the lessons, much of what they parlayed stayed with me, and throughout my life, whenever in a nearby city or back to the little town, I contacted them. When the good man who was secretary had pulled the dark green curtains back after the lessons, and we became one group, we gave individual performances. For instance, verses from the 14th chapter of I Corinthians. For years, I pondered on mine: "Love doth not behave itself unseemly, seeketh not her own." It didn't seem nearly as interesting or as easy to say as other verses; yet as the calendar changed, that verse has been of help. We recited the books of the Bible to the point where it became necessary to say them backwards, for variation. With a suggestion of pomp, prizes were presented, and once a year those beautifully designed lapel pins were awarded; and to win later the encircling gold wreath and following that, the delicate little bar to attach, meant recompense for all that memory-work. Teachers smiled; parents spoke nice words.

Our church was a tidy, wood-frame building. We stepped into a little anteroom before entering the church proper. The choir gathered in the anteroom till prairie winter weather drove us inside, to huddle near the heater until the minister gave a signal to march to our favoured spot on the platform. Emblazoned across the sanctuary wall in large, gilt old English lettering was the exhortation, "Come into His courts with Praise." It must have penetrated deeply; all these years later and I am doing just that.

THE FACTS OF LIFE

If we are to serve an apprenticeship for adulthood, we should be warned that this is the first jolt life hands you. Until I was ten I thought that our family life would stay the same, with fourteen-year-old Rene continuing to get all the new dresses that would be hand-me-downs for me and trying to be 'the boss' of me, and my younger siblings be mere family adjuncts requiring attention. Suddenly, nothing was the same! Rene took a holiday with relatives in Moose Jaw, Saskatchewan and when she came home, looked like Mary Pickford. Her straight brown hair was gone; she wore bangs and lovely ringlets. Gosh she was beautiful! Mother and Grandma made her a dress of white organdie, sent to Brandon for a wire hat frame, and suddenly, she could go to dances and have a boy walk her home. I longed to grow up!

It never struck me then, that my sister and I were very different. Did she ever run races? If so, I can't remember. I ran every race, at school and community sports days; also the broad jump and high jump, played basketball and hollered loud for the baseball team, trying to sound at least fourteen, like Rene! "C'mon, Bud! Make it a two-bagger! You know how to do it," I shouted. I could yell louder than anyone else, and led the cheering. McAuley gave this growing girl wonderful freedom to do as she liked. School made life interesting, even the boy's ever present teasing was part of the fun; and with my singing getting better and better, oh, life was good! And I was growing up.

AN ABRUPT AND HARSH CHANGE

It is late in the year 1922. Holding the mortgage on the General Store my father bought in the spring of 1920 with Grandma Wells and Uncle Percy, was Mr. Davidson. I remember him making infrequent visits to McAuley, checking on the state of the business and probably collecting a payment. One day, as I often did after school, I went up into the rooms occupied by Grandma and Uncle Percy and found Mr. Davidson having tea with Grandma. He was discussing the business with Grandmother, who was an experienced business woman even in 1922. I distinctly recall her asking him if he "would ever foreclose should times be hard, crops poor or 'bad debts' prevent mortgage payments". "Oh, Mrs. Wells, I would never think of doing such a thing," he answered. But he did.

For years, I dreamt I was trudging up the long stairs to Grandma's room over the store. Before reaching Grandma's living quarters, there was a great, dark area to cross. A few things were stored there, but there were no windows that I can recall; the boards on the floor were wide, unpainted and creaked a little; and the walls were covered only in a cheap sort of cardboard.

I was ten years old, would be eleven in April of 1923. And our family's life was about to change – abruptly and harshly.

I had sensed something was causing Mother and Dad to be talking about the store often, but what they said meant nothing to me. Mother, who had real difficulties daily, but who was not the complaining kind, had begun to spend more time in bed. She had fibroid tumours which caused her to haemorrhage. She told me that her condition worsened when we all went to Brandon in a Model T Ford. Travelling then is incomparable to now and we bumped and rattled along for several hours till we arrived at Aunt Annabelle and Uncle Will's for a couple of days. It could also be that Mother's problems began when she had three babies in thirty-three months.

One Sunday afternoon, Mother wasn't her usual self. She started out from the house and headed for a walk through a nicely treed area just a couple of blocks away. Something about her manner gave me a sense of sadness and I ran to catch up with her. When I did and said, breathlessly, "I just wanted to be with you," she said, "I just wanted to be alone." It was flattening, though not devastatingly so, because Mother never was close and warm; but I was disappointed. She walked on alone. I went back home.

There's no doubt in my mind that at that time it had become apparent that the general store was beyond Dad's ability. He likely told her little about how things actually were, and coloured whatever he did to serve his ego. I think that on that Sunday afternoon Mother knew that something was wrong and not going to get any better and she needed to nurse her feelings. By now there were bad feelings between Uncle Percy and Dad so both Mother and Grandma were caught in a distasteful atmosphere of suspicion and downright open dislike. So, Mother couldn't even discuss this with Grandma Wells.

One night Mother was in her bed across the hall from my bedroom when Dad came home, sat beside the bed and talked to her. He was trying to tell her the worst, that is, that Mr. Davidson had foreclosed on the mortgage as of that night. Was Dad trying to make it sound easier when he said, "They asked me if I wanted them to tar and feather him (Davidson)." "They", meaning the men who'd waited next door to the store to hear how Dad's meeting with Mr. Davidson had gone.

"And what good would that do?" I heard Mother say.

Caught in the downturn of business, the demands of a growing family and the inability to collect owed money for goods sold on credit, Dad had appealed to Mr. Davidson to give him more time to meet his payments. He was denied. The business was gone and even worse; the family's home was gone as well.

What now? Dad tried and tried and tried to think of some way to stay in business.

THE RESTAURANT

In the block just east of the Tin Store was an empty building. When we moved to McAuley it was a Chinese restaurant and then later occupied by a German family. The Chinese proprietors had left town without creating a lot of scandal. They had operated like all other Chinese restaurants, serving meals to travellers of that day, men who stepped off the train at 10 o'clock one morning and back on it the next morning to towns west of McAuley. Dad must have heard from the men who gathered to gossip in the General Store how the Chinese had imported a female from the city to serve some male customers. He told Mother, but Rene and I were too young to be told about it. Or so he thought. I learned it from my school friend, Susie, the daughter of the family who occupied the Restaurant after the Chinese owners moved out.

Susie's two older brothers, able bodied but not well-schooled, had told her about it; and I suppose all the boys were aware of it, what with their advanced knowledge of sex, acquired when they'd sneak into the bluff just a few yards from our house and watch Mr. Forsyth's stallion perform. We girls accepted their dictum in that and many other ways.

Susie, on the other hand, had more sexual education at home than anyone else. She told me about her brothers' 'Thing', something she said they put inside her every day! I was more curious than appalled, having no idea back then that she was describing incestuous behaviour.

Mother's distaste, and that's putting it mildly, for that family became very clear to me one Saturday, even before they moved into and out of the Restaurant. There were always chores to attend to on Saturdays and I was to keep an eye on Don, Pat and Betty. Instead, I snuck up to where Susie and her family lived, to play with my friend. Mother appeared; and she was angrier than I'd ever seen. She strode into that yard, grabbed me, and then took hold of my right ear. She marched me down the lane to our house, berating me with every step. "Don't you let me catch you with those people ever again!" Insult was added to injury when Mr. Hairsine and his team of horses went by, he obviously enjoying the little drama as I tried to detach myself.

Soon after that incident, the German family moved into The Restaurant and, for a while, attempted to serve meals. When they left for northern Manitoba, my sex education almost took a dead stop, except for a nasty classmate who, during this time when I was beginning to cope with some things that weren't so nice, decided to 'educate' me.

My friends and I had our own little group, told each other secrets and still played in the piano box left over from our move. In that corner of our back yard, we played "getting married", "having a baby", and "being grown-up". One day, the classmate, a few years older than us, broke into our private circle. "Do you know where babies come from?" Wham! With open hostility, we replied, "Of course we do!" She kept on, wanting to prove she was smarter than us. "I'll bet you don't know that your father puts His Thing into your mother and she gets a baby in her belly," she said, looking at me. "My parents have never done anything like that," I said. "Go home and ask them then," she said. Our play-acting, fun and chatter ceased abruptly, and oh, how we hated her!

Luckily, my best friend Edna and I talked about everything. She and her mother lived on a farm not far from town and it was while I visited her there and we walked from the house to the big, sweet smelling barn that my sexual education improved. Our serious talk soon ended when we climbed the thick rope swing hanging from the loft.

Meanwhile, at home, a decision about our family's future had to be made....

There were good folk in that little village who had become friends and admirers of our family; and rightly so. My parents had come from Brandon to McAuley as good citizens. Dad immediately became a member of the local Orange Lodge and the Presbyterian Church. When Dad discovered there was no ice-rink in town, and that the town council had no money for one, he volunteered to see that a rink would be built. He hired farmers to haul water in horse-drawn water tanks. The farmers sat high on the wagon seat at the front of the tank, and the patient team stood still for the longest time as the water flowed through a narrow pipe onto the tennis court. There's no doubt Dad had underestimated what he generously offered, and it was the only time there was such an offer, but we had great fun there and our family had the respect of the town.

Now, Bill Stewart, a rough old friend of Dad's, visited Dad. Before the disaster, they often played cards; in fact, it seemed to me that Mr. Stewart was always in the store, chatting with customers or sitting on the large hot air registers in the middle of the store. Bill Stewart was the most successful farmer in those parts – his farmyard and barns were lit with electricity, a rarity. Now, he offered to put up enough cash so Dad could make a deal for The Restaurant, saving us from having nothing and nowhere to go. Our family would move into The Restaurant where, hopefully, former customers would continue to deal and, an added incentive, meals could be served to travelling salesmen.

There was no more denying: The Tin Store was gone and the Big House was no longer home. Our short time in that Big House was never repeated as satisfactorily; nor did we have the regard from others while we lived there. That was far more important to Mother and Dad than it was to me. Mother felt this keenly, right then and in years to come.

CHAPTER FOUR
The Restaurant

I was eleven, my nickname was "Beanpole" and we were awfully poor. To my chagrin, I had to go with my school friends into the Big House from which we'd been evicted, to attend sewing lessons. Mrs. Margeren, the instructor, gave me an odd, questioning look once, as if she knew I was re-living my "home" feelings in that dining room. She was right. When I looked at the wall I remembered what had filled that space when we lived there: a picture of an old toper carrying home a jug of brew, which, unbeknownst to him, leaked. The caption beneath was incomprehensible to me, but my elders – friends and visiting relatives – chuckled as they read: "When ignorance is bliss, 'Tis folly to be wise."

AT HOME IN THE RESTAURANT

Kindly, slow-moving, and aging Harold Collyer and his team of dray horses transferred the large heavy household items from the Big House to The Restaurant: beds, dressers, washstand, dining room suite, including buffet, and an armchair that Mother said her Father told her "Sir Charles Tupper sat in when they were setting up the Conservative Party in Manitoba."

It was the piano that required more help than either Mr. Collyer or Dad could handle, so big Bill Thompson, nearly always available, and Bill Stewart, our benefactor, with much grunting and heaving, got the instrument safely onto a couple of planks, down the little runway and into the store section from where it was moved under Mother's direction.

The structure that housed The Restaurant faced Main Street, where the town's business was carried on. The street had two general stores, two blocks apart, faced the CN Railway and its station as well as three grain elevators. Two stores down from us, to the left, was a butcher shop and between it and The Restaurant, stood the telephone office.

It was a painful come-down for our family to move from the Big House into The Restaurant. When we'd moved into the Big House, it was given a fresh coat of paint – outside and in. In contrast, The Restaurant was an unpainted, one-and-a-half storey building with a false front, like so many small town stores in those days. The previous tenant had a solid reputation for being dirty and, poor though we were, Mother declared with certainty, "I won't move into that place until we rid it of the filth and vermin!" That meant it had to be painted with coal oil – to kill the bedbugs. The town painter, Arthur Burgess, rumoured to be "involved" with Mrs. Grist, his landlord's wife, was hired. Mrs. Collyer, who always seemed to come to the rescue in our times of need, helped out too. She used water and soap in the lower part of the building, tidying a little area for groceries and candy bars.

Filth and vermin! Mother was in no condition for such

Dad, Nelly, Rene, and 12 year old me sitting on the wooden sidewalk in front of The Restaurant in 1924.

work. Still, she and I tackled the upstairs. I was given an empty tomato can with coal oil and a brush. Though the walls and floor had been doused with a mix of water and formaldehyde by Mr. Burgess, my job was to paint coal-oil around windows and doors, along every bedstead and mattress, and then help Mother apply coal oil to the tongue-and-groove wood floor where the bugs hid. It was a very tiring, odoriferous piece of work, but only when that was done would Mother allow our beds to be made up for sleeping.

It will never be possible for me, or for anyone else, to put words to what that first day must had been like for Mother. Her health was poor and her state of mind even more painful. She disliked everything about moving into that place – the fact that it had been run as a third-rate restaurant by a family she detested for their low style of living and the filth they left behind. Not only that, there was her own need to hang on to what self-respect she could in a small town where everyone knew everything about everybody, including that our family had lost everything. One woman commented, "Oh this is such an awful letdown, they might as well leave town."

A photo of The Restaurant was taken on trip back to McAuley in 1966.

How awful it must have been for Mother as she sat in the kitchen area on the bench behind the kitchen table, asking me to help Mrs. Collyer, whose long black skirt swished as she cooked for all of us. Mrs. Bill Stewart's wonderful German cooking helped us through the next couple of days. (And would again, on our last day in McAuley.)

I still clearly recall going through the store, from front to rear, then the little kitchen that led to the shell of the building called the back shed. Inside the shed we stored a few things like the large "bread pan" of galvanised tin, the beat up old washing machine and wringer and the baby bath that was used in our family from first baby to last, then for Saturday night baths and, finally, to soak Mother's bloody rags. She haemorrhaged almost constantly now.

Over to the other side of the shed were rickety stairs that led to the two rooms upstairs. There was a landing at the top and every day the bedroom slop-pail waited there to be emptied of the night's contributions.

No one had tried to build any part of that structure with style. It was simply walls and roof, and the roof wasn't very high. One small window looked out on the stockyards and the tracks, beyond which lay the Wilson's farmland.

A partition divided the upstairs; one side larger than the other, with room enough for two beds: a 3/4 size and a single; and up by the only window stood a small washstand for our one remaining china washbowl. Mother had sold the more attractive one. The one with a spray of roses with striking black and white stripes to set it off along with its matching jug and pot we'd used while owning the General Store. She had also sold the lovely dresser.

Pat and I slept in the single bed to the left of the doorway. At the end of our bed, the floor had been cut to allow heat from the wintertime heater to give us some warmth. We liked to get dressed near the warm air coming up from the stove. It was through that hole that sister Pat's underwear fell one day, onto the head of the always present loafer sitting below. He was a jolly sort and laughed, but Pat was mortified and burst into tears.

Betty's crib was sold before we moved; now she and Mother shared a bed that was set up at right angles to the small bed. When those terrible electrical storms woke us at night, our fright at the fierce thunder and lightning was eased because Mother always lit the small coal-oil lamp and sat up by the window, calming our fears.

Most of the time, Dad and Don occupied Mother and Dad's good bed in the other room. Don wet his bed and Mother explained that "I asked Gordon to look after the boy and wake him up during the night, to help him; but he never did." Dad was probably too tired from being on his feet all day long, preparing most of the meals.

Housekeeping? Since so much has changed in our daily lives regarding cleanliness, only the bleakest of language can describe the state of things as they were. Mother had made a little quilted covering, a small modern bag to cover the box that served as a stand for the Tin Gin. It made squatting to relieve ourselves a bit easier. But the dust that collected in round tufts under our beds was visible and only once in a while was a mop used to clear the wood floors covered here and there with braided rugs. Our bedding was meagre: flannelette sheets that took all one's strength to wring out, pillow cases that lasted since Mother and Dad's marriage, and quilts made of the cloth samples from when Dad had the Tip Top Tailors franchise. Mother sewed them together and tied the finished quilt with coloured yarns. She also had a beautiful, paisley silk-covered eiderdown quilt that had been a wedding present.

The Restaurant building had two front entrance doors; one led into the grocery section, the other into the dining room; it was rarely used, probably because our dining room table and chairs filled the front of that section. The layout of the ground floor was as follows: from the street entrance into the store; from behind the glass counter into the kitchen; and from the kitchen turn right into the only long room that became a dining area for customers.

After trying to make the store reasonably clean, Dad, with the financial help of Bill Stewart, put a few groceries on the shelves that lined the west wall with the hope that his former customers would continue to support him. The really good glass showcase added a nice touch and as long as we were there it held a few chocolate bars and gum. To make a little extra money, its countertop held a "punchboard", an intriguing cardboard game that held several dozen secret prizes. Customers paid from ten cents to one dollar to lift the paper sticker and read what prize they'd won. But only patrons like Jake Waddell, the CPR head section man, could afford it. And Dad had another idea for enticing people into his store: he bought the cheapest, buff coloured postcards (1c a piece), and had me write on them: "Beans." "Give 'em Beans." "Mathie's Cash Grocery". Beans were weighed and sold in small brown paper bags. I don't recall ever selling them.

Mother attempted to create some improvement. To add a touch of home and to brighten the dreary, sparse interior, she hung a maroon velvet curtain on a wooden rod across the wide doorway between store and eating quarters. Our fine oak-and-leather settee now stood in the archway that led from the store area to the dining room. The settee was occupied throughout the store's hours: by Bill Stewart, Mr. Dobson, "Old Rockola", the blacksmith, and many others; it was so worn that it wasn't worth taking with us when we vacated the Restaurant.

Mother's best cushion, a maroon cut-velvet wedding present, was placed on the settee and soon worn out, too. How often the wooden rod holding the velvet curtain fell on some customer's head! Always a shock to the recipient. One evening when Mr. Dobson sat down on that settee, he received a blow on the head and fell over, pulling curtain and pole down. Dad and the usual gang of hangers-around laughed, Dobson saying, "I've just been given the Arch Degree", a pun on the local IOOF male club.

Without radio and television to entertain us, such incidents provided not just a few minutes jollity, they were related with relish, told and retold in The Restaurant where, summer or winter, the town's males kept abreast of deaths, births, rumoured romances and news of every sort – true or simply guessed at, embroidered each time by the teller's words and personal bias.

I recall several customers. Old Rockola, who ate at The Restaurant regularly for several months; perhaps he wanted a change of menu from Mrs. Lewis's fine table. He would eat his meal and immediately go over to the settee, stretch out, then lay his not very clean handkerchief over his face and fall into a deep sleep, the handkerchief rising with the metronome-like rhythm of his snores. "It sounds like a wet moccasin hitting a tin wall," noted Big Bill Thompson. Since everyone in town went home for supper, Mr. Rockola could enjoy the rest; but when people came back to sit, talk and smoke, he was forced to relinquish his horizontal posture and sit up. He never stayed long, returning to his work as blacksmith or to his room nearby.

One late-night customer Mother and I dealt with while Dad was away in Brandon (probably pleading with his brothers and Aunt Gladys for help of any kind), was equally unforgettable. It was a time of year when mud was tracked in from the mud road and onto the board sidewalk that ran past the restaurant. It must have been well after suppertime because Don, Pat and Betty were nowhere around. Mother was scrubbing the floor at the entrance. She was on her knees, looking tired and worn in her day-after-day cotton housedress and apron. Did Mother think I was too young to get on my knees and scrub that worn wooden floor?

I stood behind the fine glass counter that hadn't had any chocolate bars, gum or candy for some time; and behind the counter, shelves empty soon after we began our life there.

The door opened and Willy Dawson stepped in, not too firm on his legs.

"I want some supper," he said and it was evident he had been drinking, probably in the livery barn up the street just past Mrs. Lewis's house where meals were always served on clean linen and plates were full. Willy Dawson had probably been refused supper there.

Mother didn't stop putting the soaked cloth on the dirty floor. She looked at him and said quietly and firmly, "I am not making supper for you, Mr. Dawson." He stepped past her, walked unsteadily to the settee and flopped down. Knowing Mother could use the 35 cents, he repeated, "I want some supper, Mrs. Mathie," some drool slipping down his chin. Standing at the doorway from the kitchen to the store I felt a terrible sense of helplessness. Not yet 13, I was old enough to feel shame for what Mother was facing, and anger that I couldn't do anything.

"Jean. Get some sausages from the butcher, and fry some potatoes, and there's a can of corn you can open," she said.

Usually Dad was there to stir the fire in the small cook stove. Tonight, between us, Mother and I got a plate of dinner and I served it. A few cents meant so much; and since our diner was a WWI ex-serviceman, we knew he would pay.

In the dining room, positioned on a slant, stood Mother's Matthews piano; it served as a room divider, creating a space behind it for the one ice-cream table that had survived bygone Ice-Cream Parlour days. The day we moved in, I'd discovered the wonderful soda fountain at the back with its green marble top and row of fancy taps that once held syrups for drinks or sundaes. One tap was labelled, "Orange-Ice", but it had long since dried up. There were two spaces for ice-cream tubs, also empty, and a couple of scoops. I imagined customers sitting there, ordering a strawberry or chocolate Sundae, a Banana Split or even a David Harum, a fancy dish now only a figment of that era! For a short time we had a few customers who came in and ordered ice cream, however, that part of the business lost money and was soon a thing of the past.

The remaining table with its twisted metal legs was where we kids ate lunch, though there was an old, longer table in the kitchen. That table had to be kept clear at noon to prepare meals to travelling salesmen and others.

Our Mother's unhappiness at the state of things was visible to me, though she didn't talk about it a lot. Since she felt the shame of our family's fortunes with such loss of dignity, she did not attend a social group of any kind, though she did go to places where I sang whenever her health allowed (not often in times that followed our stay in The Restaurant). But her resilience continued to surface, especially when someone came into the restaurant and Mother went out to greet that person. One day it was a local farmer she didn't know. Mother's wonderful manner of cheerfulness was evident. They began conversing and when he asked if there were other children like that goggle-eyed one standing beside her, she answered in an almost light-hearted tone, "Oh, yes. I have five children." "Five!" he said, surprised. "Just building up the nation," replied Mother. I was still young but never forgot that little bit of repartee and asked her about it later on. She laughed and said it was an old quote she'd heard and thought it very appropriate.

How did Mother keep up with all the work when she was hardly able to stay up for more than a few days at a time? Rene, my older sister, had been away from the family for two years, in Brandon, at first to attend high school, then to work in Brandon's fine downtown store, Nation & Shewan's, where Mother had learned her dressmaking. Now, naturally, responsibility for any and all chores fell to me. That meant helping in the cramped kitchen, using only the same small cook-stove, and not a cupboard or counter; just a sad looking kitchen table. I cooked, served customers and made sure Pat, Don and Betty were dressed and fed. Dad, who always put on a brave face, was out in the front part whenever someone walked in, greeting them and chatting; and if it were someone ordering a meal, he'd do his best to make them feel good. Wearing his long white (most often soiled) grocer's apron, Dad cheerily recited, "You can have steak, pork chops, bacon and eggs, ham and eggs...." If steak or chops were ordered, I was given 25 cents to run to the butcher shop two doors down. By the time I returned, Dad had whipped up a fire. Besides meat, we served fried or boiled potatoes, and a canned vegetable, then rice or tapioca pudding.

FEBRUARY 17, 1924

It was brother Don's seventh birthday. I can't recall Mother going to the trouble of a big birthday party for anyone else, and that's likely why I remember this one. The guest list included eight boys. Why Mother put a good Irish linen tablecloth on the table that day confounds me, it was probably because she couldn't afford to buy anything new, even less valuable. She used her good dishes too, for the meal and dessert: ice cream and some kind of red jelly and birthday cake.

The young guests began eating the sandwiches in a quiet enough fashion. It was about time for dessert when I, their waitress, found them with chairs tilted back and feet on the table! If they'd had any manners when they arrived, that had evaporated in direct proportion to the fastness with which food was dispatched; things were getting noisy and out of hand. I ordered them to "get your feet off the table!" but wasn't getting the desired results.

We had put the desserts on a serving tray, a gift Mother had been given by the St. Andrew's Ladies Aid. It was large enough to hold eight dishes. Something wet had been dropped on the floor on the path from the kitchen to dining table, just near the piano. Mother stepped in it, lost her footing and, with a full soprano "oops", she went down, trying to hold the tray out as she fell. In attempting to save the desserts, she sat down hard, still holding the tray, with ice cream, cake and dishes scattered from the abrupt change of direction. Saddest was the tray's fractured glass that, because of our long years of hardship, never got put together again. I was sent to buy an enamel tray from MacWilliams' Hardware two blocks up the Main Street and that's what we used from then on. The broken, once beautiful tray Mother had received as a gift when we left Brandon was, in a way, symbolic of our lives since leaving Brandon – everything getting worn out or broken.

Luckily, Mother had drawn the line at using her cut glass, a wedding present from Nation & Shewan's. In addition to the cut glass, another touch of beauty remained unscathed and a part of our household as long as I can remember: the hardy sword fern, splaying its fronds out to a 4-foot diameter.

DAD'S GET-RICH SCHEME! – SPORTS DAY 1924

The annual Sports Day was usually held on the fourth Thursday of July. Everyone, from respected members of the Town council to the littlest inhabitant felt caught up in the excitement of the event. Every part of the community – town and countryside – had some part in making it a celebration to be remembered; the day was planned to show off the town while giving the farmers and their families a wonderful day off from the never-ending routine that their livelihood depended on. Jamiesons' Barbershop & Confectionery had sold ice-cream cones and chocolate bars, their booth decorated with leafy branches cut from the lovely bluff of trees behind the red brick school.

The baseball field was dragged, and bases marked with white lines; the local players were heroes and their two piece flannel suits were washed and ready for the day-long tournament. By the time Jamieson's Confectionery's had run out of ice-cream and we'd gone home for supper, we could hardly wait to hear Jack Logel bawl loudly to baseball players and the onlookers, "Batter up!" All day, the junior players worked through the draw and when the senior teams' captains did their hand-over-hand to decide which team was first up you could feel the tension rising, only to get release when the first crack of a hit gave the opportunity to holler support. Today's television broadcasts are pale substitutes for McAuley of the 1920's...but back to Dad's get-rich-quick scheme!

When it was clear that, besides the smaller communities of Manson and Willen, Elkhorn, Virden and Moosomin would also be coming, the air of anticipated pleasure could not be contained. Perhaps 800-1000 people would show up!

Persons of less optimism would not have contemplated taking on anything that might run in opposition to the local Ladies Aid Society of the Presbyterian Church. Dad did; and he did it with enthusiasm and entrepreneurial spirit. If Mother was consulted at all – and that is doubtful – she would have let him go ahead.

Dad's idea for making a few dollars on Sports Day was to increase the usual seating capacity. He crossed the street to the lumberyard and persuaded Archie Macdonald to rent him a couple of saw-horses and enough planks to create a long table. Now we could seat twenty customers at a time. He bought a half-bushel of potatoes, and I was told to start peeling. Mrs. Collyer was asked to be chief cook in Dad's place because we were going to serve cold roast beef, potato salad and for dessert, jelly and whipped cream. The tables were covered with the only good linens left in the bottom drawer of the fine buffet.

There was no refrigeration. The meat was cooked the day before and kept as cool as possible in the back shed. Mother gave instructions in how to make boiled salad dressing; and with a few chopped onions and hard-boiled eggs, the potato salad would be okay for a few hours. A dish of pickles completed the menu.

The whipped cream was the most difficult to prepare. In spite of our hard times, Dad was able to maintain his friendship with farmers who didn't owe him from the general store business. I was told to get the old bread pan – a relic of better days, it was large, of galvanised metal. Squatting on my haunches in the relative coolness of the back shed, I tried to turn two quarts of cream into whipped cream with our old eggbeater. It took what seemed an interminable time and there was one consolation: I helped myself to cream from time to time.

Meanwhile, our competition got busy. At the back lane, right across from our place, was Mr. Pateman's implement shed. He cleared it of all the machinery for the Ladies Aid and there he and other men of the congregation set up temporary tables, makeshift benches and a stove. Big kettles filled its top and the oven had room to keep pies warm. The big doors at the front and back of the shed gave plenty of ventilation. Price of a meal was, I think, twenty-five cents. Dad hoped to get 35 cents a meal at our place.

I had my own wishes for Sports Day, to run in the foot races. Like Don and Pat, I was a good runner and had won first prizes in the past. I did get away for a couple of hours and, that day, won an amazing $3.50. And was home by time to wait on tables.

Wait. Wait. We waited and waited. We drew four customers: Dorothy McAuley and her boyfriend Dan McKay and two others came, sat down and thoroughly enjoyed Dad's joviality served alongside the cold beef, potato salad, jelly and whipped cream. While we hoped with all our hearts for customers, the Ladies Aid could hardly keep up with the demand. Records would probably show they made a couple of hundred dollars, while I doubt if Archie McDonald was ever paid for the rented lumber.

That was July 1924. I was bitter then and, recording this later, it still hurts. The church that I sang in twice every Sunday and the people who asked me to sing at concerts gloated at their success, knowing they had literally taken food out of our mouths. Dad may have been terribly disappointed, but who knows? Like all other matters of this kind, he didn't talk to me about it. He would try something else. But first, he asked for the prize money I'd won.

MY FIRST PAYING JOB

Seasons were clearly distinguished one from the other in every little prairie town and when farmers began cutting their crops and threshing machines and separators emitted their strong rumbles, hums and rhythms, it was an exciting time! When the CPR "Harvest Special" brought worker crews from the east there was an added touch: strong, good-looking young men!

Before I was old enough to flirt, at age twelve, I was loaned out to be a helper on Mr. Webster's farm where the threshing crew numbered more than a dozen, and Mr. Ernie Tatum was a farmhand. Mr. Tatum was not popular with the McAuley girls and therefore had found a wife elsewhere, through an ad.

One day, Ernie Tatum showed up at our restaurant and talked to Mother. He said his new bride was due to arrive and, since he was unable to meet her train, would Mother be so kind as to do that on his behalf? She agreed and brought Mrs. Tatum home. In spite of her large hooked nose, Mrs. Tatum looked lovely; she wore a lovely grey pleated skirt and soft grey sweater and blouse, and a hat with tiny flowers. But she was not used to the hard work that would be expected of her on the farm, so arrangements were made for me to have time off school and be paid five dollars or so for my help, which the new Mrs. Tatum desperately needed.

A gang accompanied the thresher and separator. A big farmer had his own machinery, while smaller farmers brought thresher, separator and gang in; they'd be four days and worked very hard. The days were long and work didn't stop until the last meal was finished, cleared away and the table set for the early, hearty breakfast next morning. I helped Mrs. Tatum make bread for the workers' breakfast, their break and the noon dinnertime. I baked biscuits for the afternoon break, dug potatoes, shelled peas, cleaned carrots, made pies, and kept the kitchen and dining room neat and clean; and I enjoyed every bit of it. The dusty harvesters washed outside the kitchen door and slept in makeshift bedrooms in the granaries. I slept with Mrs. Tatum, the only place for me to sleep, while Mr. Tatum slept elsewhere. One night I asked her what it was like to sleep with a man. "Very wonderful!" she answered; but that's all she'd say.

Mr. Tatum was a kindly old fellow who took a shine to me, the ready and willing novice. Long gone, those days; yet I have the happiest of memories of "working out" for the first time.

When I returned home from working for the Tatums, Mother took me to the back part of the dining room and, in an ominous voice, said, "I have something to tell you, Jean." Then she told me that my girlfriend Sadie Lee had died within a few hours of contracting meningitis. Less than 24 hours later, Mel Lambert died of the same malady, and Dr. Goodman prescribed the following for all the schoolchildren and adults: to take two ounces of castor oil. The school was closed and no one was allowed to attend the funeral; schoolchildren could only stand at the gate, near the roadway where the procession passed. Sadie Lee was eleven years old; and only her family was allowed to attend her burial.

CHRISTMAS 1925

Our family fortunes had hit bottom. The grocery shelves were empty, without hope of replenishing them, and Mother was unable to keep up with any housework or mothering. Christmas was coming. The Greatest Event of the year was nearing – The Christmas Tree. We never called it concert, just "The Christmas Tree", most likely because in our little prairie town we never saw a real Christmas tree except for that one event. The CPR shipped it in, Harold Collyer and son Bill got it over to the hall where the men of the town set it up on the stage, and left it for the Ladies Aid to decorate and adorn with presents – more piled at its broad base. It was magic, it was mystery and indelibly imprinted on the minds of everyone who saw it.

Every Friday afternoon, for a month prior to the big event, we practised our choruses: a lusty, loud opening song with every student participating, and a second chorus, the Grand Finale, to be belted out triple forte. From the first hour of practice, Miss Porter's thumping the beat with a ruler on the top of the piano to Miss Isbister's well-matched reverberating accompaniment, got the adrenaline coursing. No matter if you couldn't carry a tune: sing! No matter if you didn't go to Sunday school: sing! No matter if you never got to any other entertainment except this one, you never missed The Christmas Tree; and that applied to persons in town and for miles around.

On that night of unfolding marvels, we gathered above the yellow brick store in the IOOF hall, the only space in the town big enough for all public functions. On this night it took on a personality all its own, not just from the Dennison's red and green crepe paper garlands and tinsel, nor was it only because we were all doing our own individual presentations of music, drama and drills. Every individual knew that the greatest event of the year was going to happen: Santa Claus would appear, and everyone would receive a gift. The Schoolboard Chairman said so more than once. We were all so happy, not a whiff of any local feuds in that atmosphere; only utter joy.

At home, things were different. It was typical of Mother that while she lay ill, she worried about us being left out at the gift giving finale. She asked me to bring to her the ragbag, a treasure trove that produced many a surprising bit of lace, ribbon, or just enough material to finish a made-over garment. "This is for a doll for Patty," she said, carefully cutting a remnant of white fur left from a long gone baby coat.

I watched as she cut the pattern with a razor blade, pointing out that fur must be cut from the underside, to follow the way the pelt grows. But that was as much as she could do, and I helped her back into bed. "Perhaps you wouldn't mind giving Betty your kewpie doll, with a piece of pretty ribbon around its tummy and a little feather stuck into the headband," she said, adding, "and ask Dad to find something for Don."

The next day would be the concert. I waited until my brother and sisters were in bed, then I took the white fur out and looked at it. Our old sewing machine wouldn't, or couldn't, stitch through the fur. That doll had to be ready by tomorrow! With a strong darning needle I managed to sew the coat into one piece, but it was obviously not what I expected. It needed some contrasting trimming. I pulled open the string of the ragbag and dumped its contents on the table. From better times, Grandma had worn a stole of smooth, shining black seal. Following Mother's instructions, I carefully cut a collar and cuffs, and painstakingly stitched them to the little fur coat. What a smashing transformation! Not even the best Eaton's beauty doll ever wore anything to compare with this dashing costume. When I took it to the IOOF hall the next day, and asked one of the Ladies Aid women to please hang it on the tree, not place it below, I knew she, too, thought this doll deserved a special place among the collection of toys. My sister was going to get the prettiest doll when Santa arrived.

Each year, Pat would sit with her best school friend, and each year her friend received the prettiest doll; but on this night, when Pat looked at the magical Christmas tree and saw, amid its trimmings and various toys, she said, with certainty, "The doll! That doll's for me!"

Over the years I've heard her tell about that doll; then a few years ago I learned about Don's experience that night – he didn't receive a gift. Mother was too ill to attend and Dad would have stayed home to keep the stove heated to warm her bedroom. And so my brother sat through the gift distribution, with jolly Old Santa calling out each child's name and Reverend Chalmers repeating it, while a present was carried to someone nearly crazy with waiting. Don's bewilderment and feelings of broken trust must have been profound and terrible.

Though our time in The Restaurant was bad financially, I had good times during that time as well, with friends, and in school where I blossomed as a soloist and student. When Rene was home for a short while, she played the piano and I sang – for us and for the usual customers and friends. That was an aspect of our sojourn in the restaurant that Mother encouraged and enjoyed. What strikes me as most memorable is Mother's self-possession through a variety of incidences that must have been sorely trying. Tougher times were still to come and we developed a philosophy that eased the pain of poverty and that saw us through the Great Depression. I doubt whether we've ever enjoyed such robust laughter as when Mother made herself a petticoat from a flour sack and inadvertently cut the garment so that the sack's label, "The Seal of Purity," ran right across her seat. On another, somewhat ironic occasion, when Mother again sewed herself a petticoat (this one made from a bleached sugar sack), the name and slogan of the sugar brand, "Sweeten it with Red Path" appeared on the front!

Nor have I ever heard us sing as we did every night after

supper. Too poor to own a radio, I turned from the supper table to the piano and we sang through our very own repertoire, having great fun when a song took some very high notes, and Pat, with the best soprano, stood on a chair in an attempt to reach higher and higher. One song reached a climax with a high C, and she would actually put one foot on the table as she attempted that note.

There were good times, and we all survived. That is not to say that poverty is good for one. Each of us was scarred, and each of us has responded uniquely; we have dealt with that part of our lives in ways that is reflected in how we live and deal with our personal and public lives.

"You can't unring a bell," was a favourite saying of an old friend; and acceptance of difficulties seems to have been a part of the theme of my growth years.

Miss Porter

Miss Porter's voice could make us quiver in our seats and her voice could shrivel her students with fear or indignation. "Jean, don't look so innocent," she said to me once. "It doesn't become your personality!" Was I ever embarrassed! On one occasion, when we were all to write something about after school, Edna wrote about "getting the cows home on horseback". What a picture Miss Porter made of that; and how Edna blushed when Miss Porter said, "How smart you must be, Edna, to get the cows on horseback!"

Marjorie Baird was shyer than Edna or me, so when "Old Porter", Edna's nickname for our Grade VII teacher, asked sarcastically, "Marjorie, what's that thing on your shoulders?", meaning her head, Marjorie thought she must have meant a bug, and she turned her head this way and that, trying to brush off the creature. We smart-alecks laughed at her expense.

The boys in our class were so full of tricks in those days. One bitterly cold winter day, John Chalmers brought a handful of snow in and tried to make it stick to the thermometer. If the thermometer hit a certain low, school would be closed. Alas, the teacher discovered his plot. John was reprimanded and we stayed in our seats.

There was always rivalry between Dorothy Herberts and me, and I felt she had the edge on me because her father was on the school board. Often our hands shot up simultaneously. "What is the meaning of the word, 'catastrophe'?" Miss Porter asked our literature class one afternoon. I'd been reading Anne of Green Gables, the chapter where she walked the barn ridge pole on a dare, fell off and broke her leg. That chapter was titled, "A catastrophe". Up went my hand and, darn it, so did Dorothy's. Ken McAuley, seated behind Dorothy, whispered something in her ear. After a nod from Miss Porter, and with confidence, Dorothy said, "A catastrophe is a large toad." I laughed out loud, so did Miss Porter, then the entire class. Dorothy's chagrin was balm to my heart.

On another day we were asked to write a business letter. It was easy for me, with my grocery store background, but poor Wilson Waddell was flummered. Finally Miss Porter suggested, "Write for a piece of music to a Winnipeg store." Perhaps his Scottish family played Scottish tunes on their gramophone, for Wilson's letter asked for a song entitled, "A Roman in the Gloaming." Which was really about a couple roaming...in the gloaming! Wilson was so self conscious that I tried not to laugh.

"Oh, didn't we think we had the world by the tail in those days?" I wrote to Edna years later. "Both you and I have reached a very different plane, haven't we?"

Being a 'town' kid, one of the most exciting things for me was to get an invitation to visit with a country friend. That meant a ride in a van! For those who were transported to and from school in a van everyday it was a matter of course, but for me it was a significant event. With advice from my Mother to "always remember to be a lady", and my nightie tucked neatly in my schoolbag, I looked forward to the change of place and the lovely feeling of my school-mate's hospitality. According to where their homes were situated, students grouped at the school gate, waiting for their transportation. Imagine how different it was from racing home and looking for a piece of bread and jam, and doing house chores, to climb into a van and find a place to sit on one of the side benches. This is where I learned that there was nothing more intriguing, even shocking to me, than looking at the rear end of horses, something my friends blandly took for granted. After all, didn't they see all those animal characteristics every day!

I have warm, fond memories of visiting at the Matthew McAuley home. When Hazel and I got home her oldest sister Dorothy greeted us with a big smile, and said, "Well, you are going to have to sleep on the parlour floor tonight because the threshers are here." Everything was fun: we stood looking at the threshing machine, ate a huge supper, did our homework and had a good sleep on the quilts and blankets. Mr. and Mrs. McAuley were the kindest people you could ever know. Her special talent as a seamstress was evident in the always up-to-date dresses her daughters wore. When 'fugi' silk first came out and Ethel and Marjorie appeared at the next dance in new dresses of that fabric, they were the envy of the rest of us.

Mrs. Baird's Scotch scones, baked on what she always called the 'girdle', meant a great visit with lots of good food. Marjorie and I were close friends the years of 1922 and 1923, and she invited me to spend most of my summer holidays there. I was too young then to have any romantic notions, but a few years later when Jack was a dashing "sheik" – that was our label for him – I did have a crush on him.

It was only when Dorothy Herbert asked me to spend a night at her home, that I had mixed feelings. She and I were friendly rivals in the classroom, but it was her father whose stern, strict discipline gave me some trepidation. Coming into The Restaurant one day, Mr. Herbert grasped my chin, looked directly at my mouth and asked, "Are you wearing lipstick?" Perhaps I wasn't used to such scrutiny. As we went home in the van towards her home, Dorothy explained that her father might seem gruff, but not to let it worry me.

UNDER A NEW MOON

I wonder, do people still say it's unlucky to look at the new moon through glass? I know of a person who still goes outside to look at the new moon.

We were in Grade Seven when the Ladies Aid had a strawberry tea on Mrs. Wright's lawn and about a dozen of us played on the lawn when it was over. There were June bugs that night when Gregor asked if he could walk me home. "Sure," I said. He was a really nice guy.

When we got to our gate, we stopped to say good-night. I knew he was going to kiss me, and somehow I wasn't ready for that. How do you get out of a situation like that? Miss Porter had recently taught us about the different phases of the moon so, just as Gregor leaned toward me, I turned my head, looked at the evening sky and, just missing what would have been my first kiss, said, "I wonder what phase the moon is now?" Gregor never walked me home again.

During our teens, however, boys were a hot topic for Edna and me. Especially the good-looking fellow, Charlie, that took over the CPR station for a while; he was the man of our dreams, but Dave was nice, too. He was Charlie's assistant. We all sat at the supper table together, eating Edna's mother's delicious cooking and trying not to giggle too much because we hoped Charlie would give us a smile.

THE MCAULEY HOW-DO-YOU-DO-CLUB
ANNUAL SHOW & DANCE
IOOF HALL
FRIDAY, MARCH 17 8 PM.
GENTS 50 CENTS, LADIES 35 CENTS, CHILDREN
FREE
LUNCH SERVED AT MIDNIGHT
COME ONE, COME ALL!

Innovation wasn't a word to be afraid of in our town, so to assist in raising money without the austere reservations of the Ladies Aid Society who held an annual bazaar where they served refreshments like egg sandwiches, we younger women created a semi-religious club and gave it a breezy, welcoming name: the "How-do-you-do-club!" We co-opted the fine talents of a local citizen who, being Anglican, had no church to attend but gladly became our leader. Mrs. Leppert was one of those natural organisers and she taught us how to work together, how to engage public participation, how to perform and, best of all, how to do it all gladly and with good intent. We made our own costumes and they were astounding: yellow clown suits with black dots sewn on, the long sleeves and necks ruffled, topped with tall cone-shaped hats held on with chin ribbons.

At every evening we sponsored, we bounded on to the stage singing our jazzy theme-song, "How do you do, everybody, how do you do? It's not your face that's fair, nor the way you comb your hair, how do you do, doodle doodle do, how do you do?" Following that, we stood in a semi circle, addressing someone we'd singled out, a good member of the audience like Mr. Hairsine, or Doctor Goodwin. By the time we'd greeted half a dozen, we swung into, "I miss my Swiss, my Swiss miss misses me", with suitable antics; and by then our natural exuberance got our feet moving with "Five foot two, eyes of blue…has anybody seen my gal?" and I could step forward flinging my arms and legs to left and to right in perfect rhythm, while my partner urged me on with "Yeah kiddo!" and the audience clapped in time with us.

They loved us, we loved doing our thing, and we certainly made money. With our semi-social qualifications we put on dances – and in our town everybody danced, and danced with everybody else. When my girlfriend was paired with my little brother as they walked under an arch of paper roses, I was afraid she'd be unhappy but she was game and smiled when they walked down the length of the hall to where lunch was being served. I wasn't quite as pleased when, during the box-lunch auction, I drew an old bachelor to share my lunch with, but he was happy and Mother's glance told me to be a good sport.

Dances started smartly at 8 pm, went till 11:30, resumed at 12:30 and ended usually around 2 am. Appetites were keen and no wonder! Everyone there had worked all day, with farm lads having hurried to scrub up, change clothes, harness buggies, drive in and park their horses and vehicles, take the stairs to the second floor of IOOF hall two at a time and never even sit down between dances. That meant our midnight lunches had to be hearty.

We, too, had put in quite a day, cutting the Dennison's crepe paper for streamers, making big rosettes, hanging our decorations gracefully and making sure we left enough orange paper to paste in the shoebox with the light bulb tucked inside for the Moonlight Waltz.

Bessie McCauley's family farm was on the edge of town, which meant we could walk there, so that's where some of us met to prepare the supper. With fine-tuned organization we made canned salmon and egg salad sandwiches, enough to fill two orange boxes. Two tall cans of salmon cost 35 cents and eggs were right there on the farm. Kraft Miracle Whip wasn't around for another twenty years; we used tangy home-made boiled salad dressing, and bread was home-made since we hoped to make money and McGavin's bread made in Brandon and shipped out was 35 cents a loaf. As we cut the bread and mixed the filling we caught up on all the doings of the day, having lots of laughs while sneaking a nibble. We shared the donations of cookies, cakes and pies. Our cakes were left in pans for safe transport to the dance hall.

Bessie's brother, Foster, came in from chores, saw us and said, "Hey, how about it?" Bessie and her brother were good dancers and just as we began singing, "The sheik of ara-aby" Foster and Bessie did a smooth foxtrot down the length of the long farmhouse kitchen. It was a cameo moment.

Obliging males carried pails of water from the nearest pump (Mrs. Lewis') a block away, up the stairs and filled the wash boiler, which we prayed wouldn't have any soapy flavour this time. Wood for the little stove was the gift of the IOOF. When every crumb was licked up, some kindly males walked back to the pump and brought water for washing the heavy porcelain cups, saucers and plates with the familiar cloverleaf

From left; Mother, Father with Betty on knee, Don, Pat, me behind Pat, and our Aunt Mavie cousins Betty on her knee and Alice behind, 1926.

design, ones the Ladies Aid had lent to us. I've never had more fun fund-raising.

The experience we all got from our Big Event didn't make the treasury bulge, but Mrs. Leppert, our leader, had another idea: we could do "craft work" for the annual bazaar. The older girls were serious and did nice needlework, but Edna and I sat as far from them as we could while we tried to make a fancy lace-trimmed powder puff that wore a label, "You can pat my back!" And the puff was tied with pretty ribbon to a thin stick, wound with ribbon. We never got ours finished, and our giggles didn't help; but Mrs. Leppert's oatmeal cookies and tea made for a great evening.

A newspaper clipping from 1925, reads as follows: *"Though confined to the church kitchen and Sunday school, while what pioneer feminist Nellie McClung called "the heavy work of moving resolutions" had to be left to men, in their own groups women learned to conduct meetings, make decisions, handle vast sums of money, organize and train other women."*

Those days cannot be revived, and more's the pity!

MY FATHER

Was there anyone like Gordon A. Mathie? Dad exuded endless optimism with his smiles and chatter. He was well liked; no doubt how he survived the disappointments he faced, but, unfortunately, it did not bring his former customers to this location. The grocery aspect of The Restaurant had long since ended and our only income, from serving meals, was dwindling too.

There was another cruel twist while we were in that tawdry, unkempt place. A travelling salesman from Brandon who had known Dad when the Third Street grocery was flourishing, stopped by for a meal. He returned the next night, and then again, making himself comfortable on the oak settee while he and Dad chatted. Dad seemed in better than usual spirits. I was asked to play the piano and sing. One song was "The Sunshine Of Your Smile". I recall putting all my emotional ability into my singing. The man nodded and complimented me, while Dad smiled and said something about my talent being 'part of Mathie gifts'. Dad was feeling so good that later that night when he told Mother that the fellow was an agent for Pioneer Grocers and was in town to open a Red & White grocery store in McAuley, he was almost ecstatic, rubbing his palms together in that way he did when he was excited. Dad hinted that he would be given that business. Mother was quiet; but her weak physical condition was always noticeable. I was pleased and really hoped we'd soon be enjoying better times.

How shocked, embarrassed and terribly down-hearted we all were when Dad learned from one of the fellows who always had the latest local gossip, that the new Red & White store was opening down the street and the franchise would be given to Jack Lawrence, the butcher just two doors down from our place. Of course, the deal was made with someone with financial resources. Did Dad ever say how he felt about that? If he did to Mother, she never passed it on to me. That man never showed his face to us again.

It was the worst thing we could have heard. Dad, always on top of events, hid his deep disappointment from me, but when he and Mother faced it, they knew we were even deeper into our own personal depression. Bill Stewart, the generous backer we'd had when the Tin Store was lost, probably declined further assistance – if Dad asked for it. As far as I could tell, Bill Stewart and his kindly wife never held it against Dad that he couldn't repay the loan they made when the Tin Store was gone; and no further money was loaned or given.

January 27, 1926.
WORLD-SPECTATOR, MOOSOMIN, SASK.
For Sale
A well established Grocery and Confectionary Store.
A good turnover, doing a strictly cash business.
$1800. will handle.
Apply to G.A. MATHIE McAuley, Man.

Reading the ad that my Father placed in the local papers, I still feel one of those often experienced shivers of bodily discomfort. Why? Dad was kidding himself and hoped he could kid someone else, too. Only a few customers came in the front door and asked for a meal, and when they did it was a small panic to put a meal on the fine oak dining room table.

Clearly, Fortune wasn't smiling on us. Dad's brother-in-law, a manager at Pioneer Fruit in Brandon, arranged for Dad to work as a travelling salesman. But that didn't work out either; so, in early 1926, we knew we would have to get out of the Restaurant. But to where?

Dad, the "retired grocer", a title he gave himself to salve his injured pride, managed to pressure a farmer, Mr. Kelsey, to repay an outstanding debt from the Tin Store days (No doubt, the loss of the Mathie & Wells general store was due to too many bad debts; a dynamic Father never had to deal with in Brandon). Payment would come in the form of a modest little cottage which would be set behind the house that Old Matthew McAuley and his daughter Mary lived in. Another small debt would be repaid with an old granary that would be hauled into town, set into the vacant lot between Pateman's Machine Shop and the Post Office, and become a tiny grocery.

But temporarily, before our new home, the small cottage, would be delivered, our family required some kind of shelter.

CHAPTER FIVE

The Orange Hall, an Old Granary and a Small Cottage

My friendship with Edna is what ties together any stories I have about McAuley.

You sure had to give Dad credit for being surprisingly ingenious. With the latest turn of events, we no longer had a home. The restaurant business that had slumped to nothing was finished. The mini-depression that began in 1922 brought hard times to many in our little village. The farmers were able to stave off the worst because they could meet the simplest needs of life with a cow or two providing milk, cream and butter or, when absolutely necessary, by selling a few bushels of grain at one of the grain elevators. Horses helped with farm work and transportation. We, however, had nothing. No income, no home and, what may have seemed like to some, no future.

I was the eldest at home. Mother was flat on her back most of the time, with the foot of her bed tipped up with empty tomato cans – the only treatment to halt the constant bleeding. Then Dad announced he'd found a place to live and we'd be moving.

THE ORANGE HALL

I was thirteen when we moved from the awfulness that was life in The Restaurant and into The Orange Hall. Whereas the Independent Order of Oddfellows (IOOF) owned the large, two-storey yellow brick store and the town's only hall big enough for concerts, dances and gatherings of all kinds, the Orange Hall was smaller and humbler in appearance. As I recall, the one storey, one door, one room building had a church-like feel to its frame. A curtain blocked off a corner of the hall; I mused that this is where the Organization stored its secret books and robes. At the other end of the room was a platform that ran from one side to the other. When our little kitchen stove was brought in and set-up, there were seventeen lengths of stove-pipe between stove and where it disappeared into the chimney.

By this time, Mother had sold for a few dollars whatever furniture we could do without. I remember how painstakingly I wrote, at her direction, a description of her lovely cut glass water set, then taking it down to the tiny Post Office building, pinning it to the wall alongside other notices there, all the while hoping no one would buy what was one of Mother's few remaining wedding gifts. No one did, and it remained in the family.

Into the Orange Hall went the dining room suite, a buffet, a couple of dressers, one of which Mother sold while we lived there, three beds, a cot, a washstand and the piano.

Privacy. With only one room in the Orange Hall, it could have presented a problem. But at that time in our lives, we Mathies didn't blink an eye when all that separated beds from dining table was the old curtain Mother rigged up and hung on a wire from one side of the narrow platform to the other. She created 'walls' between our beds in the same manner, beds that she and Dad placed slantwise on the platform. Pat and I slept together, while Don had a cot, referred to in Manitoba as a 'Winnipeg couch'. Betty had a smaller cot and Mother and Dad still had the nice white enamel with brass trim double bed. What thoughts they must have had when they were first married and purchased that bed! The bedroom china, of course, had its place; a bowl and pitcher stood on the little washstand, the companion piece under the bed, that is, when it wasn't perched on its stand – in use. The good neighbours living just a few steps away offered the use of their outhouse.

We were very poor. I don't know how we even had enough to eat, or how we were clothed, because our only subsistence came from Dad's small set-up in the wood granary. He continued to be 'the grocer', donning his now stained white apron each morning, winding the strings around twice before tying a knot in the front. In that scanty space he sold whatever he could find a few dollars to buy: a bag of sugar, some bags of beans or salmon and a few boxes of chocolate bars.

It was mid-winter and Dad's morning routine went like this: start the fire, pull on his pants, socks, shoes and by now unravelled, jumbo-knit fawn sweater; and, as he reached the door, carefully place his felt hat on his head. That hat was the last vestige of earlier times when every item in his wardrobe was nifty. It was a soft, pale grey Fedora, with matching grosgrain ribbon band trimming the brim, the hat tended, year after year, with such care; and when you consider how many times a day he put it on, you have to admire the manufacturer. Dad never, ever went out the door without wearing that hat.

"Time to get up!" he'd call from the door, and then go outside for an armful of wood for that measly old stove. When he returned, he was ready for his tea. To the right side of the stove sat the old brown teapot with a bent tea-strainer hanging from its spout.

One day, on a particularly cold morning, there was a noticeable difference in the usual routine. My brother hadn't filled the wood box the night before. There was just enough kindling to start the fire and get hot water boiled for his tea. Before going out, Dad set the teapot where it would keep warm and went outside for wood. "I called you kids," Dad said again and maybe three or four times, annoyed that none of us had gotten out of bed. We huddled closer when he couldn't close the door quickly because his sweater and a chunk of wood were entangled. When he returned, he leaned forward to drop the wood in the box and our comfort was forgotten as Dad's worn sleeve snagged the wire of the teapot strainer. There was a crash; we heard a scrambling, his howl and then something that galvanized us into action like bullets from a gun. "Damn!" Dad roared; and we leapt out of bed, but not carefully enough to keep our balance. There we were, clutching the wire that held the curtain, but it left its moorings and for a few moments it seemed that Pat and Don and I would catapult over the edge of the platform and end up on the floor below.

There was an unspoken rule in our family about language: speak freely, be careful about gossip and don't use swear words. We had never heard our father swear. Dad knew that, too. Now, we were terrified; we didn't know just then if it was from not having fallen over the platform's edge or from the shock of hearing that word! (Very sad, too, was the loss of the old teapot, because there wasn't even twenty-five cents to buy a new one at the time. Eventually, of course, it would be replaced.)

Dad's attention, diverted from his personal calamity by our commotion, and our unseemly appearance, tickled my sister's funny bone. She started laughing, Dad picked it up and then we all laughed together; it was a family joke for decades!

How would the present generation of young people deal with the scarcity of what, nowadays, are merely everyday comforts? Could they have any fun over the simplest of family situations such as being struck dumb because your dad had said "Damn"?

1926 McAuley, Manitoba

I am 14 now. The family has squeezed into the small cottage. Rene lives with Grandma Wells in Lumsden. Don, 9, sleeps on a Winnipeg cot nudged in the small bedroom that has Mother and Dad's double bed pushed up to the east wall. Eight-year-old Pat and I sleep in a 3/4 bed and youngest sibling Betty has a small cot squeezed in that room.

Blurred memories of our day-to-day life come back, with only a few clear details. Many a time I ran next door to gasp out, "Mrs. Collyer, come quick! Mother's fainting." Mother's fibroid tumours continued to cause haemorrhaging and we didn't have the money to call for a doctor. I recall Mrs. Collyer's long black dresses, how she lifted the skirt from around her feet and hiked after me to help Mother into bed and make tea to revive her. Then she and I placed wood stumps under the foot end of the bed to elevate Mother's legs and waited, hoping that the bleeding would slow up. In a few days, Mother was up and around, weak and thin and not very active, but always giving us the impression that life couldn't be better.

This was nothing new. When, during one of our bitterest moments, soon after the mortgage was foreclosed on the Tin Store, little Mrs. George McAuley called out from her

The cottage in McAuley.

upstairs window over the harness shop, "Sorry to hear of your troubles, Mrs. Mathie," Mother called back, "Thank you, Mrs. McAuley. Yes, it is bad, but life is sweet." And we continued to walk towards the station.

Did Dad discuss the state of things with Mother? If so, not in front of us kids, or to us. We lived in close proximity to each other, each of us alone, except for Mother and me. We shared local gossip, the housework and taking care of the three young ones.

Trying to put a finger on it from a distance and an entirely different lifestyle, we were a family only in the sense that we were under one roof (except for Rene, who only lived with us for a few months in 1925). Dad got up first, lit the small kitchen stove, made a pot of tea and, when the store was red-hot, he made toast by taking the lid off and holding the toaster over the fire. When she was feeling strong enough, Mother cooked porridge; I made toast for myself and Don, Pat and Betty.

Each of us kids scrambled to find decent clothes for school; we developed ingenuity in putting together a mix of clothing. Even Don, the lone brother, could trade a garment once in a while, and again Mother would come up with an idea that saved the day. She was never far apart from her training as a seamstress, which gave her insight into how to put fabrics, texture, colour and design into a reasonably good appearance. Thus, Mother's sewing machine did more than sew; it gave each of us kids a measure of well being. Once, she ordered khaki cotton fabric from Eaton's and made neat outfits for Pat, Don and Betty; and for me, a nifty broadcloth dress and hat from a 48 inch wide yard of material.

All our worldly goods that remained intact fit into the cottage. Mother's piano was an adornment to any room, as well as the fine oak dining room suite. But we were very poor. I was hurt and embarrassed when the cheeky minister's son, Doug Chalmers, taunted me one day when I was walking home at noon from school. "Mathies live in a shack!" he said in the hearing of the gang of us sauntering homeward. "It's a dump; not big enough to swing a cat in." I was too upset to think quickly enough and remind him that the church manse that he lived in was only theirs because it was donated.

It could be that Don heard that sarcastic remark and did something that made Doug Chalmers angry. "I'm going to kill you, Mathie," he screamed at Don, only eight at the time, then chased him. Years later, when I was a guest speaker at a McAuley Reunion, Lehman White, our neighbour and Don's buddy, asked about Don. "Tell him," he said, "that I still remember the wonderful times we had. Especially the time that Doug Chalmers threatened to catch Don and kill him, and I was able to run between them, throwing Doug off his stride. He lost his balance and never caught Don." When I conveyed that message to Don, he said, "Yes, and Chalmers would have killed me if he could have caught me. He was the meanest guy I ever met."

One night I wakened to hear a commotion. It was around 4:30 a.m. Dad asked me if I could find a nail file. Fuzzy with sleep, I got up and tried to rummage through the dresser (the only one left now, since Mother had sold her good one). Then I realized that Dr. Goodwin was in the other bedroom, and Mother was having some kind of physical difficulty. Dad had lit the stove and asked for a basin of boiled water. We never had dressing gowns, so I stood there in my nightie, but didn't go into the bedroom because there was no room for me. Dr. Goodwin paid no attention to me, merely telling Dad that Mother would have to stay flat in bed and we must get some means of raising the foot of the bed 8 or 10 inches. The other children slept. Perhaps it was Mrs. Dobson who came to see Mother, and I suppose I was making them a cup of tea when I heard Mother saying, "Dr. Goodwin said he thought it was a placenta; but I know it was no placenta. It couldn't have been." The way she said it clearly meant that it couldn't have been any such thing because there hadn't been what was necessary to create it.

I was visiting with the Cole family near Elkhorn in the summer of 1927, at the request of son Bill, who had met me in April when he and his sister and cousins had come to McAuley to a dance. Few farmers had cars, so it was exciting to have them drive to McAuley one Sunday afternoon and have Bill be attentive to me. My visit with them in the first two weeks of July faded when Bill realized how poor I was, which became evident when they took me to the annual summer fair in Brandon. With no money, they paid for my every meal, show and ride, and it dampened Bill's ardour; I was keenly aware of his growing disdain. What could I do? Ask him to drive me home? He was avoiding me by this time.

Then a short note came through the mail. It was from Mother.

> *Dear Jean: You will have to come home immediately.*
> *I need your help. Dad has got a job in MacLeod's store*
> *in Rocanville & we are moving there on July 15.*

It seemed the fates had shifted in our favour.

Bill drove me to the CPR junction where the train stopped, if informed of a passenger. He helped me step up onto the train steps, spoke a toneless goodbye and we never met again.

Rocanville! We were moving to a town that had always given us frivolous flappers an aura of glamour. It had a larger populace than McAuley; and when a carload of Rocanville boys appeared at our dances they seemed more sophisticated, always well dressed, with a touch of naughtiness. Very proper mostly, with the exception of a few, one of whom asked Katie Carefoot, sitting next to me, for a dance. She coolly refused and told me, "I'm not dancing with anyone with the smell of beer on his breath!"

I was pleased we were going to Rocanville, yet conscious of my close friendship with Edna Lewis that I'd be leaving behind.

MY BEST FRIEND EDNA LEWIS

We lived in the Big House when I first met Edna. She and her mother lived just a couple of blocks away (though a block is not the way to describe space in the little town). Edna's father had found work in the Birtle, Manitoba, Indian school. Mrs. Lewis was housekeeper for a bachelor, Mr. Forsyth, and his small home was on a rise of ground up from our home.

I was 9; Edna was 10, so we were in different grades at first. Later I was promoted and we ended our schooldays in McAuley in the same grade. By the time I moved across the hall into Grades III and IV, we were pals. Edna's mother doted on her, a trait that Edna understood and was not averse to using to advantage. Furthermore, Edna's mother was an agent for the then California Perfume Company (later, Avon). Small wonder then, that our passionate love for cosmetics took root then and there, in the Lewis house, where Edna and I tried all the wonderful samples Mrs. Lewis had at home – perfumes, soaps, powders and lipsticks, which came

Me and my best friend Edna, about 1924.

in many fruit flavours: peach, apple and raspberry. We were especially thrilled to use the "Raspberry" lipstick. Once, when we were driving over the sand plains on our way to St. Lazare with Lyn, the boarder, we kissed him and asked, "does it taste like raspberry?"

Unlike me, Edna had a bedroom of her own, where she hung the never-to-be-forgotten wall hangings from the Pompeian cosmetics company, one especially glamorous, of Mary Pickford, seated and wearing a gown of white organdie, pondering the long-stemmed red rose in her hand. This was, for me, simply delicious: to visit Edna and discover another world, slightly too exotic for my home, where my older sister was bossy and my mother always busy or ill. In that milieu I put in my days and nights, but in Edna's home life took on a colourful flavour.

We also clipped the coupons from *True Story* magazine, addressed an envelope to some place that might as well have been on the other side of the world: California. We put our dime in the envelope, sealed it and, in a state of euphoria-like anticipation, took our letters to the post office, praying they would get to their destination, and that our request for a sample of lipstick and powder be mailed to us. We knew we were too young to be seen with make-up, but what a great way to be glamorous and with a touch of naughtiness! There was a problem, however; only the American magazines had coupons, and only a few people – older than we were – ever got their hands on one of them; and by the time we saw them some pages and coupons had been torn out. But if we promised to keep secret where we got the magazines, we could keep them long enough to read some of the remaining stories that were plain Out-of-Bounds, like: "She knew she was doing wrong" and "He said he would do right by her", or "Painful Afterthoughts." Edna said she hid her precious copy under the mattress. I never dared to take a copy home.

When the Pompeian order arrived, I was in a daze. The

3-foot long Mary Pickford was there, too. The panel hung by my bed for years but got lost in the moves from the restaurant to the Orange Hall and finally, this small cottage Dad procured through an unpaid debt.

Edna's next home was at Wilbert Jamieson's farm, and it was during my visits there – overnight and on weekends and Sunday afternoon – that I learned the difference between our ordinary table and superlative baking and cooking. Never did Mrs. Lewis serve anything that wasn't cooking at its best. My mother did nobly just getting the noon-hour dinner ready for us.

There were animals at Wilbert's farm. Though I knew nothing about horses or cows, Edna and her mother made me realise their worth; and when it came to the world of cats, Edna made it easy to understand what strange, beautiful creatures they were; she usually had more than two, sometimes five.

To be given a Sunday afternoon visit to the farm was utter joy. The big, clean barn had a swing and the barn's high, pointed roof meant you could push off till you almost touched the floor of the hayloft. Camie and Gregor Jamieson and Joan Catley were just a mile down the road, and were

Edna, Gregor, Jean and a neighbourhood friend Laverne Poole.

often there. Joan was older than the boys and her mother seemed always to need her around the house. We played together with a lightness of heart that was still childish delight, the joys of later life to not bear any comparison. When Mrs. Lewis came out the kitchen door and called us in to supper, we would wash up at the kitchen sink, mop off the good sweat (which mother always corrected me to say "perspiring profusely"), be seated, hear Grace, and launch into one of Mrs. Lewis's feasts, always a finale of pie or richly iced cake, sometimes both. We restored our energies walking me back to my home in town, about a mile away, and once in a while Gregor or Camie hitched up horse and buggy and we travelled the gravel road into town.

A picture taken at the farm on one of those idyllic afternoons is of Edna, wearing a pretty two-piece printed gingham dress, Gregor (biting his lip as the picture was snapped) and me, wearing a yellow 'jumper' dress over a white blouse – one of Mother's always great make-overs. Mother had renovated a dress, removed the sleeves and somewhere found a piece of black velvet ribbon to give some shape to my then scrawny build. (Mrs. McWilliams, a resident of McCauley, knew of our circumstances and, from time to time, gave Mother a dress or jacket she no longer wanted. They were always high class garments Mrs. McWilliams had worn when she was a secretary in Winnipeg before her husband Alex wooed her, bringing her to our town.)

Mr. Lewis had probably negotiated a deal that gave Mrs. Lewis and Edna their next home in McAuley; and now that my friend and I were a few minutes walk apart we saw each other every day and often at night. How could we have known that, following our impending move from McAuley, we were closing one girlhood area of our lives, to be regarded as our own sweet and wonderful meeting, a rooting of the friendship tree we took with us and shared all our lives?

MOVING

Upon my return from the Coles', Mother and I found boxes somewhere and packed our household belongings. Dad had arranged for a man in Rocanville who trucked to Brandon to stop and load our furniture, including the 2'x2' wooden box that held the beautiful cut glass watering set and other fancy dishes. Wherever we went, that box was special and we were careful not to drop it, even though it was wadded with torn bits of towels and sheets. When, during our time at the restaurant, the McAuley gas tank caught fire and everyone evacuated to school grounds, I carried that heavy box from where it was stored under my bed.

Mother's best friend, Mrs. Dobson, visited while we packed. She and Mother had shared a relationship in which both were experiencing difficulty. Pat and Betty said goodbye to friends and Don's constant pals said it was too bad he was going away. I had dinner at Edna's several days prior to moving.

What still touches my heart is how Mrs. Bill Stewart asked our family to have dinner with them on our last day in McAuley. She knew we had nothing, not even a decent meal left, and she served a typical fine prairie meal of meat and potatoes with wonderful gravy, and then put a bowl of something I'd never seen or tasted on the table. "This is cabbage coleslaw," she said; and to this day I taste that piquant flavour remembering her kindness to us. Mother was very quiet during that meal, and possibly I noticed it because my siblings were talkative and hungry. Mother had always cognizant of our McAuley downturn: we had come there to the first good house she'd had since her marriage and, after losing that home, our status dropped as low as it could get.

I have wondered if the job at MacLeod's in Rocanville was made available through Dad's sister Gladys, whose husband, George Laing, was the Manager of Pioneer Fruit in Brandon.

Dad's reputation had decreased with his continued bad luck; and all the travellers whose route started in Brandon would have been known to Laing. It could be they told Uncle George of Dad's predicament and that he then used his influence to help Dad find this new job.

In any case, Dad had been hired as clerk for $65 a month, with a house as part of his employment. He received an advance and was to begin July 1, 1927. At 45 years of age, Gordon Mathie was back behind someone else's counter.

CHAPTER SIX

Rocanville!

Moving to Rocanville didn't mean going from rags to riches; but it was a swing into a more secure existence. And then, surprise! The boys were terrifically interesting, my piano playing and singing were not only in demand; they brought a new dimension of pleasure as well as general approval by admiring friends and citizens.

FIRST DAY IN ROCANVILLE

We left McAuley, Manitoba, on July 15th via CPR train travel, destined for a town that, though only half an hour away, would shape our destinies for the next few decades. Mother had somehow scraped together enough money to pay our fares, probably borrowed from Mrs. Dobson or Mrs. Stewart. There was no group of well-wishers to bid us

Me, in the summer of 1927.

Godspeed and there was little excitement for the family.

I was in charge of getting Don, Pat, and Betty dressed, and packing our clothing and enough cutlery to get a meal ready. Each of us carried something: a bundle or box and one old black suitcase from Dad's days as a bon vivant. Our household furniture and other belongings went by Harry Mitchell's truck that morning.

When we got off the train in Rocanville each of us must have sensed from the upgraded station that we were on a new level of life. Mr. Masters, the station master, took pride in the grounds that included green grass, with borders of glorious dahlias and gladiola. His young daughters raced up and down the platform on tricycles, flaunting their ringlets and nice dresses.

There were few cars in Rocanville in 1927 and Dad had been there for just a couple of weeks, so it was understandable that there was no one to give us a ride from the station to our new home. Dad met us and, though he walked us to our new home, he seemed different. Now he was at his boss's beck and call; anxious to return to the store.

It was dejavu all over again: Brandon to McAuley; McAuley to Rocanville. We walked to our new home under the watchful eyes of locals. "That's Hunt's," Dad pointed out. Mr. Hunt owned the butcher shop. That's where we were to buy our meat, not from the competition – Sandy Roth.

The house Mr. McLeod provided for our family had been appropriated from one of his debtors. It sat on a full-sized lot and years before we moved in, someone had given the house a coat of rather pale green paint. The door and windowsills still held remnants of a darker green and the four steps needed bracing.

I don't remember if we approached it from the back or front. From the front it looked not too bad, though the narrow veranda floor sagged at the south side. After the living quarters in McAuley we would have been pleased with anything. Beggars we were. Choosers we were not. If Mother disliked that house – and she said that to me when we walked through the back yard – she never let anyone else hear her criticise it.

When Dad returned to the store, Mother and I applied ourselves to emptying and sorting, getting beds made and creating some order in the kitchen. I remember being very busy with an underlying excitement. By 11:20 Mother asked me to leave my work and go down to the store for food. I got bread, butter, jam, sugar and salt, oatmeal and flour and felt better as I carried those things to the house. Mother was tired out; she'd worked hard that morning. At noon she said, "Jean, tell the children to come in."

What a clear, pleasant memory I have of going to the front door, looking out at Pat and Betty playing with Merice Campbell and Mary Brownlee; Don, too, had found a friend. They were already happily settled into a new environment.

By the time Dad got home, Mother was resting. Our neighbour, Mrs. Hunt, came over and offered help if we needed it.

MacLeod's Red & White General Store

If you counted the basement, the store was two-and-a-half stories. The basement was used for storage, the ground floor held sale merchandise – groceries, shoes, dry-goods, school supplies and farm supplies like salt blocks for cattle – and the MacLeod family lived on the third floor, which, true to Mr. McLeod's Scottish background, was a real saving.

The job of clerk demanded a strong, willing worker to handle the hundred-pound-sacks of flour and sugar that farmer's wives ordered; and it needed quick, agile hands to carefully handle the produce those wives brought in to balance their household budget. Dad had those qualities and something more; he had personality, something the clerk he replaced apparently lacked. If Dad found it hard to be cheerful – as he had every right to be – no one could have detected it. His greeting and pleasantries while he put up an order with a willingness to please his customers were right at the top every minute of his working day.

Week days began at 8.30 a.m., with an hour for lunch, a ten-minute walk each way, and from Monday to Friday, shops were open to 6 p.m. Thursday afternoon off at 1 p.m., and then came Saturdays, and that meant being on tap until the last farm wife had ended her visit with friends and returned to pick up her order. It was often Dad tidied the store, swept the floors and walked home at midnight or later.

Before the disaster of Mathie & Wells, Father dressed well and in Rocanville, even after many years of bare existence, he could still be natty. On duty in the store, and as soon as he got home, he would hang his old blue weekday jacket on a hook, and then his suspenders – never a belt – were visible, holding up trousers, bought in good times, of dark blue serge.

AT HOME IN THE MCLEOD HOUSE

The main floor provided a parlour, dining room, and a closed staircase that led to the two bedrooms above. There was no hallway; the bedrooms were separated by a make-shift wall. Mother and Dad's fine bed went into the front bedroom and, beside their bed, stood a little table that once looked good – before our several moves had chipped and scratched its finish. Vividly I can hear Dad winding the old clock each night as he prepared for bed. At times Don slept on a cot in their room, sometimes downstairs.

There was room in the back bedroom for an old bureau. To hang clothing there were some wire hooks, and we had the only washstand, matching the bureau.

How would we ever have managed without the cubby hole, that space under the staircase? When something couldn't be found it was usual to look through the jumble of things stuffed inside. Mother had never done housework before her marriage; she probably did reasonably well before she had any baby, and early on after that, when there was some household help.

There wasn't another piano as gracefully stylish as Mother's Matthews; and if we had nothing else of quality, our small parlour created a sense of style that no drab surroundings could lessen. Beyond that, all that remained of the good furniture (the rest sold out of dire need) were two couches and one small table, its top cut like a 3-leaf clover, with brass beading around the edges. (Rene later cut one leaf from it and took the table to her Beauty shop).

The cut glass water set adorned the top of the buffet, and for quite a few years a decanter also rested there. Once, when I admired the etching on it and its stopper, Mother said, "That was always on our buffet at home when I was growing up; and," she added, "it was never empty."

An old, second-hand heater was brought into the dining room for warmth when winter made it necessary to add to the heat from the small cook stove in the kitchen.

A doorway separated the dining room from the kitchen, the room that saw more activity than any other part of the house. The usual rough table and a couple of unmatched, worn chairs sat next to the north wall. The table, purchased for a couple of dollars, never wore a tablecloth, just the usual oilcloth that could be wiped clean and, when making breakfast, the wood surface was just fine. Its one drawer held cutlery, small tools, stray pencils, shoe-laces and bits of cardboard.

Ours was the last house on that block; and a 2' x 4' window in the kitchen brought daylight into the room as well as a wide view of the old barn in Hunt's yard which sat far back from their house, probably because his work as a butcher meant that the decrepit Ford he used to transport slaughtered animals held odours his housekeeper wife disdained.

Every house had a pantry, even the shoddy, shabby old

MacLeod house. Some thoughtful person, probably a carpenter, had taken one corner of the kitchen, walled off four square feet and installed shelving, leaving the rest of the kitchen with a modified "L" floor space and creating an alcove for the sink and water pail. The old grey water pail had to be kept full from our neighbour Hudson's or Scott's pump, and we used the dipper more for ladling than for drinking, because one of Mother's rules was to drink from your own glass, and the table was never set without a full jug of water and glasses.

Perhaps no other item revealed so metaphorically how our family functioned as the "roller-towel" that hung on the west wall, drab and seemingly always dirty. Our only real, close contact with each other took place in the kitchen. Each of us lived our separate lives, with little parental control, but each of us took a grab at the roller towel created by Mother from striped towelling, ends sewn together. It rolled quickly when grabbed by wet hands in search of a clean, dry space. Roller towelling didn't come with matching face-cloths and if other families had wash cloths, well and good; ours had disappeared in the years since there was barely money enough to buy a towel let alone a wash cloth.

The roller towel was still quivering from Dad's quick face-and-hand-wash when the rest of us joined him in the kitchen each morning. The towel never froze, even when it was -40 outside, but it was cold enough to cause wishful thinking as you swung it, rattling, over the wooden roller, rubbing yourself awake with its roughness. Dad never had any competition in getting the old stove red hot in minutes. By that time, the towel was beyond any sense of warmth or dryness. It hung as if ashamed of itself, sodden and soiled.

Calendars were free, so we always had at least one, displayed on nails someone hammered into the drab, unpainted wall here and there (we didn't have money for Kalsomine), giving us a small measure of artistry.

Breakfast was eaten in the kitchen, sometimes at the table, school mornings by the stove. Whoever got up first, scrambled outside for the bottle of milk from Park's farm, lucky enough to have the taste of cream from the top of the bottle for cereal. Porridge was a mainstay, cheaper than packaged cereals. One exception was Shredded Wheat, the biscuit layers separated by a cardboard, which could be cut and shaped to fit in the sole of a shoe that showed a hole. Dad had to wear boots because he was on his feet from morning to night, and we kids had to have shoes for school, so Mother, whose shoes were all old and worn, was glad to make use of the little cardboard dividers that needed only a bit of shaping.

1927

Dearest Pal, Edna:

Gosh. This town is so different. Mother and I have been trying to get settled but she is still unable to do much and that's why you haven't heard from me sooner. There's one nice thing about the change: Dad works in a nice general store so we can get shoes and dry goods as well as groceries there. That's a pleasant change. You know how bad things were for the last five years. We kids all went to Sunday School on the first Sunday we were here and we got some stares when we sang. You should see the church here! It's much bigger and the choir can meet before the service in a room of their own. And the organ! It is something else.

My younger sisters and brother have made friends right away, and a few of the girls my age have been talking to me – mostly asking questions. Seems strange, here in this town where I don't know anyone. It was so nice to walk over to your home, at any time, knowing your Mother would invite me to stay to eat; and of course I did.

I've been downtown to the post office for the mail but it's not a friendly place like McAuley. Get this, Edna, a cranky old woman is POST MISTRESS. A woman! People waiting for her and her assistant to sort the mail start yakking – same as ever – but gee, this old dame opens the wicket and lays down the law! "If you don't quieten down," she shouts, "I'll clear the place out!" Slam, bang! She closes the wicket. I'm too new to this bunch to make any move but the other girls giggle and a couple of guys warble and make faces. The store owners look in and leave. They have their own Post Box; I don't know any of them except Mr. MacLeod, my Dad's boss. I look at him and say hello but he's surprised and just looks at me. This town is bigger than dear old McAuley. I've seen a lot more gals and guys; some give me a friendly look and I'm grateful for that. Oh well, when school starts it'll be different. Oh gosh, I miss you!

Excuse the ink blotch. Next letter I'll use some new pen nibs. Must dash and run to the station with this. Good thing my Uncle Will is baggage man and will see that this letter will get into the right mail sack.

It would be great if you could come for a visit. CPR fare from McAuley to Rocanville is 35 cents; or if you are working on the telephone switchboard, the local phone office will send a runner for 25 cents. Please try to come soon; I could sure use a chinwag with you, asap. Love and kisses, your lonesome pal.

P.S. Don't forget to look at what's printed on the back of the envelope: SWAK (sealed with a kiss).

FRANK SCOTT, THE GOOD LOOKER

Until that day in August 1927, my reaction to boys was only mildly exciting; but on that prairie summer afternoon, walking from home to downtown, there he was, this young god, pushing the lawnmower, frowning at the cull blades and thick withering grass, looking neither right nor left. Oblivious to my slowed pace in hopes he'd take his eyes off the grass, and give me the 'once over'. He just pushed and dragged the mower.

Friends we'd made since moving to Rocanville had informed us of the town's Who's Who, so it wasn't difficult to place the Scott family in the hierarchy. Mr. Scott was a partner with John Barrett in the better of the two general stores, and the Scott house, with its three and one half stories and broad lawns on either side, dominated the local scene. The Scott family had just returned from a month at 'the lake', then named Carlyle, so that's why the grass required all Frank's attention. Mr. Scott, widowed in 1921, had married again and now, Frank and his sisters, Marjorie and Sheila, had a stepbrother.

"...Oh boy, Edna", I wrote, "you should see some of the sheiks; they are nifty and good dancers and I'm singing "Lay My Head Beneath A Rose" this Friday night at a concert. Rene is playing for me. Wish me luck, kiddo."

EARLY 1928

Dear Edna: I know you've been waiting to hear about Christmas in this place. Well, kiddo, I guess I'll never get over the concert we always had in McAuley and it's because that one was for the whole town and countryside and in this town is just for the church. I mean the United Church. There's a little Anglican Church here, too, and a Catholic miles away, in a little area called St. Marthe but only one Rocanville family goes there.

The CPR supplies the evergreen tree to the station agent and it's loaned to the church for the Christmas concert. I had plenty of singing, too, as a soloist and with the choir; but oh, Edna, it was nothing like the dandy songs our whole school sang to open and close the Christmas Tree Concert in McAuley, where you are and I am not.

Well, here's something nice to tell you: When a guy asks you if he can carry your skates home after the night's skating you know he's got something in mind. And this swell-looking guy has eased out the guy who lives next door. His name is Frank Scott and he's just so handsome! And he's one grade ahead of me at school. Guys dress up more for school here, too, and so do we femmes. Now that my Dad works at a general store I'm getting some really nice clothes and Mom keeps that Singer sewing machine humming with some really pretty things. She's even designed and made an entire outfit for me; yeah! A winter coat with fake fur trimming and a natty little cloche-type hat to match. It's considered smart to leave the top two buckles of your overshoes undone, and with my skinny legs that's OK with me. Can't take time to tell you anymore right now, but next time I'll give you a picture of what the dances are like here. Oh, how I miss the old IOOF hall and the Grist orchestra...!

THE KITCHEN STOVE

The icy winds of winter made it necessary to protect the back door where someone had thoughtfully added a little shed, big enough to hold the washing machine and just enough room for two to cuddle for a few minutes before saying Goodnight. Some nights were too cold, and it was OK to ask the boy friend into the kitchen, hoping the fire in the beat-up cook stove hadn't fallen through the grates. Mother never had a good stove like most women. They had big, black and chrome "ranges" with at least four stovetop plates, a warming oven with chrome-trimmed closing cover, a copper hot water reservoir, a fancy chrome shelf on the left side and a fine oven.

Our oven door had been harshly used, probably by some

heavy-footed male warming his galoshes, or loading it with damp wood. If anyone else had a broken oven door, I never saw it, and for as long as our family stayed together, when we wanted to warm our frost-bitten toes, we took a piece of wood and propped the door open. Many's the past midnight I sat there until the fire fell through the burnt out grates, sometimes with company, and one coal-oil lamp over on the kitchen table. Mother always called softly when she heard the back door to the kitchen letting us in. "That you, Jean?", and I'd answer at the foot of the stairs, also quietly, "It's me, Mom".

There were times when our greeting was omitted. The year I played the female lead role in "Baby Mine" (a Samuel French, New York play!), we took our production to several out-of-town platforms; and the night we played across the valley in Spy Hill, I didn't get home until after 2.00 a.m. After the performance, there was a dance for which I'd played piano.

That night, as she always did, Mother had put an iron in the middle of the stove, covered it with the old black cake pan,

Showing off in front of the Edna's house.

leaving it for me to warm my bed. There was still enough heat in the iron that it needed a piece of towel wrapped around it, but in my state of exhaustion I didn't feel the iron burning the skin of my right shin, where it left its mark for the rest of my life.

There was another thing about that stove and its place in our family life. If someone came in the back door and slammed it and the cake you put together was in the oven, not only would the cake fall, the oven door would leave its moorings and fall to the floor. A family joke we enjoyed for years after was when, having warned brother Don there was a cake in the oven, and he affected fear, and crept through the kitchen into the dining room, whispering, "Don't make a noise. Jeannie has a cake in the oven."

LETTER TO EDNA 1928

It's about time I picked up my pen, wiped the nib (this one isn't as scratchy as the previous one) and let you know how things are going. The school principal is a man; and listen to this: he teaches French! We have lessons from a book that I thought was LEE PREIMIER PASS! Dumb kid from the sticks, huh? It is pronounced 'luh prem-yer paw.' Get it? Makes me wish I'd listened to those French boys we danced with in McAuley. Mr. Hoffer's pronunciation is so cute when he shows us how to say, for example, window in French: "fen-tetre". Wait till we have a visit and I'll try my French on you, especially since you told me those guys from St. Lazare are squiring you McAuley flappers. Ooo la la!

This town is so different from little old McAuley; and you can sense the snootiness about it. Being so new, I know most of my schoolmates have lived here quite a while, so I don't butt in when they brag about their family history. There's one place where I shine and that's wherever there's singing. Mr. Schwanze, the church choir leader, has to be careful that he doesn't offend when he leaves out all those sopranos and picks me to do the solo. When one of them complained about not being asked, the organist said, "Jean does it so well because she makes it sound easy." Don't mind telling you that family of that other jealous soprano thinks they're the cat's meow!

I sure was knocked for a loop when I found out that we had to go outside school to use the toilet. After the nice warm steam heat and flush toilets in Rutherton School, this was a let-down: just an old wood two-holer! Have to say, though, that the boys here are spiffy! This school goes to Grade XII, so they're older and most of them townspeople, though there are a couple of handsome farm guys, too.

RELATIONSHIPS WITH THE OPPOSITE SEX

The process of my physical and mental development was a heady time. Sexual attraction overtook reasonable thinking. It felt good, especially since, in my case, there was no parental control. A relationship with a male high school student was real and assuring of self-importance; it coloured life with excitement, newness and adventure. The mores of the day included a lot of "don'ts" and we cruised out of line for the sheer pleasure of being naughty.

Until our family moved from McAuley to Rocanville, I easily navigated relationships with the opposite sex. The dances from age eleven on were innocent of anything to worry about. Only if you weren't asked for every dance would you feel any insecurity; and since neither of my parents attended the dances as some parents did, I was on my own. It was a time of healthy, carefree living. No one could have convinced me or my girl friend that it was an era that, in later life, would seem more like an old fairy-tale. The world of school, Sunday

School, church and the 'How-do-you-do Club' *couldn't* change, *couldn't* be lost forever because you didn't want to lose anything of it, even though you longed at times to be grownup.

At 15, in a new town, life's pace quickened.

I don't suppose I was different from other children in wishing...wishing for nice things to happen, like hoping Mother would comfort me when I felt physical pain. Or wondering if Father would ever say more than, "Just do it like a good little girl." I longed for and wondered about that quite a lot.

That wishing and longing for recognition from my parents that I'd experienced as a child never went away. Quite the opposite, it grew stronger. When the indistinct line between childhood and puberty arrived, the child in me was unaware of how strong this desire had become; and by that time, the lively, headstrong, selfish young woman I'd become was guided by a strong force inside. I felt its pull in anything that required feeling, whether it was the glorious rhythm and sounds of music, getting top marks at school, or winning the admiration of people – old and young, male or female. Ahhh, the admiration of boys! That made everything blissful, terribly exciting and even a bit frightening.

Mother did give a mild word of caution occasionally and too late. Mother was 'old hat' in every way; particularly her own girlhood was directly opposite to this daughter's. Mother respected her parents as I, Dorothy Jean, never did. Though I loved Mother and was on good terms with her, we weren't confidants; that left me to follow wherever my wishing and yearning beckoned.

Actually, I thought this was fine. I was free to flaunt my natural sexiness, flirt with the boys who gave me the slightest come-on, and make my own decisions. Dad disapproved through Mother, but there was no real communication between them; and because he saw how well I was appreciated by those who listened to my fine voice, if he had any hope of directing me, it was far too late for him to advise, let alone order. I was a free-thinking, free-living, and gifted, clever, attractive female.

Another, more serious, friend wrote in the ubiquitous autograph album: *"The future lies before you like a path on fallen snow; Be careful how you tread it, for every step will show."*

At 15, I leapt into that untrod path like a new-born gazelle, pleased at the flurries I made when I dashed from one exciting moment to the next with a natural exuberance and vigour. I loved how my energy affected my friends or foes. If Mother offered a mild remonstrance, it didn't even go in one ear or slow my vivaciousness; and this despite our near-poverty situation.

It was due to Mother's special talent with her sewing machine that I developed such a wonderful confidence. Other girls ordered from Eaton's and Simpson's catalogues; but no one wore such pretty dresses for school or dances, and no one ever had a winter coat, designed by Jean and completed with a one-of-a-kind chapeau. It was this that held Mother and me together: the fine style and finishing of everything she did and the compliments I brought back to her bridged the otherwise open space between us.

Dad Turns Pentecostal

In McAuley, our family had attended church as a family before our fortune collapsed. In Rocanville, Dad, who had a beautiful tenor, didn't attend a church. In Rocanville he was just a clerk, an employee of Mr. McLeod – a leader in the church where we kids attended Sunday School. Our parents had a lot of pride; they had started out with everything in McAuley, then lost it, but not before they'd established a reputation and were accepted by the community. In Rocanville, they were poor.

My mother grew up in the Anglican church; Mother loved

the liturgy, and whenever she heard the phrase, "Father, Son and Holy Ghost", she genuflected. There was no Anglican church in Rocanville, and since it was beneath Dad's integrity and dignity to attend the United Church where he was thought of as 'poor old Mathie', he joined the Pentecostals. In other words, Dad became a Pentecostal by default. Pentecostals were disciples of Amy Semple McPherson; and in Rocanville, it was Mrs. Strong and her daughters who started Pentecostal meetings in the basement of the Farmer's Building, a beautiful three storey, red brick building in town. Mrs. Strong was glad to have Dad join a group that included another 'saved man', Sid Frost. Though Dad perhaps wasn't completely satisfied, he took it on. Once, when he told a family friend that "I've been to the Pentecostal church where we believe we must be born-again," she replied, "Oh Gordon; we must live our faith by example, not by being saved!"

Everybody I knew went to Sunday School, church, then an evening service and afterwards, went out to Park's or somewhere to smooch. A few times my friends and I attended the Pentecostal service. The music was something else! The Pentecostal minister's lovely daughter, Audrey, played piano; she could improvise a hymn, and the other older daughter had hair that made her look like Mary Pickford; all the women wore long white dresses. What I thought was wonderful for my mother, who never had a sister, was when Dad invited the minister and his wife for dinner. It was a bitterly cold day, and guests had to dig their way through deep snow to get to the house. As the back door opened, this woman called out "Hello Sister" to my mother in a warm voice. My mother had never been called Sister before; and I could see that this was one little starry moment in my mother's life – that small, but friendly, greeting. I knew she was touched; even so, I was infuriated; I felt the Pentecostals were competing. Our minister pondered that he hadn't done something right that these people started this other church. There were never more than up to fifty, mostly thirty-five or so, with a membership of perhaps two dozen. Mrs. Strong was married to one of the well-to-do citizens who didn't attend. Some of the boys from town, including, at first, Frank, made fun of the group. When they attended a service and sat in the back row making little comments, Mrs. Strong brought in 'little Miltie', Mr. Milton Hyde, the town policeman. He looked at the rowdy boys and said, "I have to warn you; with my authority: Your behaviour is improper and cannot continue. Either you behave, or leave!"

GOING STEADY WITH FRANK BALDWIN SCOTT

1928. The heady atmosphere of Rocanville to this fifteen-year-old secret reader of *True Story Romances* left me breathlessly excited when I had a 'steady' who, in my opinion, was terribly good-looking. Sauntering down the board sidewalk towards home, I'd hear his signal, a soft whistling of, "My Blue Heaven: When whippoorwills call. Ta tata ta ta..." followed by my answering with the second line: "and evening is nigh; Ta tata ta ta...". How could we have known that, forty years later, when it was sung at our wedding, the song would still be popular!

Frank & Jean, going steady!

Sunday afternoons were special. In the morning both of us attended St. Paul's United Church Sunday School; I was in Mrs. Rook's class, Frank in Mr. Rook's. We both played in the only Sunday School orchestra ever to perform there and both sang in the senior choir: I sang soprano, Frank sang bass. That left Sunday after church for a bit of smooching, unless, of course, Mrs. Rook or someone else hosted a modest party in town; or we all piled into a couple of cars and roared to the Park's home a mile out of town where, in spite of thirteen children in that family, there was no lack of marvellous food whenever our gaggle of kids showed up. We'd done well by the hymns at church service, now we could let off steam with other songs like, "Five foot two, eyes of Blue, but oh, what those five feet could do! Has anybody seen my gal? Yeah!"

We sang in harmony, since we all read music, and better harmony has never filled my ears since those impromptu concerts when we shook the rafters with: "If you were the only girl in the world and I was the only boy, nothing else would matter in the world today...I would say such wonderful things to you, there would be such wonderful things to do...." We girls and guys stood close as we poured rich young voices into every song. You knew your paramour got the message if he gave you a surreptitious pinch when the song reached its heart-thumping finale.

In the spring of 1928 Frank struck a deal with his father: he would do his share of work in the garden if he could have the family Chevrolet on Sunday afternoon. About two o'clock every Sunday afternoon, the Chevy would make its peculiar chug-a chug-a chug sound in front of our house and away we'd go. As long as we were home for dinner we were free for a couple of hours to get out of town onto the gravel highway and head for either Moosomin or McAuley.

Frank always looked well-dressed; and small wonder. The Barrett and Scott General Store, owned by his father, had a separate men's clothing section that included farm work or dress style. When two-tone shoes were 'in', Frank's brown and tan oxfords were very smart, balancing nicely with his light wool suit; but it was the way he wore a well-crafted Fedora hat, its brim trimmed with grosgrain ribbon, that attracted me. I'd noticed this before we went steady. Walking down Main Street one day, I saw and watched him across the street, walking in the slow, lazy gait he affected, hands in both pockets of his jacket and head topped with that grey Fedora. He was the very epitome of what every young man ought to look like!

Though the United Church Young People's Society provided good times both in the church basement and even better ones in various homes, it was the Friday night dances that were the peak of our pleasure. The IOOF hall had a platform for an orchestra and a reasonably good floor. Women, young or older, sat on benches around the walls, while the men stood near the hall entrance. Foxtrot, polka, or a waltz? When the orchestra began to play you knew immediately; and the males fanned out towards their choice for each dance. Oh, the sighs of pleasure that followed an announcement that "the next dance will be the Moonlight Waltz!" And, indeed, a moon shone overhead, courtesy of the decorating committee who had fashioned one by cutting a crescent moon-shape out of a shoebox, covered the hole with orange crepe paper, and tucked a light bulb inside. When all other lights in the hall were turned off, partners danced, cheek-to-cheek, under a make-believe moon. It was magic!

We all knew that good things must come to an end, yet we were subdued when the orchestra leader announced the last number, a waltz: "Home Sweet Home". Arms locked with your own Fred Astaire, everyone found her coat on the small, off-stage row, all the while humming "Walkin' my baby back home". With pleasure for the night, and fondness for the partner, we left the hall, ready to saunter down Main Street to Happy Young's Chinese restaurant, for a midnight lunch break, where Frank, unfailingly, ordered Boston Cream pie for thirty-five cents and paid for my standing order for a Denver sandwich.

MATHIES IN 1929 (Kodak camera picture, probably taken by Pat's friend Edith Hunt)

There we are, our entire family, and it's the only picture that ever caught Mother and Dad and each of their offspring, including my sister Rene, over to the right, giving her baby daughter Rosanne her bottle. Rene hadn't wanted to participate in the family photo.

It's a Sunday afternoon. Dad has this day at home and we can have a picture taken by our neighbour. Good. I am still wearing my good black crepe dress. My siblings played with friends nearby and Mother felt too unwell to be in the picture. She always wanted each of us to look nice, and had a good deal of self respect. When this picture was taken she

Family photo 1929. Rene is hiding in the back with her baby.

116

hadn't had her hair washed. "Hair," she often reminded her daughters, "is a woman's crowning glory." In a prairie town, mid-summer 1929, bath water and hair washing waited for the rain barrel to provide soft water and if it didn't, hard water turned soap into curds. An occasion like this, to have a family portrait, couldn't be ignored, so I coaxed Mother to put on her one good dress, a printed cotton of orange, beige and brown. Don found a clean shirt, while both Pat and Betty happily posed in tidy looking cotton dresses, Pat adding a necklace and Betty cuddling a doll. My dress was stylish, its hem of diamond shaped embroidered black crepe, bought through MacLeod's store, which was unusual. I wore a necklace and, visible on my third finger left hand, the fake diamond ring, from Woolworth's 5, 10 & 15 cent store in Regina, given in troth to me by Frank Scott, my boyfriend. True to form, Dad was top and centre, wearing a Sunday shirt with braces, holding his ever-present pipe and looking good in his old but stylish straw boater.

When this family picture was taken, the MacLeod house had been treated to a coat of stucco. Store owners then had to collect debts in a variety of ways, and a family in nearby Spy Hill owed a sum of money to MacLeod's store, long overdue. With a trade in cement, they were reined in and asked to use their professional stock-in-trade and reduce their debt by giving this old, unpainted structure a facelift. They finished the house and gave us a back-door step, but refused anything more when asked if we could have a cement walk from our front door to the board sidewalk.

What might have been lawn was left to dry up, with only tufts of grass that showed dry brown earth where we created paths both front and back and to the ubiquitous backhouse. A few yards of green grass sprouted along the south foundation, and it was there that Mother sat sometimes talking with her friend and neighbour, Mrs. Cline. Both Mother and Mrs. Cline were lady-like women; neither was given to small talk. Mother maintained her dignity and self-respect at all times in spite of obvious economic circumstances; and it's probable that their friendship was based on an unspoken understanding of each other's day-to-day coping. Mrs. Cline's husband was a veterinarian and a good one, so everyone said; but it was also opined that he too often 'fell off the wagon'. The picture still vivid for me is of those two good women, seated on the cool green grass, chatting, with now and then having something humorous to laugh about.

Not seen, but providing something to pose on, are the worn wooden steps that led onto the veranda. Most verandas had neat picket borders, but Mother's love of plants meant tin cans or clay pots with greenery; and she actually got climbing ivy to grow and wend its way up the supporting pole to the right of the posers.

But the McLeod House in this photo wouldn't be our home much longer.

FRANK B. SCOTT - AFTER BECOMING MR. SCOTT THE TEACHER

Frank finished teacher training in Regina, Saskatchewan in the spring of 1930. After pocketing his certificate, paying the final month's board and bidding his boarding-house roommate of the past year "So long" and "Good Luck!", Frank caught the CPR train to Moosomin where his father met him and the two drove the eight-mile gravel stretch of No. 8 Highway back to Rocanville. Years later, Frank remembered how he'd expected a warm handshake and congratulations from his father, and how disappointed he was when, instead, his father only patted him on the shoulder and said, "You're home again." The elder Mr. Scott was not unfeeling; he merely acted in the manner of his day.

Sometime In Late Fall, 1931

We moved from the McLeod house after Dad was fired; apparently, Dad had repeated some gossip about Mr. McLeod which somehow found its way back to Dad's employer; and that's why he was fired. At first we lived in a cottage across from the Scott house, but had to move from there when its owner, Dan Reavie, sold it. Then we moved into the 'Roth house', named after its owner, the butcher, Sandy Roth who had moved to Vancouver. Dad set up another 'grocery' in a vacant store and it really seemed that there was some light at the end of a darkening tunnel. The following story reveals his mood!

It is Sunday morning, the day Dad gives himself a careful shave. He sets a mirror on the dining room table, propped up with a book or a dish – whatever he could find. The razor strap, a lifelong possession that always hung from a hook or nail either in the kitchen or bedroom, now hung on a doorknob and, holding the strap in one hand and the razor in the other, he slowly and methodically sharpens the razor. Next he fills the kettle with water, gets a brisk fire going, and when the water is hot, he pours the old enamel washbasin half full. Now it's time to lather his face. With a towel over one shoulder, he sits down and begins his careful ritual.

Who knows what we kids thought on that Sunday morning as Dad sat at the dining room table, razor in hand, chin well lathered? We were children and behaved as such, one of us initiating a game of teasing and chasing. Don, Pat, and I were the worst, racing around the table till we bumped into it. "If you kids don't stop, I'm going to cut my throat and throw my head in the ash heap," Dad said, as the mirror fell over. "And then I'll be hung for murder!" We stopped, and began to laugh at the outrageousness of his statement – a laugh that still returns whenever we recall the incident.

If he was anything, Dad was a talker. After Rory McLeod had fired him, Dad used his wits to sell an idea to a few men whom he knew had some spare money. His pitch was this: lend me some money, about $50.00, and I can set up my own business. You can get your money back in no time, in the form of groceries you or your wife will buy from me.

We were still living in the MacLeod house when I'd overheard such a conversation Dad had one evening with Guard Strong, one of the community's well-to-do farmers. Just one doorway from the MacLeod store there was a vacancy. It was rather small in comparison with MacLeod's General Store, but it held room for two counters, with room between them for boxes tipped to show produce as well as Dad's hoped-for clientele. "When you lose a job, you got to make one, eh?" he said cheerily when asked how this one might go. But did he ever consider Mother's financial status when he made such statements, about her never having any cash?

Our house was run the same as always: food enough to eat, coal delivered for the furnace in the good basement; we were comfortable enough. I was 18, Don 14, Pat 12, and little, quiet Betty just 10. Our home looked reasonably decent because, again, the elegant piano stood in the parlour area, along with a cloverleaf table that held Mother's still attractive sword fern and our oak dining suite, including the matching buffet with its oval mirror and linen drawer that, by now, held little except, as always, Mother's old, empty grey purse.

"Do you remember that Mother never had a dollar in that purse all the time it lay there?" Patricia recalled years later.

Of course I remember! How could I ever forget that time, especially how hard it was for Mother, whose empty purse I tried to fill one April 16th, on her fiftieth birthday. Dad was away and I worked in the store alone. The cash drawer held fifty dollars and I took out twenty-five, wrapped it and presented it, inside a poetic card to Mother with, "You deserve this." When Dad returned and discovered what I'd done, he demanded she return the money; and she did.

That Mother could use something new was evident.

My brother Don belonged to the Boy Scouts, led by the Anglican parson. Don had a fine voice. I shall never forget him walking through the back door singing, "There was a bee-I-ee-I-ee..." and other rousing ditties he learned at Scouts.

One day, Don happily announced an upcoming banquet and said, "Every Scout is to chaperone his Mother to the church basement." He obviously looked forward to it. Mother said nothing; and I should have been ready for her response when I said I was pleased she and Don would attend. She didn't reply with bitterness, exactly; but there was an edge of resignation. I persisted. "Don will be so happy to have you there," I said again and again. "And isn't it nice that the Anglican minister got Don interested in going to Scouts and singing, too?"

"I've made up mind, Jean; I'm not going," she replied quietly. Tonelessly. Though she didn't say so, there was the reality of her wardrobe. The only thing she could have worn that night would have been an old black skirt, something she'd likely 'made over' from the yearly box of clothes relatives sent us. Her only blouse was made of some cheap yellowish silk, certainly not her choice of colour or fabric; and probably because there wasn't enough material, the pattern fell far short of looking good, so different from all the beautiful things she turned out for me. Her only pair of black oxfords was beyond any improvement with shoe polish; and her shoes would be noticed as she descended the steps into the lower hall of the church where guests sat at tables. Mother didn't wear earrings, and her hair was grey and straight, brushed back softly from her face with a little bun at the nape of her neck.

Furthermore, that year's guest speaker was Dr. Monroe, the provincial Minister of Health. A couple of years prior to the Scout's banquet, when we were still living in the McLeod house, he had come to see Mother. We had hoped he would prescribe some new treatment for Mother's constant haemorrhaging, but he only repeated what we'd been told by previous doctors: "the fibroid tumours are the sole cause of her bleeding. There is nothing I can do; only surgery will fix it."

Did Mother perhaps wish to avoid being seen not only by good citizens like Mrs Barrett and other well-dressed women, but Dr. Monroe as well? At the time, right up to the night of the affair, I kept asking her to "please go." Only years later, did I understand Mother's reluctance; her wish to not be seen by women dressed in their finery; Rocanville's social register was even more stratified than in McAuley! And, since Dad no longer worked at the MacLeod Store, Mother had no evening apparel to wear.

Did we ever discuss it? Did I ever try again to coax Mother to attend another special Rocanville event? If so, I can't recall.

And while the business flourished, the state of Mother's health took a toll...and I fell in and out of love....

BOB BARNES

Bob Barnes played the piano! (I did too, in 'The Melody Four', a usual small town dance band that included Warren Rook as leader, Blake Schwanze, and Ted Hunt on clarinet.) Not only that, Bob was the handsomest member of his band. From the first time he smiled back at me from the platform where he performed with the Fraser MacPherson dance orchestra, I was in love. This should have been the nicest thing that could happen except for the fact that I was dating Paul DeCorby for the past few months. Paul was more than a little fond of me. I liked him a lot, not only for his French good looks and personal style, but also for his generosity in taking we scatterbrained flappers wherever we asked to go, even sitting on the sidelines as we danced the night away.

On this night when the orchestra broke for the usual midnight lunch hour, Paul and I strolled down the street. There was a new store under construction, and we sat on the saw-horses. We were quiet for a few moments, and then Paul said in a poignant tone, "I love you, Jean". If he'd said it a few hours earlier, I might have responded with some ardour, though I didn't want to marry him; but now, when his declaration demanded a response, I was in another place, with Bob Barnes giving me heart bumps.

"Remember, Jean; always be a lady"; Mother's words came to mind. I've never wanted to hurt people and that scene would have been sweet and lovely if I'd been able to accept his proposal. I couldn't. Not wanting to confess I was crazy about the good-looking piano player I'd just met, I responded with a weak, "Paul, I do care about you; but let's leave it at that." His response was gentle, dignified and uttered quietly. "For now, Jean," he said in his French accent. I felt a small sense of relief and a larger craving to get Bob Barnes near enough to touch.

When I returned to the hall, Bob Barnes asked me to dance. It was heavenly! Afterwards, he wrote his address on a tiny piece of paper, and I told him I'd be in McAuley when the orchestra was scheduled to play there. In his delightful, educated British manner and my impetuous Canadian we

Me and Bob Barnes, 1931.

123

entered a heady romance.

"You have no idea how pleased I was to receive your letter...and we will make good use of the time when Fraser McPherson gives me a few minutes off...and I'll see you at the end of the dance for certain..." he wrote in fine handwriting in his first letter. I had, of course, written him immediately! It was love as I'd never believed it could be!

Now, I could brag to my Rocanville girlfriends. They all knew how mortified I'd been when Frank Scott jilted me. "You ought to see Bob! He's gorgeous...," I raved; and they listened with wide-eyed curiosity. Mother understood and even seemed pleased that my new boyfriend was British. Bob had sought his fortune in Canada, but had arrived when the Great Depression swept through everyone's life; making a living was a perpetual challenge for him. He played with the orchestra and did bits of office work for a lawyer; from time to time, he got a "remittance" from his family in England.

When September came, I expected to return to school. It was a shock when Mother told me I couldn't because there was no money for anything. My only earning power was in planning for the occasional dance and perhaps working in McLeod's store when there was a sale. It should have been a time to leave Rocanville, head for Regina or Winnipeg and find work. But Bob Barnes was on my mind, day in and day out. I dithered. I spent a week at a time with him, staying at the MacPherson home, or at his boarding house. Full of life, lots of energy and good looks, brains to burn, but completely rejected, I lost those few months of a time when my energies should have been geared to productivity; and I paid for that dearly, later, when Frank Scott returned and I threw Bob over for a reason I hate to admit: Frank had a job as teacher and Bob was as poor as the proverbial church mouse. Bob was so broken up when I chose Frank over him that he drank his sorrows away until good friends put him on a train and boat back to England and I never heard from again.

WOMEN'S WEAR

It was surprising when Mr. Dave Shaw opened a Ladies Wear store in the vacant space next to the little store Dad was running at the time. Entrepreneurs were rare; the Depression was in its early mean stages; yet Dave Shaw, son-in-law to a local widow with 'means', rented space, brought in dresses, shoes and some lingerie and asked if I would work for him.

This time it wasn't just the experience in groceries that came to my rescue. I had inherited Mother's extraordinary taste for style; and Mr. Shaw was generous in his compliments on my ability to sell, particularly because the great twice-yearly catalogues from Eaton's and Simpson's were tough competition. Then the Victoria hospital notified me that I could commence training August 18, and to Mr. Shaw's regret and not a little of my own, I gave notice. That was my first and only job of that kind.

LATE SPRING 1931

Dear Friend Edna:

I know that "dear friend" sounds serious; well, it is. You know I had such hopes that when Frank came home from Normal School and then got hired to teach, we might continue with our romance and even get married sometime. Might as well give you the bad news: there IS no romance, Edna. I have to admit I'm feeling pretty bad. I'll try to get down to see you and give you all the unhappy "dirty details", as we say. Being a teacher gave Frank quite a boost in status and popularity with the girls. Yep. We didn't call it quits, our romance just faded away. The good news is that I've been accepted by the Victoria hospital in Winnipeg, to start August 18, I'll have a couple of days visit with you before I go.

It was true. After a brief reunion following his return from Normal School, Frank and I had gone our separate ways. I was living at home, not attending school, looking after household tasks as Mother was in bed most of the time and my siblings needed looking after.

There was no boyfriend in my life in the summer of 1931. Just a few months earlier I had jilted the nice English chap, Bob Barnes; and though I still ached for a relationship to resume with Frank Scott, he had established himself as a 'Don Juan' and there were plenty of young women in Rocanville who made it clear to him that he was just what they wanted. The two daughters of the post office owner, in particular, made a play for Frank; and he liked this new adulation, for here he was, Frank Scott the teacher, about to begin a job in a nearby Finnish colony. It was unusual to get a job that quickly, in fact, two of Edna's friends who had teaching jobs, received no salary; their board was their pay. But Mr. Scott had clout and Frank's job awaited him.

I was crushed when Frank turned away from me. While he'd been away, he'd written nice letters; and I wore the 15 cent Woolworth ring and really thought we'd get married. We were having sex and you didn't have sex unless you thought you'd eventually get married.

July 1, 1931 was The Day to go to Moosomin for their Annual Sports Day. Moosomin, on the Main Line of the CPR, was to us an exciting town, bigger than Rocanville; it had a nicer Dance Hall and church, so I found it more than a little disappointing that I had no boyfriend or anyone else to bum a ride to get to Moosomin. Pat, now 14, had entered into a new phase, going to dances and enjoying male attention, so she was especially keen to go to Moosomin July 1st. She convinced me to walk over to Shelton's, a British family who had one son, and ask if we could catch a ride. Sheltons were well enough off to have a touring car, since he had a steady job on the CPR Section crew maintaining the tracks. My question surprised Mrs. Shelton; was I rude? I realized we'd had no contact previously. She hesitated, looked around and asked Mr. Shelton, and when he said quietly it would be possible, Mrs. Shelton smiled and said they would be leaving in half an hour. I ran home, told Pat, we found some duds, dressed, put on a little make-up and arrived at Shelton's in time.

Upon our arrival at Moosomin, Pat went her way and I was lucky enough to meet an admirer who asked me to stay for the dance and be his girl. I wore an ankle-length, soft green voile dress Mother had sewn. To the simple pattern Mother sewed a long, 4' deep flounce that went from my shoulders to below the knee like a long apron, back and front. It looked pretty and the voluminous skirt made it swell for dancing. Pat got home somehow, and Bill Rust, who I'd dated occasionally since Frank gave me the cold shoulder, got a car and took me home.

But now there was no other big event until Rocanville's Sports Day, three weeks away! Life in a small town on the Saskatchewan prairie at that time of year was dull, dull, dull.

Rocanville 1934, 'Chorus Line'.
Sister Pat fourth from left, I'm fifth from right.

Rumour had it there as new male in town. I was intrigued. A new, unknown guy! How to meet him? There might be a way.

Rocanville had a nightly ritual: when the CPR train arrived every evening, all citizens, young and old, turned out. Mr. Sinclair and son, Lindsay, loaded the mail sacks on their cart and took it to the Post Office for distribution. The ritual of crowding into the small area in front of the mailboxes was like following holy orders. Once the mail had been distributed, and the place was empty, my friends and I began our regular walk around the two sides and end of Main Street, gossiping, giggling and looking for some kind of excitement. Not to forget that we femmes were being scrutinized by the men who sat in store doorways, looking us up and down, while they waited for the Regina Post. The Fates whirled around us. There was no Guardian angel to warn me, and I would have given short shrift to anything like good advice. Though I am not exactly sure, I must have met the new guy in town then, probably in the first week of July.

The 'new guy' was Bill Mohart, a baker for Pinkerton's Bakery & Confectionery; and I picked up on him — that's the best way of putting it. He didn't choose me; I put myself forward. Like someone knee-deep in mud, trying to get one foot out while the other foot drags you down, I began a relationship that was as bad as anything could be. It is the most difficult thing to relate, and every word of it still hurts; but it is part — too much a part — of my life; and I will try to record it.

Bill responded to my plies and became my 'steady' within a month or so. By the time I left for nurse's training in the Victoria Hospital, Winnipeg, my romanticising had reached the point where I believed he'd be waiting for me when I graduated three years hence in 1934.

CHAPTER SEVEN
Endings & Beginnings!

Mother always hoped for the best for me and, in her own way, she tried to help me realize it.

AUGUST 1931

I was to begin training at the Victoria Hospital in Winnipeg on August 18th. The morning before, my mother and I were up very early to be ready for the trip with the local trucker, Mr. Mitchell and his son, whose business took them as far as Brandon a couple of times a week. Mr. Mitchell knew we had little money and offered a ride if I understood that their truck's cab was not very comfortable and was really meant for two passengers. I was slim as a reed, and needed that ride so I accepted. Mother got the cook stove going and we made toast on the top plate. When it was time to leave, she put her arms around me and said, "Take care. And now you are away on your 'beloved nursing'." For a long time, I wondered why she said it that way.

It must have been very difficult for a woman of my mother's upbringing to have a child like me: a strong-willed, impatient-for-life, ungovernable and a boy-hungry female. She and my Uncle Percy had been brought up in an austere household, with very English traditions. Both Mother's parents were well-educated and Mother often quoted her father's belief that, "children should be seen and not heard." My behaviour was the opposite extreme and I know now I took advantage of her reluctance to curb me. Her farewell, with its mention of my referring to training as "my beloved nursing", may only have been her way of tempering what lay ahead. Perhaps she knew how rude the change would be for a perpetual romantic like me. Once in a while I thought I felt a little envy and pleasure at some of my unbridled antics. But who knows? As my story weaves its way to the present, it becomes clear that the Fates ruled otherwise.

There were two reasons I'd chosen to enrol at Victoria Hospital. The program accepted trainees with Grade CL standing and it seemed a good thing to enter where there already was a former school friend. (That, I found out soon enough, made little difference; my friend was in her senior year and as soon as I had unpacked my few personal items, she told me that we would have little to do with each other – that was a rule and rules here were strictly followed. She did let me go out with her to a friend's home a few times, but in the hospital we were not to communicate.)

We'd left home at 6:30, arrived in Brandon by one o'clock; from there I caught a train to Winnipeg, found my way to the hospital and with a terrible feeling of entering the unknown,

'Probies' Grace, Ida and me, 1931.

I was ushered to the top floor where all probationers slept. Without further ado, I was told, "You'll be downstairs for breakfast at 6:30, and shown to one of the wards by 8:00. Just be neat, and follow the orders of the senior nurse on your floor."

My bed was near a door and next to my bed was a chubby, friendly girl. That was lucky because both of us needed someone to talk to. I slept, woke the next morning, washed my face, pulled on the blue denim, front buttoned dress, then the starched white bib, tucking it around my waist with the full starched white skirt. The practical, no-style white stockings and solid white oxfords completed the uniform. Then we 'probies' – student nurses on probation – took the elevator to the basement dining room. We were hungry for food and anxious about ourselves, and oh, we were so far from home and all that it meant.

Routine for a probationer unused to strict schedules and plain hard work came as a shock, and another aspect of training was the business of seniority: every day, week, month or year you worked there gave you power and respect over anyone junior to you. We ate, worked and slept with that reality.

There were no pre-duty classes to orient us to the new environment and radically new services for the neophyte. From Day One, we were on our feet and up at 6.30 a.m., breakfast in the basement dining room, then upstairs and on duty in the wards, with but one order: Do what your ward supervisor tells you! This was hard work, with no pay. And the coveted nurse's cap wasn't ours until we'd proved we could handle the physical, mental and psychological demands that were part of our training.

Not long, and I hated the imposed drudgery that made us so tired that when we got off the wards we headed straight for our attic bedrooms where, niceties forgotten, we threw ourselves onto our beds and slept till another friendly trainee shook us awake for food or to go on to the afternoon shift. Notwithstanding the fatigue, nauseous odours, startling procedures and subservient treatment, I did manage to pick up on the good aspects of training. And besides, I had experience from caring for mother and my younger siblings when they were ill.

Apparently I did my job too well; I was told I was somewhat "too sympathetic", and after a high score on a test, that "Either you are very bright or you cheated." I was too startled to reply; and the matron knew cheating wasn't my style!

Dear Edna: Can't write much because all of we 'probies' are so darn tired when we get our afternoon break; have two hours to dash downtown and back and then right back on duty till 8 o'clock. Hey, you didn't tell me you've got a crush on Jim. Sounds to me like there are some hurdles in the way. Oh well, someone said it a long time ago, "The path of true love never did run smooth." Hope your romance is getting hotter. I had a few dates before coming here but hey, and migosh, I'm never going to meet anyone as long as I'm working like this!

Bill Mohart was no longer in the picture. Soon after my arrival, I received a letter from my sister Pat. "Don't believe any more what Bill Mohart tells you. He's running around with everybody and now it's Marjorie Scott," she told me.

Dad's phone call came on December 4, 1931; the day I was awarded my cap, the sign that my probationary period was over.

"You have to come home," he said.

"Is it Mother?"

"Yes."

"Is she worse?"

"Yes, worse than ever."

My head swam with this news.

Dad continued: "I have arranged for someone to meet you at the CPR train in Moosomin; but you are to see Rita Strong and ask her to lend you the money for your train ticket. I'll repay her Father. You must come home right away."

Rita gave me a hug and the necessary train fare. We had been friends since 1927, and small town people know all that needs to be known about other townsfolk, so she could trust me. I dashed up to the top floor, packed my few things, thankful that my sister Rene had sent me money just a few days before and I had bought a cheap black winter coat, a black felt hat, galoshes and gloves, all for $25! Then I lay down on my bed and cried while the probies not on duty comforted me. I didn't know if I was crying to get out of the unpleasant seniority system or whether I knew, instinctively, that I might never return and resume training.

When I disembarked in Moosomin on that bitterly cold afternoon, my driver, his cutter and horse were right there. I snuggled under a fur blanket he provided and we made our way back to Rocanville.

Dad was waiting at home, and my siblings were keeping warm by the stove. Dad and I went upstairs where Mother lay in the smaller bedroom. She was wan and thin, almost skeletal. Still in my nurse's uniform, I was a bit pompous.

I don't think anyone had been taking food to Mother, in fact they hadn't been getting regular meals either, so the first thing I did was get some help from my sisters while Dad got a roaring fire going to cook a dinner. I took hot water upstairs to give Mother a bit of a wash, but it was chilly there and she was so weak. How were we going to find some way of getting Mother back to good health?

"Has Dr. Campbell seen Mother lately?" I asked Dad.

"Yes."

"What did he say?"

"He just examined her and said I'd better have you come back home."

I asked Pat to go see Dr. Campbell, tell him I was home, and request that he call. He appeared the next day and as he left he spoke to me by the pantry door. "...fibroid tumours," he said quietly, "but they are not malignant; and won't become malignant." With that, we carried on as before.

It wasn't too difficult to keep food on the table for our family; but what made for a lot of hard work for me was the washing. We never had anything other than an old, second-hand washing machine that had to be worked by hand, and a washboard to rub things clean. In addition to Mother's rags was brother Don's ever-smelly wet bed. The one respectable 'baby bath' was constantly used for soaking things in cold water prior to the hot water & soap treatment. My days were a blur of clearing up after breakfast, starting the washing and getting a good hot dinner on the table for my ever-hungry siblings who hurried in from school at noon, ate and, within moments, asked for more mashed potatoes and gravy and such.

My mother had only a few good friends in Rocanville. Her manner was warm and friendly, but reserved. Poverty, and the intolerance of Rocanville's strata-conscious citizens, had bruised her self respect. Mother drew back from mixing with the women who ran the church group. Fortunately, two near neighbours, Mrs. Hunt and Mrs. Cline, often visited with Mother. I'll never forget Mrs. Hunt speaking to me after one such visit. "Oh, Jean," she said, wiping her eyes, "Your Mother was such a good friend to me."

"Was?" I replied. "Mrs. Hunt; Mother is going to get better...."

Not long after I'd returned home, Bill Mohart came knocking at our back door, looking sheepish, full of excuses for his behaviour while I'd been away in Winnipeg. He looked at the photograph of me in my nurse's dress and cap that I'd brought home with me from the Victoria Hospital. Later he stole it, an omen of a pattern to come.

Let's look at this candidly: I was without any male attention and hadn't ever consulted either parent about my romantic fancies. And thus, in spite of my resolve to have nothing further to do with Bill Mohart, I wasn't done with him yet.

> *Dear Pal, Edna: Haven't had time to sit down and pen you a line. My Mom is worse than ever, so I had to come back home. She's unable to be on her feet at all, so weak, and of course my sister and brother are too young to handle things the way they are now. Thanks to your Mom for getting the message to me that you got married and now live on the farm. At the time of scratching this quick note, all I can say is I wish you much happiness and when things are better here we'll have a visit. Sure would like a heart-to-heart chinwag with you.*

MOTHER'S HEALTH WORSENS

Mother's illness worsened that winter and her health became the most immediate matter. Dr. Campbell refused to accept that nothing could be done. "Mr. Mathie," he said when Dad claimed he couldn't afford treatment, "I don't care what it takes; your wife must go to Brandon hospital to see Dr. Bigelow (a specialist) as soon as possible." Dad paid Dr. Campbell his two dollar fee and said "alright; contact the specialist".

Friendly customers, the two Johns brothers, who were then courting future wives in Brandon, offered to drive Mother to the CPR station and to let me go with them as a passenger to Brandon. Preparing Mother for train travel must have taken all my time because I didn't have any supper that night; we had to be ready early in the morning.

It was an open vehicle, but Mother was well covered with blankets, a makeshift stretcher was made, and Mother was passed into the baggage care where, by good fortune, our Uncle Bill Mathie was in charge. The train ride would be four hours.

By the time the Johns brothers got me to the hospital, it was time to give blood for a transfusion. That was soon done, and I asked Gladys Herman, the special nurse hired at five dollars a day to look after Mother in the hospital, if she could order some food for me. She said it wasn't possible and I knew that meant waiting till I got to Uncle Will and Aunt Annabelle's. As I walked downstairs, I felt weak, and little bits of silver blurred my vision. "I have to sit down," I told her. Just then the Matron, on her way up, asked what was wrong and when told I'd not eaten for 24 hours and had motored from Rocanville that day, she said, tartly, "She needs a glass of hot milk." That was it and that was all. I left the hospital and walked along the streetcar tracks to my aunt's. The next morning, Aunt Annabelle said that she and Uncle Will had looked at me sleeping and "we nearly called the doctor." I'd been so deeply asleep, they were worried.

Dad gave blood for two transfusions, I gave three and Uncle Lew gave one pint. It was wonderful to see the effect of the blood transfusions on Mother. For the first time in years, her eyes sparkled and her spirits rose. Mother went from the hospital in good shape to a laboratory downtown where she was treated by therapeutic X-ray. During this time, she stayed at Aunt Annabelle's. When asked what it was like, she said "It wasn't unlike being in a sawmill...with a loud buzzing." Mother took it well, while another woman from our town couldn't stand the sounds of treatment.

Within several weeks, Mother came home; the next two treatments were given one month apart. During one of those times, while Mother again recuperated at the home of Uncle Will and Aunt Annabelle in Brandon, Bill Mohart, now employed in Boissevain, visited her. Mother was surprised but impressed. Bill, not wanting to accept my having told him that "there's nothing between us!" and "I never want to see you again!" hoped Mother might persuade me to let him back into my life. She told me later how pleased she was that he drove in on his day off to see her, and that "I told him that Jean mustn't feel she has to marry. And he agreed with me that you must feel free to live your own life."

Dad's store business suffered devastatingly due to Mother's healthcare and related costs. Dr. Bigelow was paid, Gladys Herman, RN, was paid, the CPR and the X-ray laboratory were paid, and a part of the hospital bill was paid. Ten years later, after I wrote a stinging letter to the Hospital, their bills ceased.

Whenever I could, I worked again in Mr. Shaw's Ladies Wear Store. One day, when I went downtown, I went into Dad's store. By now, there were no groceries to sell, the shelves had been empty for several months, and only some melted butter, that Dad had probably given credit for to some farmer's wife, lay smelling on the floor of the little room at the back. Mrs. Campbell, the doctor's wife, came in with her grocery list.

"Rice," she read.

"Haven't got it," Dad replied.

"Tea."

"Haven't got any."

"Barley."

"Haven't got it."

I stood by the second counter, searing with shame. But what made the scene so unbearable was that Sid Frost and another man let out a loud guffaw every time Dad responded.

Finally, Mrs. Campbell folded her list and quietly said, 'Well, I'll have to go somewhere else."

Dad may have had a couple of those items, but if he gave them to Mrs. Campbell he wouldn't get any cash: it would only be applied to his account with the doctor. For decades, I had a recurring dream: I stepped into the store. I knew that if I turned my head even slightly to the right or left, all the shelves would be empty.

Then the hospital wrote, asking me to recommence training, and I was in a dilemma. Did I want that profession? I pondered my various reactions to nursing and finally decided it wasn't what I wanted.

What would my life have become had I returned to Winnipeg and completed my training? Years later, and especially when the Great Depression took us into its malevolent cesspool, I questioned that decision and realized that my artistic sense would have been threaded bare had I gone back.

After Mother's third treatment, she haemorrhaged terribly, which Dr. Campbell said was normal; and soon the bleeding completely stopped. She had a new lease on life.   Now, it was the Spring of 1932 and it was time for a break. I asked Mother if she'd mind if I visited my good friend Edna in St. Lazare. Edna was expecting a baby; I wanted to assist her. Mother said yes.

On the way to St. Lazare, I stopped in McAuley to see Edna's mother, and was invited by Miss Porter to sing in a cantata at the church. Miss Porter was eager to have me step in, and gave me a solo part. Mrs. Lewis missed having Edna at home and she told me how distressing it was when Edna became pregnant.

Reg, Edna's husband, came to McAuley and drove me to their farm outside St. Lazare. Edna was so glad to see me, as was Reg's brother, Paul, with whom I had a good relationship.

Edna and I soon caught up, but only once did we talk about

her pregnancy. We were sitting by the creek, our bare feet cooling in the weed-green waters, when I asked her whether she hoped for a boy or a girl. "I wish it were neither," she said slowly, in a terribly sad voice. On May 24, Edna went into labour. Reg raced across to Birtle to get the doctor. "She's going to have that baby all by herself," he told me. I, too, sat helplessly outside her bedroom, Edna repeatedly declining my offers of help; indeed, she had the baby alone, without making a sound.

We had no baby clothing, or baby food, but we soon made up for it by using ingenuity that led to comic relief. Once, when I visited a nearby store and ordered Kotex, Reg's brother, the owner, said, "Kodaks!? Why do you want Kodaks?" Not funny at all was this: pigs found and ate the placenta which I'd buried over by the tracks.

Edna's baby was born on a Thursday. The following Saturday, when the baby was two days old, Paul and Mrs. Lewis and I went into St. Lazare to shop and then to the local movie house where Noel Coward's "Private Lives" was being shown. When the movie concluded we walked out on to the main street and who was there, walking toward me, but Bill Mohart?! I was shocked. But there he was; and that same old Ford coupe of his standing next to the curb. He had driven all the way from Boissevan, where he worked in a bakery.

"Your mother thought you might like to come home for a few days, since you've been away for a couple of months," he said.

"I can't," I replied. "Edna needs help with her newborn and I don't want to leave Mrs. Lewis on her own." Mrs. Lewis, however, said it would be alright if I went home for a few days; she would manage.

It is painful to write about that particular Saturday night. And it is a copout to say, "if only Mother hadn't told him where I was." Why didn't I just tell him to get lost and leave me alone? Of course Mother never knew or suspected that this man had a strange side; she liked the fact that he had paid her a visit when she was recuperating in Brandon. Furthermore, she knew I was still at loose ends since Frank Scott had jilted me. But did she anticipate the outcome of our evening together?

Throughout the long, tiring drive from St. Lazare to Rocanville, and for several more hours in his parked car outside the house, Bill appealed to me with maudlin, tearful pleas. "Jean, I can't live without you...Jean, I'd go though fire for you...Jean, please marry me and I promise, I will...."

I was exhausted and all I wanted was to go inside and sleep – like the family inside. And so I said "yes" to Bill's proposal.

Bill left early the next morning; he had to start baking as soon as he arrived.

I faced Mother on that Sunday morning and told her the news; she was pleased and showed it. Since my parents had married on a June 19th, Mother and I both thought it would be pleasant and romantic for Bill and me to marry on that same date. With that, wedding plans were underway.

Dad, who was always very tired on Sundays, did not participate in the discussion. To be honest, Dad took little to no apparent interest in anything we kids did; I had no warm, father-daughter relationship with him. So, it was up to Mother and me to look after all the details. Everything would be done simply. "I always like to read Wedding Reports that refer to 'a quiet but pretty wedding'," Mother confessed.

June 19 would be a Sunday, so Bill was to arrive on Saturday after work. The local church minister could only make it at 9:30 a.m. because he had two other preaching commitments that day, one at Prosperity at 11:30 and another at Spy Hill in the afternoon. Mother planned a nice lunch to follow the ceremony, which would take place in the parlour. Extra chairs would be borrowed from our friends and neighbours and, because we needed a really nice chair for Mother to sit in during the ceremony, we asked Mrs. Stewart, the rather sharp-tongued postmistress, if she would lend her good occasional chair. "Of course," she said, sounding a bit pleased.

Dearest Edna: Now you have a little boy, and I am glad I was there to be of some help. Thank goodness your Mom came, too. She is now a Grandma, and I guess she'll be as good at that as she is at everything else. I just hope the little fellow is doing well, and that you are, too. Now we have shared another milestone in our lives. Having said that, Edna, you'd better sit down 'cause I have some startling news.

When Bill and I drove back to Rocanville, he gave me a woeful story of how terribly he missed me and he even said he couldn't live without me. I wasn't impressed at first, but this avowal went on long enough to make me want only one thing: to get out of his car and go to sleep. When he said he'd "go through fire" for me, I told him I'd consider his proposal. And, hang on to your hat; I told him I'd marry him!

Looks like we'll tie the knot at the end of June. My Mom is pleased. Bill always impressed her because he had steady work and he was polite to her.

Am I excited? All I can say right now is it looks good to me, to settle down. But there is always going to be a little sadness that Frank and I broke up. First love, you know. Just wish you could be here, my old pal.

WEDDING PLANS

This was the first time I had seen how good Mother was at planning. She bought two chickens from a local farmer and hired the Woods twins to come and clean. My dear friend,

Doris Masters, was happy to play "The Wedding March", cousin Isabelle MacTavish of Moose Jaw would sign the register and my 14 year old sister Pat would be my bridesmaid. Custom was that the churchwomen's group gave every bride a shower in the church basement; mine was to take place a week prior to June 19.

We had no telephone in our home, so long-distance calls were handled by a runner bringing a message that we were to respond to. Bill phoned a week before the wedding date.

"I can't get to Rocanville," he said.

"What's the matter? All the plans are made for our wedding on the 19th."

"I just can't get there. I can't make it."

"Why?"

"I can't find any place for us to live."

I went home and reported to Mother that Bill could not come. I took the news without much feeling; but Mother was clearly upset. "You go back and phone him and tell him no matter what, he's to be here and we'll have the wedding on the 26th, a week later than planned."

What was I thinking? The guy was trying to free himself of marriage and, not only that, I wasn't even upset. But he and my Mother knew each other better than I knew either of them. When I told Bill that "Mother said I am to tell you that no matter what, you are to be here for June 26th and we can find some place to live after we're married," he didn't argue. But the churchwomen were confounded: Were they to give me a shower or not? It never happened, but friends and Dad's customers sent some very nice gifts.

Bill arrived Saturday, June 25th, having driven with a fellow who didn't know he was going to a wedding and more than that, be Best Man! My cousin Isabelle had already arrived. The house looked better than usual, the Woods twins were to help tomorrow, too, and Mother seemed in her element, with a dandy lunch ready, even without any refrigeration for those dainty little jellied chicken salads.

I went to see my former employer, Dave Shaw, and bought a neat, yellow, two piece summer suit and a small-brimmed, white Panama hat. Another customer said he could even include a little lily-of-the-valley with the beautiful maroon peonies that were to be my bouquet.

JUNE 26, 1932

I am 20 years of age plus two months. In everything I did I felt self confident, almost too much so. I say that because, since puberty, my daily life was based on my own decisions; neither parent made decisions for me. Mother was tolerant; Dad was ignored even when, on the evening before the wedding, he said, "Nobody has asked me yet." I was coming in the back door and he was going out as he spoke to me. I looked at him quickly and walked past. That was our only contact.

Everything connected with the wedding was between Mother and me, and for me it was something with a bit of attention and glamour. If Mother had ever asked me if I knew what I was doing, or cautioned me about the serious implications of tying my life onto a man – a man I didn't know much about – would I have said no? But she was all for it, perhaps hopeful that I would settle down and 'be a good wife'. And, possibly, she hoped that my marriage, with a real wedding, would help her get over her disappointment that Rene, her firstborn, had eloped. Rene's marriage had come apart and Rene had been forced to ask if she could come home with her new baby just after we'd moved to Rocanville. For a number of years, Mother raised her grandchild.

Mother looked just right that morning. She had bought a knitted suit in Brandon before Dad's business had gone broke from the expenses of her medical treatment. Mother had been married in a brown suit, and here she was wearing the same colour for her daughter's wedding.

Guests began arriving soon after 9 a.m. while Pat, Isabelle and I dressed upstairs. Sixteen-year-old brother Don wasn't interested in anything pertaining to the wedding and sauntered off into the trees near the house with a rifle for shooting rabbits. He wore the daily shabby overalls. Dad looked neat, wearing what Pat referred to as his 'pink' suit. Mother said everything was in order and sat down in the loaned occasional chair.

Pat, in a green voile dress, sat beside me at the top of the stairs, with Dad on the second step down. Doris began the Wedding March. I had asked her to play the longer version and later was told, "We thought you were never coming." Down the stairs we walked, through the hallway, past Mother's large fern set back against the hall door; and then towards Bill, who stood close to the piano in the parlour, facing the guests, his astounded Best Man and Reverend Ingram nearby. Bill looked scared and suddenly I felt a sense of alarm. Pat's buttocks trembled as she stood beside me, holding my bouquet and her own. We gave each other one quick look.

"Dearly beloved," the Minister began.

Can I still get out of this? Can I stop him? I looked at the thirty or so guests in the dining room area and at Mother, who looked so serene....

The next thing I knew, the ceremony was over and our witnesses, Isabelle and the Best Man, were signing the register. Bill and I turned around and became part of the crowd, shaking hands with our well-wishers. There was no hugging in those days.

Mother had used this opportunity to reveal her talents and style: on the dining room table stood what was left of her own and Grandma's 'Bridal Wreath' china. The Woods' twins, who had squeezed into the dining room for the ceremony, now obeyed Mother's orders, bringing in plates and serviettes and all that was left of Mother's linens; then cups and saucers, some borrowed; and the food: buttered buns, jellied chicken salads and pickles…. Mother sat in that lovely chair and poured tea.

Bill had paid Reverend Ingram his ten dollars before his almost immediate departure, but where Bill disappeared to after that, I don't recall.

After introducing Isabelle to a few people, I sat in the parlour area with her, Doris and Mrs. Rook. It was then, caught up in the excitement, I got a sharp little chicken bone in my throat and struggled to get it out without making a scene. I was afraid I would choke; but it came out. (The sensation of having a bone stuck in the throat, recurred for years; I even consulted a doctor, but no cause was ever found.)

Since Bill hadn't found a place for us to live, I would remain at home for a couple of weeks, when he would come and take me back with him to Dauphin. Now, he and his Best Man, left – but not before the Best Man had let people know that he really didn't know Bill very well and thought he was "just coming for a weekend, not for a wedding I was to take part in." There was some disappointment when guests were told that they wouldn't be able to wave us off.

Mrs. Rook's Senior Girls Class St. Paul's United Church, Rocanville, June 1932. Mrs. Rook is fourth from the left in the back row, I'm third from left in the front and Marjorie Scott is third from left on the top row.

The house was suddenly empty.

I changed into a good dress I had bought while clerking for Dave Shaw: black with a small floral pattern and a small jacket of plain black that tied neatly under my bosom. I asked Isabelle if she'd like to go to Sunday school, and with her usual pleasantness she said she would. Pat and Betty, Isabelle and I attended St. Paul's United; and I have a picture of us and other members of Mrs. Rook's class taken that morning.

One day, as Isabelle and I talked about Bill and my marrying him, I said in defence of him, "Well, in comparison to his tall brothers, he's small." Quick as a shot, Isabelle responded, "Yes. So is poison!" Later on, she might have considered how right she was.

CHAPTER EIGHT

From Miss to Mrs.

Naivete, uncontrolled: that was I. Getting married was a new thing, to be sure. Anything more than that was mysterious coupled with inexperience and my own dealings with whatever happened. It never dawned on me that I might not be able to handle this unknown new life; I really thought anything was possible. But from that time on, I was to learn that I had put myself in a situation where impossibilities were my daily experience; and I quickly realised something was wrong. This was obvious from day one.

LIFE IN DAUPHIN, MANITOBA
JULY 7 1932 – TO MID-JANUARY 1933

Dauphin was a bigger town than Rocanville, with a solid Main Street and bustling businesses all the way up and down. The bakery where Bill worked was on a corner, with large windows displaying enticing confections. When I was introduced to Mr. Lepphart, the proprietor, he was very cordial, though surprised Bill had never mentioned me. He took me into the bakeshop, offered me a fresh cookie and said I was welcome there anytime. I never told him how Bill embarrassed me anytime I did go there. Usually there were a couple of fellows standing around watching Bill and making casual conversation. That changed when Bill made a rude remark to me, once asking, "Hey, Jean, you need to go to the bathroom?" I wasn't aware that I had passed wind, but Bill and the guys thought it was really funny and laughed while I felt dreadfully uncomfortable and walked out.

Bill had been renting a room from an elderly woman on the second floor of her little home. In addition to the one room at the top of the stairs there was a bedroom with a bed and dresser. That was it. We were allowed to get water downstairs and use her toilet. Our landlady shared with me her recipes and allowed me to use her washing machine. Everything about my life took on a different daily, nightly and even hourly way of handling my attitudes and feelings inside this new tide that was my marriage to Bill, one with an undercurrent of uneasiness from the beginning

Now, I was a 'housewife'; and none of this new life had any semblance to the free style of my former home. We ate together, sometimes went for a walk after Bill woke from his regular sleep that started at 8:00 a.m. and lasted until about 4:00 o'clock and conversations didn't go beyond his day's work. Soon I felt a new and frightening bondage that I didn't want to acknowledge; but it was there like that bone in my throat on our wedding day; and this one couldn't be choked down or dislodged. How to deal with it?

Next door were wonderful sounds: a jazz band practised there, one with a very good pianist. I had the urge to walk over and somehow get involved, even tell them I had been pianist in Rocanville for the Melody Four, a small orchestra... Every rhythm that wafted over caused in me a pulsing sensation; then I remembered where I was and why I dare not try to make friends with the musicians who were turning me upside down as I listened to songs I knew by heart.

I must tell Bill about hearing this jazz, I thought, and finally one day, I did. "I'd like to introduce myself...," I said at mealtime, knowing I was on unsteady ground.

Bill showed his displeasure and his new role as a husband. There was no doubt in his voice and manner that I'd better not have any involvement. The answer was "No."

What? Never in my life had I been refused to be associated with anything musical. Disappointment and hurt added to a bewildering frustration. And I knew there was no chance that I could meet that band; Bill didn't dance. There was only one other way to satisfy my need for music and desire to meet other musicians.

Bill didn't object when I told him I was going to go to church choir practice; it was then that he revealed that he was a Catholic, smirking as he added, "I was even an altar boy." Shock number three, or was it fifteen by then?

One of the kindest church ministers I ever met welcomed me to his congregation, later inviting me home for tea. I was so relieved, and also impressed with that family's kindness. Tea with them was a little ceremony, trolled into the parlour on a tea wagon with linens, sandwiches and iced cakes. Then began a procedure I had to get used to: Explaining that bakers worked at night and thus slept during the day. Though they seemed to accept it, I felt uneasy. Did they believe me?

Some release came when I was invited as a choir member to sing at a local concert. When I sang "Somewhere a Voice is Calling" the audience's response sent my blood pounding. One of the soloists with a fine baritone asked if I'd sing with him and I readily agreed. That evening I made several new friends and went home happy.

There was little use in trying to make that evening sound good to Bill. I couldn't even let my new found pleasure show; as I described the singing, I disguised the depth of my happiness. It didn't work. Bill warned me not to get too friendly with any of those people, adding, "I've heard some things about them and don't want you associating with them!" An inevitable estrangement was already underway.

I did develop friendships with musicians; and met the male pianist from next door through friends of his. The small-town girl in me was too naive to realise this was asking for trouble, after all, music had made its demands on me since childhood. Bill the Baker would take second-place and, though I didn't know it then, it was happening with a force I had never controlled – didn't know how to and seemed not to want to.

1932

Dear, dear friend Edna: How is the baby and how are you? This town is really something! Bigger than Rocanville and McAuley, with a really good church choir. I've been soloing at a couple of lovely concerts where people were swell to me. Wish I could say that everything was smooth with Bill and me. He doesn't go with me to church or anything else, even when a dear old lady who knew my parents back in Brandon asked me to dinner last Sunday. So I went alone. Seemed strange. He gives the excuse that, being a baker, he starts work in the evening. I know the people I visited thought it really odd that he didn't go with me. Sorry to have to tell you that sometimes he says things that hurt a little. That's enough of that. Please drop me a line and if you have any pictures of the baby, I'd love to see them. Your rather lonesome old friend, Jean.

MORE TROUBLE

A family related to people in Rocanville were especially kind after I introduced myself to them. Mrs. Batty, a sister of Mrs. MacLeod in Rocanville, had recently lost her husband. Jessie, her daughter, was a few years older than I, and we became warm friends. As well there were two brothers – nice, handsome lads. Their home soon became a real source of pleasure for me.

One Sunday I enjoyed a great dinner with them, again excusing Bill. "Would you like to come to church with us tonight?" Mrs. Batty asked. "We're Baptists."

"I'd love to," I replied. Surely Bill wouldn't mind that, since he knew the family, had met the boys downtown. Mrs. Batty, Jessie, Syd and I cleared away the dishes and walked several blocks to the church where the hymns were vigorous. "Pray without ceasing, pray on!" has stuck in my memory; perhaps because of the extraordinary happenings that were later a part of the evening.

"We always have a cup of chocolate after church," Jessie said, "so please come back home with us." That sounded fine, and it wasn't that late, so we walked back, singing and joking about needing exercise after sitting so long, then chasing each other as we approached their home. Afterwards, Jessie walked home with me, saying Goodnight outside our door rather than going in and waking Bill.

Bill sat at the kitchen table.

"Oh, you're up." I said.

He scowled. "It's about time you got here," he said, then added, "you and Syd Batty."

"What on earth are you talking about?"

"You and Syd Batty. I saw you. I heard you. I followed you guys; I was down the lane from you." And then he stopped speaking.

I attempted to straighten him out by telling him what a lovely dinner it was and that "you should've been there."

"I don't want to hear about it. Shut up!"

This frightening scene continued for well over an hour: my trying to convince him to believe me, protesting that he was all wrong, reminding Bill that "Syd is engaged."

Bill finally got up and put on his jacket. I quickly put myself in front of the door and said, "You're not going until you speak to me."

He put his hands on my shoulders and threw me away from the door. I staggered a few steps and fell as he slammed the door and went off to the bakery. Neither of my parents had used physical punishment on me, nor had I ever been manhandled. I didn't go to bed; I sat up, in shock, waiting for morning to come....

I had lived in Dauphin since July; now it was late fall and Rene and her little daughter took a bus from Rocanville and arrived in Dauphin.

What a wonderful change! We talked, ate and laughed

together like I hadn't done for half a year. Bill was aloof, gruff and not at all a kind host. Then one day he was rude to me and shoved me as he spoke. My sister came to my defence and told Bill to stop treating me like that. "You shut up! If you say another word I'll throw you and your kid out...right out in the yard in the snow!" he responded. Both she and I were startled and frightened. Bill went upstairs and dressed in his white baker's garb for work. As soon as he left, my sister and her little daughter got fully dressed for the long trip back to Rocanville, leaving that afternoon. That round went to Bill.

My Dear Friend and Confidant:

How are things down in the valley? It is very much colder here so far north of home, but the people are nice and the movies are 'way ahead' of anything at home. Does Harry Davis still show old movies in the basement of the Welwyn drugstore? That's where I saw that great war picture, "All's Quiet on the Western Front". I think that was the only time Harry got a good film. But for 25 cents, we shouldn't complain.

It sure makes me feel older and different when people call me "Mrs." Sort of a more respectable status. How does it affect you?

Guess I might as well give you the state of things, Edna. So I'll quit beating around the bush. Things are not going well. Before marriage, I thought of Bill and me in a cozy little home and sharing things like having people in for tea or supper. Perhaps I took too much for granted, though I have to tell you that I never saw the side of Bill I'm seeing now. Of course, this little house we're renting isn't much. I wanted a couple of easy chairs but we have only a Winnipeg couch besides our kitchen table and two chairs (and our bed, naturally). I don't earn any money like I could back home playing for dances and helping when MacLeod's General Store had a sale. I could use some woollen underwear and a good winter coat. But all that is not as important as his way of being rude. Guess I'm not able to understand how anyone can be like that, even though growing up with a brother and sisters we were argumentative and sassy with each other.

Can't write anymore, kiddo, because I have to get this to the Post Office, which is downtown. There's a really good Chinese restaurant here. Maybe I'll have time for a cup of coffee and get back in time to have supper ready. This letter is strictly confidential. Up to now I haven't told my Mother. She would be so disappointed. When you write to me better not mention anything. He is possessive about everything I do. Hope my next letter will be cheerier. S'long for now.

LEAVING BILL – JANUARY 1933

What a naive, unthinking young woman I was!

I had already left Bill Mohart twice because of the way he treated me. Before running away from Bill now, for a third time, and this time back to my family, I had never really planned ahead. Bill had taunted me by telling me he knew where I was and with whom (even though he was invited to join me but chose not to); now, as I stayed with friends in Dauphin, I was afraid he would discover my whereabouts and that would mean a repeat of other troublesome scenes. I asked my dad to send Bill a telegram that would inform Bill he could contact me only through the lawyer we had met with in Dauphin after one of our altercations. With the few dollars I had, I bought a ticket, leaving one bleak morning on the CN train. That trip gave me plenty of time to wonder where my life was taking me. The train stopped for about an hour at Neepawa and I sat, looking out the window, feeling lost and rudderless, wondering what to do next. Turmoil mixed with relief and the hope that Mother and Dad and my siblings would make everything better. Up to that time, every difficult situation was handled by some weird faculty of optimism derived, no doubt, from my mother's attitude that surfaced at the worst of times.

In Brandon, I changed to the CPR train and was home later that day – January 13, 1933.

I think my family was glad to see me. Mother had been anxious for me to marry Bill, and though she was sorry and hurt it hadn't worked out, she was sympathetic. Dad had little to say. Sister Pat was glad to see me and there we were again, sharing that old bed. Betty was still my 'little sister' and not as close as Pat. As for brother Don, he lived in the same house with us but had little to do with his sisters, except for talking about local happenings at the dinner table at noon, or the supper table at 6 o'clock.

In 1933 physical abuse of one's wife was frowned upon but no one considered that the perpetrator required professional medical treatment. Nor was there such a thing as 'counselling' in those days. The minister who married us did come to see me, and he appeared to be sympathetic, but the only time he showed any concern was when he asked me, "what do you intend to do now?" to which I said, "Get a divorce." With that, our conversation ended.

JANUARY 1933 (6 MONTHS AFTER MARRIAGE)

Dear Friend:

Do I ever need to talk to you! I've been back in Rocanville for a few days. After two terrible happenings, I left my poor little home and asked to stay at a friend's until I could contact my family and find a way back home.

When I wrote to you a couple of months ago things were

154

not too bad. Then I went alone, to have Sunday supper at Batty's and, again, Bill declined the invitation....

Edna, what I'm writing is just the way it happened. The Battys said they always had hot chocolate after church, so I thought it would be OK to go to their place before going home. To my surprise Bill hadn't gone to the bake-shop. He was sitting at our kitchen table when I returned home. When I saw him I knew trouble was looming. After some pleading by me, he sneered, "Oh, you and Syd Batty. I know. I saw you. I ran down the lane watching you after church."

I was stunned at his accusation. I protested that I had had nothing to do with Syd. Bill became abusive and then refused to look at me or speak to me. When he put his coat on, I ran to the front door and stood with my back tight against it and my arms out flat. I said, "You're not leaving here until you speak to me. You must know what you're saying is wrong." The next thing I knew, he grabbed my shoulders and threw me away from the door and across the room where I fell on the couch. Then he left.

Edna, this is awful to tell you, but I have no one else. My sister is six years younger and the other one even younger, so I don't want to go into the gory details with them and it hurts both my parents to talk about it.

Anyway, I cried and cried. When it was daylight I put on my coat and walked down the back lanes to Batty's. I didn't want anyone to see my face or my red eyes. When Mrs. Batty opened the door she was shocked. I went in, cried some more, and told her what happened. She sent Jessie to get Syd and when he appeared, she said, "Syd, you must find Bill right away and tell him he is completely wrong." (Syd is engaged to marry a girl who lives just across the street.) Mrs. Batty coaxed me to have some food and we waited for Syd to return.

It was noon before he came. He said he caught sight of Bill and tried to catch up to him, but Syd had followed him from one building to another and finally cornered Bill in the Pool Hall. When he asked Bill what he meant by saying something about me and him, Bill's quick reply was, "I never said any such thing! She's lying!"

But I am sure they believed me. Jessie offered to walk home with me. When we got there, Bill was upstairs sleeping and refused to be wakened. I started to pack my clothes, to go anywhere just to get away from him, and when he knew what I was doing he plead with me to forgive him and promised it wouldn't happen again. Jessie said she thought she should leave so we could patch things up.

I wish I could say that's what happened. Within a couple of months he had treated me so badly that I again ran to stay with a friend. When my friend and I went to collect some warm clothing, Bill was at his job, but he'd left me a short note, in which he plead for forgiveness and instructed "Jean, bury me in my brown suit." I put the note in my pocket. Jessie saw that I was OK and left. Unexpectedly Bill showed up and refused to let me take my clothes. I left in tears and walked back to my friend's home. We all agreed I must have the right to my own clothing and this time I took a friend's advice and went to see a lawyer. Mrs. Batty and Jessie came with me. The lawyer agreed to hear our case and ordered Bill to be in attendance. I knew nothing about the law, or how it worked with a suicidal threat. The lawyer gave Bill a dressing down for his treatment of me, said Bill must allow me into our house and, in addition, he said with legal emphasis, "Mohart, you are a rotten husband; but I want you to know that I could have you arrested for leaving this note where you suggest suicide. That is illegal. I could have you jailed. Don't you ever try that again."

Well, Jessie again came home with me and there was a repeat of the promises. I was hopeful. I went to a nice store and bought some really good woollen underwear, charging it to Bill. The next time there was more hurt I packed up while he was at work, went to a neighbour's and the next day took the train home.

Oh dear friend; this has been so heart-breaking; and not just for me – it's hard on my family, too. You know my family. They are kindly, decent people. They welcomed me; but Edna, can you believe it, the townsfolk are judging me harshly. Nothing can be worse than coming back to this town without a husband. I may have been an A-student, and the most popular singer in town; but to be a married woman without a husband is to be the blackest of all sinners. Only one of my former schoolmates, a close friend, considers me worth speaking to. Thank goodness I can still count you as a dear friend. This is a really rocky kind of situation. Wish I could tell you there might be a way to happier times. For now, I'll just hope and pray there's a way out.... Love, Jean.

ROCANVILLE AGAIN

Within a week, Bill showed up in Rocanville. Apparently, his boss had fired him when he learned that Bill had been mistreating me. Now, Bill wanted me to take him back. Standing at our back door, he wept and begged. I told him I didn't want to have anything more to do with him. "That's alright, Jean," he threatened. "I'll ruin you and your whole family."

And try he did! He made the rounds on Main Street, talked to anyone and everyone who'd listen, in one breath saying, "I should have kicked her out sooner; she was having sex with lots of guys!" and in the next breath weeping loudly and saying, "I just want her back."

In my dad's little grocery store it was difficult for Dad to control the situation. Always a man who abhorred quarrelling, he was upset and confused and quite unable to know how to cope now that Bill had an audience and he, Gordon Mathie, was the father of the runaway bride. Bill, meanwhile, was warmly encouraged by all and sundry; in a small prairie town caught in the doldrums of winter, the exciting gossip spread quickly. My former employer, Dave Shaw, was so distraught by Bill's weeping that he implored Dr. Campbell to "please help Bill". But Dr Campbell merely replied, "Pay no attention to him. Those Germans cry over anything."

Bill had told outright lies to my friends and me but I didn't have the insight to know that he was a liar; worse still, he was a liar of a kind foreign to my family. From that time on, and for the rest of Bill's life, I would be confronted and confounded with his flagrant abuse of truth. Only many years later did I learn that he was a pathological liar, a person who skewed truth to suit himself at any and all times.

After exhausting every sympathetic ear, Bill tried a different tactic. He drove his noisy Ford roadster around and around the block and each time he passed our house he created a loud THRUMMMM! I can't remember if my Dad ever tried to stop him.

Day after day, the noise continued, till, one day, I'd finally had enough. With Mother's permission, I went outside and invited him to talk things over. He quickly shut off the motor; and once more he was in our house and back in my life. My dad said little, Mother wanted an end to the noise and, hopefully, a fresh start; and I, without any feeling of romance or caring, went along with what seemed the only way to put a semblance of peace to my own and my family's daily life.

But now there was a new crisis. Uncle Percy phoned to say that he could no longer look after Grandma and could he send her to Rocanville? Of course Mother said yes. Within a week, Grandma arrived in such poor health that she had to be carried from the train to our home. The single bed was set up for her in the parlour for the first several weeks. It was the middle of winter, so her bed had to be in a warm room.

One night Dad came home, bringing the icy air in with him. Grandma's mind was wandering most of the time by then. When she heard the commotion, she sat up and said, with fear in her voice, "Who is that?" Mother and I tried to quiet her obvious terror. "Don't be afraid, Grandma, it's Dad," I told her. "It's Gordon, Mother," echoed Mother.

Grandma raised herself to a sitting position and shouted, "Gordon? Gordon Mathie! What are the assets and what are the liabilities? Don't let him in here! I know him of old!" Mother tried to reassure her. It was a scene that none of us will ever forget. Grandma was reliving the last days of "Mathie & Wells", that failed business venture which had caused a rift in the family from that time onward.

The small house was crowded with me, Grandma and Bill all living there now; and it was agreed that Bill would go to live with his family in Melville, Saskatchewan while I remain at home to assist Mother in caring for Grandma.

How little had changed! Now, in 1933, life continued to be about hoping to make ends meet, stretching each dollar to its limit, mending every item of apparel, using ingenuity in providing meals and never throwing anything out no matter what its outworn condition. Dad's business was deteriorating, yet it was our only means of support.

Mother left it to me to take care of Grandma, and from the time we took her upstairs I spent most of my time with her. She required little care. She had lost all her mental power, a great change for a woman who was able to take over her husband's job when he died in 1910. We had no communication anymore; but a change occurred in her in the last few days of her life. She cried out when there was light in the room, so I pulled the old green blinds down; but even coming into the room with the coal oil lamp made her waken from her state of insensibility. Raising her skinny arms she would cry piteously, "Oh! There's another wave! Won't someone please save me and my poor baby?" Grandma was reliving her passage across the Atlantic, when she and The Major had come to Canada to start life anew.

This continued for the last 48 hours before she quietly went to sleep. I couldn't believe she was gone. I checked her breathing with my head close to her mouth; I used a mirror to see if there was the slightest bit of life still moving within her, but it was over. I went downstairs where mother was on her knees washing the kitchen floor. "Mother," I said, hesitatingly, "Grandma is gone."

Mother got up, dried her hands and we went upstairs. Weeping, she walked over to the bed and took Grandma's hands in hers, crying audibly as she did so, saying, "Oh, you poor, poor dear. You have been through so much."

Mother was the Executor for Grandma's estate. Grandma had received $120.00 in back-dated Old Age pension a few months previous, arranged through the kindness of a friend she had known in better days (Mr. Wilde of Moosomin). His letter to the government stated that "Mrs. Wells rightly deserves pension, more than anyone I know." It was a lot of money in 1933. The Old Age Pension was a pittance and a Means Test had to be carried out by a government agent. This woman, who had braved a variety of tribulations and trouble, would have suffered again if she had known the indignity of 'accepting' welfare.

Now Mother sat in the kitchen, the cheque in her hands. I stood over by the door to the dining room. Dad stood nearer to Mother. She was very quiet, sad and seemed reluctant to speak for a few minutes. Then she said, "I have told Mr.

Douglas I want him to make the coffin." Billy Douglas was a carpenter and, according to my brother Don (who experienced Douglas's dishonesty), a scoundrel; however, my Mother commanded respect with whomever she dealt and she trusted him to do this special work with skill and honesty.

Money! I didn't take long to say to Mother, "surely you are going to get a really nice dress, something cut velvet, like Mrs. Pinkerton wears to church."

Mother shook her head and murmured, "No. I don't think so." Then she said, "I am taking twenty dollars for the purple velvet I want the coffin covered with and the other money will cover the cost of the cemetery accounts, the Death certificate and such."

"Mr. Schwarz (the local undertaker) came to me this morning thinking we would need him and I told him we were taking care of it otherwise," Dad said.

I went back into the dining room and sat down. Mother had some money and she wasn't going to treat herself to anything! I was filled with bitterness, but there was work to do. Uncle Percy was called from the local telephone office, and he said he'd come from Broadview. I asked Mr. Ingram, the local United church minister to please come and talk to Mother about the service.

It was after supper that Dad spoke to Mother in the kitchen, asking her to let him have $100 to make a little money. She questioned him about putting the money into something speculative. He was persuasive; telling her that he would buy white sugar at a certain price and in selling it would make another $20. This is hard to record: Mother gave him that money and to the best of my knowledge, his plan failed. I know that mother had nothing from it.

To save money, we held Grandma's funeral in our parlour. Dad and Don and Billy Douglas carried Grandma's body down the stairs and I heard a couple of bumps as they tried to manoeuvre the turn in the stairs. Mother and I had dressed

Grandma in a fine black silk dress. I made sure we took her rings off before she left our home. I played the piano for Grandma's favourite hymn, "The King of Love my Shepherd is…"

Now that Grandma was gone, I had to decide if I should join Bill who now phoned with news that he could have a good job as baker in Glenboro, Manitoba, if I would go with him and work as kitchen helper and waitress in the adjoining restaurant. He would earn $75 a month and I would earn $25. Room and board was included. Okay. We were there within a week.

GLENBORO MAY 1933 – SEPTEMBER 1933

I don't remember how we got to Glenboro but I think by train. I was 21 and very thin.

Bill and I had a bedroom one floor above the store, a makeshift room with only a bed, a washstand and our suitcases. The tin roof allowed heat to create an oven in that room which could become so hot that I could not bear to touch the metal frame of the bed when I took time off after noon dinnertime for a much needed rest. There were violent electrical storms that summer. Crouching under the window, I wondered if we would be electrocuted by the lightning and earthshaking thunder; I often felt I couldn't survive.

Bill's work ended with each day's baking; mine was from dawn to after dark. I was to work along with the wife of the proprietor in the kitchen, cooking, baking pies and cakes, washing up all the dishes from the family kitchen and diners', laundry and ironing. When necessary I was needed to be a sales clerk where baked goods and confectionery meant filling ice-cream cones, making sundaes, and serving at mealtimes.

There was an electrified washing machine and iron, but I did all the work by my strength and my hands. Every wash meant seventeen shirts had to be laundered, hung out to dry, brought in from the clothesline, each one sprinkled with water, rolled up and ironed with flat irons as soon as possible to avoid mildew that developed in hot weather.

Mr. & Mrs. Cline had constant disagreements and one never knew what to expect. It got really testy when son Russell disagreed with his father, manoeuvring it so that he got his mom's attention. That quickly turned into a spat between the parents. In everything, Mrs. Cline held the upper hand. Dud attempted to sound like the man he wanted to be, with sputters of protest that were swept away with a few curt words by Mrs Cline. Russell's pitiful immaturity completed the weak connection between the three. Yet I am sure they would stand together if accused of any lack of affection of each other.

There was another Mrs. Cline in town who filled me in on their background. Whenever I could, I visited her and she always made me feel welcome. Of course I knew she wanted to hear the entire goings on at the downtown store; and perhaps it gave me an outlet for the narrow, mean routine. Mrs. Cline understood my profoundly dismal life.

The work was sheer drudgery and I was worn to a frazzle; what kept me going were people I befriended. There was something nice about chatting with the bank manager as I served him. Another gleam of light in that terrible summer was the traveling salesman who was a cantor in a Winnipeg synagogue. I was never so tired that I couldn't sing and when the man with the glorious voice played and sang, we changed the temperature and ambience from stupid, mean and tawdry to the rarest of sounds – he with his soaring tenor and I with my fulsome, easy soprano.

Another restaurant customer, a strapping, good-looking bus driver, offered to introduce me to some people whom he felt I would enjoy meeting. He was right. His girlfriend Vesta Sampson invited me home to meet her mother and two sisters. Vesta explained that her friendship with the bus driver was platonic though he'd prefer otherwise.

Mrs. Sampson loved telling stories about her late husband, his love for her and the girls, and his wonderful way of coming home with beautiful things for them and for the house. When I commented on the striking beauty of the rose patterned carpet, she relished telling me how happy they were, without sadness. Her pride in her eldest daughter having been associated with the dashing young Brandon doctor who drove a Stutz roadster made for a wonderful tale. Vesta told me how, when the doctor was killed driving his fast European car, her sister heard about it on the radio, rushed to his apartment and cleared it of all her belongings.

I was at their home one hot afternoon when three of my former friends from the Victoria Hospital who were visiting in town, called to see me. That was an uncomfortable hour for me. They were now far along into nurse's training and looked well and happy; I was married, working as a servant and not happy at all.

We worked in Glenboro without a break until one September day when Dud and Bill had an argument that ended with Dud firing Bill. It happened an hour before noon. Bill found me in the kitchen and said I should go upstairs and pack our things since we had to get out immediately. There should have been relief on my part, but coming as it did out of the blue, it felt tragic; for the first time ever I had earned 25 dollars a month and hadn't spent any of it. I felt sick with the same old haunting fear that I was out in orbit, alone, poor and with only the worry of how to make a living.

Bill and I were paid off – his monthly pay of 50 dollars plus mine at 25. We walked across the street to the Chinese restaurant to have dinner. The kindly owner smiled and told us he had a turkey dinner ready; Bill enjoyed the food, but I was unable to eat. We caught the bus, passed the day in Brandon where I spent a few dollars on a pair of black kid pumps, silk stockings and a cute little black satin hat with tipped brim over one eye. Then we caught the CPR train back to Rocanville.

ROCANVILLE AGAIN!

My family's home was crowded and Dad didn't like it. Once more it was agreed that Bill would go to his home in Melville and look for another job. I stayed home, easily fitting into the same routine that always existed. The difference now was that I had a little savings of my own: a total of $150, more than I'd ever owned.

I again found temporary work in Dave Shaw's Women's clothing store. Dad's small grocery store was just about finished; with no cash reserves he could not order stock to keep the business afloat. I was half-happy to be with Mother and my sisters, not wanting to link up with my husband again.

Mother and I had some happy times during this stay. We

A 'true' friend, Doris Masters, bottom left, I'm behind her.

looked at Eaton's catalogues, saw some lovely fabrics, and ordered red silk with tiny white dots for a formal-style dress and green corduroy for a jacket, skirt and cloche style hat. In a parcel from our relatives in Moose Jaw there was a good piece of black and white cotton tweed. Mother made it into a svelte, body-fitting jumper to which she matched a little blouse of black and white rayon, and then finished the combo with a large scarlet satin bow, the blouse and bow from the surprising contents of Mother's ragbag. When I wore that to a local dance I was aware of many eyes on me; and the frowns of old women, looking on.

My life outside of my family wasn't at all the same. When Mrs. Scott gave a shower for Dorothy Miller, she invited every town girl but me. To have 'married' status was okay, but only if you had a visible husband; and I didn't. Jean McRae's wedding, to an RCMP fellow from the town where she'd been teaching, was such a wedding as hadn't been seen in Rocanville. She asked Mr. Ingram to have the wedding party turn around and face the audience! My sister Pat was asked to be one of the servitors at the reception following the wedding, but I, who had been Jean and her sister Mary's close friend since 1927, was not invited to any of the functions! In so many petty ways, I was made to feel distinctly uncomfortable.

Once again, a girlhood friend remained kindly. Doris Masters and I picked up the same good feelings we had about each other, in spite of her sister Jean's cold and stuck-up attitude; a kindness I never forgot. (In 1999, shortly before Doris's death, I wrote her a letter to tell her that "...you proved to be the truest friend I had when I really needed one, and for that kind superhuman gift one is always thankful.") But I was adrift: no future for work, no future as a wife. Doris understood, even suggested that I get back to school, get my Grade XII and go to Normal School so I could become a teacher. We talked about this often.

In March 1934 Doris took me to stay with her in the one

room she rented from the Finnish family in Kaukanin. How generous that was; and probably against the wishes of her parents and her sister Jean. I remember baking for our week together, offering to pay for expenses. We shared a week together in which she took me to school and let me play with her students. We went to a great supper at Knutala's, where young Percy, her student, played his violin and I sang to the wonderment of his family. He hadn't known anyone who could sing like I, and I thought his talent would carry him far.

Hindsight indicates I didn't know how to pick up the reins of my life and direct it right then and there. Was I really so numbed by the Depression and so weak in my ability to look ahead and make plans? Seems like that was the only way to read it.

Then Bill wrote to me from Melville. Someone he'd known since boyhood had money to invest in a baker's oven, compensation from having lost a leg on the CNR tracks in Melville. Bill thought it was $4000. Would I send him the money I had saved? With some misgivings, I took that money, went to the local CPR station and transferred it to Bill. He notified me once only, after the job was set up.

From March until July I didn't hear from Bill, and then he sent me a gift.

One of the enticements to going back to my husband was his uncanny way of sending me something pretty and of good taste. He was illiterate and his vocabulary was unlike what I'd grown up with, yet he could pick garments that had real style and quality. In August he sent me a tan cotton skirt and a pink crocheted blouse. Doris admired them, telling me later that when she reported it to her mother and sister Jean they asked with obvious distaste, "And Jean wore them?" Oh ye, of little understanding! Of course I wore them. The Masters family, who were CPR people, had no idea, as our family had since 1922, what poor meant. And I had few things to wear.

Though I accepted the gift; I still felt no strong desire to link up with Bill again.

I looked at the options. That word wasn't even heard of in those days. Doris knew I could become a teacher; and she offered to add a few dollars to whatever I could find. It was an exciting thought, but for naught. In fact the only money I could think of might be from the business Bill was now involved in. What to do?

Mother would feel better if I'd return to Bill although she did want me to make up my own mind. I recalled that our time in Glenboro as a married couple hadn't been too bad. Bill hadn't been physically cruel, but it was a business alliance, nothing more; and we were civil to each other. I'd made friends with a couple of families who weren't interested in making friends with him, or he with them. Balcarres was unknown to me; it was a railway junction for both the CPR and CNR; it had at least twice Rocanville's population. Still, meeting new people in new areas always interested me.

In late summer, my sister and I talked about my future. We still shared the old wrought-iron bed. Pat didn't want me to leave home. But she was still young; and what did she know?

By September some decision had to be made. Doris was back at her teaching job. There was nothing for me to do in Rocanville, not even in Dad's grocery store, which, by now, was almost finished – the shelves were bare, and the few farm women who brought their butter and eggs in were all that kept him going. Dad had never been able to cope with anything more than serving over the counter and, perhaps, displaying some produce. Now, the butter he'd taken and left in the shed at the back of the store melted or turned rancid; and the only regulars at the store were his Pentecostal cronies, Sid Frost and Mr. Herman. Even Dave Shaw couldn't give me work; he'd hired another woman.

Then Bill sent a letter saying the bakery was "doing well" and would I please come and live with him again in Balcarres.

This is a part of my story that is more difficult to write

about because I'm trying to sort out my thinking about it. I really didn't want to return to Bill. I knew there was never going to be any desire on my part to continue in a relationship that held nothing for me; and perhaps he knew that, too. But what to do? Where to go? And how to disentangle myself from my own self-inflicted predicament? In the middle of the Depression any new venture that offered some economic security couldn't be tossed off without weighing the good with the-not-so-good. To join him again, I reasoned, was a new chance to have some subsistence. We had no telephone, and because using the local telephone office meant whatever was said was food for gossip, I penned Bill a short note and said I'd be on the CPR train on September 15.

It was one of the few times Mother broke down in tears, wishing I could stay home, saying as she wept, "Oh Jean, these bitter years; it's been so hard, so hard." She was wearing that old fugi silk dress that was originally rose-pink, and then dyed black, with an embroidered red rose with green leaves at the right side near the hem. I stood with sadness right to my core.

CHAPTER NINE
Balcarres: Breaking Away

The short train trip gave me the dejavu feeling of when the minister read the marriage service and I was thinking to myself I might be able to stop him right there. But it was a beautiful September day and we hadn't seen each other now for six months.

BALCARRES, SEPTEMBER 1934

Bill met the train, waiting for me on the platform. We walked to the store. More dejavu; this time like leaving the train when the Mathies arrived in McAuley....

My new beige skirt and pink knit top with brown oxfords gave the on-lookers in Balcarres something to take in with their morning coffee. Bill looked neat and, as we passed the stores, I noticed he was sort of showing me off. Compared with many small towns dotting the prairie, this one looked busy, with the longest Main Street I'd seen.

The bakery was in the centre of the business section, with a busy garage and service station on one side and a barber shop on the other. Its large windows looked across at an attractive general store. There was a small counter just inside the front door, with four booths on the east wall; from that space we walked into a kitchen with a large black range, the standard kitchen table, and a few odd chairs. The baker's oven, working counters and a home-made stand for wrapping bread filled the rest of that room. It appeared to be a good, viable business.

The partner was about to serve a young fellow a meal right there in the kitchen. Apparently he ate his lunch there every day. Boiled potatoes, canned corn and a good steak were served while introductions were made. I asked where we'd live and then Bill and I went out the rear door and up some steps to a room above the store.

There was room for a bed (we slept together) and a Winnipeg couch; and the window looking out on the street added a smidgen of colour. With dry goods ordered from Eaton's, I made a clothes cupboard on the wall space across from the bed, and some pretty curtains. We also had a little bedside table and one chair.

Although there really wasn't a "honeymoon period", I found it very pleasant to be in a new town. Within a few days, I felt a sense of optimism. In the front shop I was happy to be selling goods again across the counter. It was always easy to meet people.

When I went to my first church choir practice and was warmly welcomed, there was more reason to smile. I was recognized almost immediately as a valuable soloist, both at church and at the local dances. Having moved from McAuley, a mere village, to Rocanville with its well-defined social strata, and now to this town that sported two railway stations and a greater variety of business than I'd ever seen, my interest grew and with a sense of pleasure.

Twenty-two years of age, married in a kind of a way, healthy, vigorous and with music swirling in my head unceasingly, I let the less exciting things float off and into the background. Not to worry if your husband doesn't accompany you when you're invited out or asked to solo at the local dances. Balcarres was way ahead of anything I'd seen. Here, at every dance, and during the brief midnight lunch break, there was music or other entertainment. For example, Len Purdy did gymnastics on his athlete's bar, and I sang "Sing me to Sleep".

Previously my singing was appreciated, in Balcarres it was received and applauded joyously. I was involved in a delicate balancing act, unaware of danger. From time to time, I sensed that Bill wasn't pleased that my friends and my doings were separate and apart from our daily life. Which was true, and for good reason.

It was only a few weeks after I arrived in Balcarres for this 'fresh start' with Bill, that a new friend, Mabel Decker, invited me for a walk with her one evening. Getting acquainted with the layout of Balcarres was on my mind, and I said yes. We had walked for an hour or so when Mabel asked if I knew that Bill had vehemently denied that he was married. Surprise! Then she said, "Well, Mother and I talked it over and we think you should know."

"Know what?"

"You've met my friend, Nora," Mabel said, in more of a statement than question.

"Oh yes, we've met at church, and her brother who works at the Post Office; he eats his noon meal in the store from Monday to Friday."

"Yes," Mabel confirmed. "And Bill vowed to everyone, especially Nora, that he had never been married. He even said he'd marry her, and now she feels just awful."

Nora and Mabel had been schoolmates and confidantes since childhood; and now I knew how shocking and hurtful my advent on the local scene must have been to Nora. I, too, felt more than a little discomfited as Mabel and I walked back to the downtown, each of us aware of a mood that was opposite to the beginning of our walk.

Mabel's disclosure of Bill's off-key romance took the glow off my new-found second attempt to relate to Bill Mohart as my husband. The old tug at my own deeper instincts surfaced once more, nagged at me to retain my own personal integrity in the face of his evermore obvious lying which I now knew was as much a part of him as breathing.

That evening there was no alternative: I had to face that creature who wasn't in the least upset or concerned. He knew that I'd been fully advised about his romance. We had just a few words about it and, rather than quarrel, it was brief and cold. No apology from him, just a self-deprecating smirk when I said "it's too bad I had to know only now, not before I made the decision to come here." His defence? "She chased me."

FEBRUARY 15, 1936

My new career began on February 15, 1935, five months after I'd joined Bill in Balcarres. One day I was the wife of Bill Mohart; the next day I was just a homeless young woman with no money or means of support.

On the night of this sudden change in my circumstances, I'd reunited with Bill after three separations in our two year long marriage. That evening, I'd been one of the entertainers during the midnight lunch at the dance. Bill didn't dance, but he came and sat with the family who'd befriended me. Bill left after the entertainment, saying he'd have to begin the usual bread-making. "I'll see you later," he said. He didn't compliment me on my singing; however, didn't seem in a bad mood. I danced with good friends and then the Deckers and I walked home together, their house just across the main street and through the lane, easily visible from our upstairs room over the bakeshop.

Bill wasn't working. He'd gone to bed. I undressed and crossed the room, carefully lifted the cover to slip into bed, when his foot caught me hard and knocked me against the wall. "Nothing but a goddamn whore. Hope you got all you were looking for," he yelled.

From the moment his foot touched my stomach, everything changed. Fright, surprise, revulsion and fear startled me: *body and mind sent a strong message: get away from him; run! Get out of the room; you must get to Deckers' home. Wait! You're barefoot, in only a nightie. It's two in the morning, it's a Prairie winter night. Put your coat on! It's in the cupboard by the door....*

"Whore! Goddamn whore! Sucking up to anybody!"

Ignore his screamed accusations. If he keeps talking, you can get your coat off the hanger and slip it on....

But the sleeve's lining made a sound and Bill jumped from bed, grabbed me as I stood at the door, now wide awake. *Don't let him think you are scared*, I told myself as I reeled across the room, falling against the bed. I stood up and, coatless, headed for the door; but he was too quick. He slipped the key into the keyhole and locked the door. "Can't get out!" he shouted defiantly.

"I wouldn't mind being locked in here with a man; but I hate being in here with a maniac!" I said calmly. He stopped muttering and returned to bed while I remained near the door, looking out across Main Street. *Yes, the Deckers are still up. No use; can't jump from window, the street is twenty feet below.*

I moved to the couch with its pillows. And there I hunched for the next few hours, waiting for Bill to wake and go downstairs to the bakeshop.

I know what I am going to do. I pull on warm clothing and overshoes and walk to the street where Mr. Speers, the council appointed policeman, lives. His wife greets me with a surprised "Hello".

"Is Mr. Speers home? Could I please speak to him?" He is a kindly man and I don't like asking him to do something I know is distasteful.

"I've come to ask you to please accompany me to my home...because I am leaving...and I need to take my clothing with me," I stammer. "I've been through this before...and I know that I need your help."

Mr. Speers shakes his head in wonderment, mutters, "hard to believe..." and I know that I must be clearer. Must share the details.

After a few minutes of quiet and dreary talk, he says, "I'll come with you."

"I have a little trunk I'd like to take; do you have a cart we could put it on?" I ask. "Yes," he answers and we set off. We don't meet anyone along the way.

Upstairs, in the room that is our bedroom, I pack as quickly as possible while Mr. Speers sits on the couch. Suddenly, the door swings open and Bill rushes in. "Don't go, Jean. Please don't go," he begs. "I'm sorry. I'm sorry."

Seeing Mr. Speers' face softening, I turn from my little trunk and face him. "Bill. Last night you had nothing but terrible things to say to me. You called me a whore and a hussy and flirt...and you kicked me right here, in the stomach, and then you locked the door. You accused me of things you know I haven't done. You know why I'm going," I say firmly. "I am not going to live with you any more."

Mr. Speers sits on the couch, sadly shaking his head, but I know he believes me.

"Bill," he says, in his policeman voice, the shock of a few moments ago gone. "You're going to have to leave."

Still weeping, Bill leaves and I finish packing. Mr. Speers carries my bags down and at the bottom of the stairs I thank him and start towards a friend's home blocks away.

What is written here took place in 1935. Saskatchewan was then in the depth of the Great Depression. Times were just plain bad, anyway you looked at it. In some ways, it helped people bond, but there were grievous gaps when dealing with sociological suffering. No one had heard the term, 'Transition House' and there were no shelters for women who'd experienced abuse. Women lived and were judged by their community's standards, and abusive married men had little to worry about, since everyone remained passively silent when family troubles happened. Gossips had a field day; talk was cheap and without any consequence. The women who were hurt suffered, mostly alone, or if more fortunate, in the seclusion of family or a close friend. To leave one's husband was nothing less than sinful, bringing down the scorn of others and even the loss of friends. Then there was the awful problem of finding work...of any kind.

FINDING WORK

I have left Bill for the fourth time.

I have no job, no bed to sleep in and not a dime to buy food. Much as I enjoyed being known as a soprano soloist, that wouldn't earn me a cent; but I was young and strong and reliable.

I'd done plenty of housework and I knew how to work. The only work I can get is housework. The pay is poor but with the usual bed and board; if it's hard cleaning you can hope for a few dollars extra. Somebody will know of work and the only way to find out is to ask who needs a hired girl. So, I start looking.

A few households in that small town were presided over by women with $10 a month to spare on hired help, so I let it be known that I was available, and in a few days I had three offers: the Anglican minister's wife, the school inspector's wife and the 16 bed hospital.

The school inspector's wife and I were friends; we sang in the same choir week after week. When I told her I had two other offers besides hers, she said she'd wait, since she and her husband were going to Ontario in May and she'd like me to do her house-cleaning and painting while they were away. The hospital job wasn't available for another six weeks at least, so I went to the minister's wife. At the front door of the old, two-storey house just near the small hospital, she and I made a deal: if I cleaned the house from basement to attic and did the regular work as well as prepare three meals a day, and at least one wash-day a week, I'd earn $8.00 per month. She said the church would pay for it. "It hasn't had a good clean-out for some time," she added.

Before we talked, my pride had to be reckoned with and definitely pushed aside. Like the people of the town and local farm folk, Mrs. Hart knew I was always in demand at concerts and in the United church for my fine soprano voice. But she knew, too, that I'd walked away from the local baker because of his treatment of me and she was not stupid when we met now, when I needed any work I could get. With what dignity I had left, I said I'd gladly take her offer and would be there tomorrow morning.

"I like my tea brought to my bed," Mrs. Hart said in her new "boss" voice. She explained that the Reverend would deliver her morning tea to her bed, and that he'd also bring their terrier who would be allowed to snuggle under the bedclothes with her.

Was it then that I noticed for the first time her dull, thinning hair, how drawing it tightly back into a bun gave her face a nasty pinched look, a look that was as cold and friendless as the tone of voice with which she now addressed me?

A hired girl, in those days, was expected to do every kind of work pertaining to feeding and or cleaning humans and livestock as well as the house. If you carried water in, it was necessary to carry it out, in another state – from bedroom, bathroom, kitchen and again, barn, if necessary. While breakfast was being made, water was warmed in the stove's reservoir for toilettes. Then there was the tin boiler, at least a seven-pail capacity, that had to be filled and kept hot for the washing of dishes, people, walls, floors, clothing, chamber pots – all in a seemingly endless sequence. And, as in every household, the stove was the fiercest enemy until you taught it who was boss.

Furthermore, the hired girl slept where she worked; she was, in a sense, her employer's prisoner, with rarely a chance to sleep in and certainly no government scheme to aid her when she was let go or quit.

Preparing the first meal, I found that there was only one kitchen basin for all chores – from washing carrots to bedroom walls.

Mrs. Hart was a slave-driver, too, and I wanted to gain a good reputation as a worker, so, when the Reverend announced that they would be transferred in three weeks hence, I asked if I would still be needed. They said yes, and with that, the house got the cleaning of its life. That is, until one day, when her demeaning attitude, coupled with her orders, bit me too hard.

A pleasant young fellow knocked on the kitchen door one morning and, though Mrs. Hart could have answered the door herself, she sat in the dining room nearby. I suspect she preferred to have callers ushered into her presence. The caller was a young salesman. We began a conversation, interrupted in a few minutes by Mrs. Hart, who ordered me to stop talking and bring the caller in to see her. Embarrassed, but aware of her rights, I asked the young man to follow me and, in his presence, Mrs. Hart angrily and with pomposity said "get on with the dinner and the wall, floors and woodwork washing." She topped off her orders by slamming the door shut between me in the kitchen and she and the young man. I was enraged.

Dinner was always at noon. I emptied the washbasin of suds, rinsed it and went to the basement for potatoes.

When I returned upstairs, I heard her ushering the fellow out. Come what may, I thought, I cannot work for her for another day, or even another hour. I put the paring knife down, undid my apron and walked up to my room, tucked a few clothes in a sheet, walked downstairs and opened the front door to leave. I hadn't worked a full month yet, nor been paid even one dollar and knew that I might not get any pay at all if I left now. I turned, saw my employer sitting alone with her wire-haired lap dog and stepped outside. I closed the door firmly and sadly walked toward the gate. Just as I reached it, Mrs. Hart flung the door open, her eyes mean and hot, and yelled, "You come back here! I want those potatoes cooked for dinner!"

"In that case, Mrs. Hart, you'll have to peel them yourself!" I said with my last bit of courage.

A good friend allowed me to sleep at her home that night, though I had to share a bed with her snoring houseguest; and the next day I went to see Mrs. Harring, the school superintendent's wife, and was hired. Mrs. Harring paid her hired girl $15 per month.

A few weeks later, the Reverend Hart found me and paid me for the exact number of days I'd been their hired girl. I never saw Mrs. Hart again.

Working for Mrs. Harring

Mrs. Harring and I knew each other from the church choir. She was a woman of strong, sturdy, yet attractive build, and her good contralto voice matched her figure. Sometimes we sang duets, and our voices blended well. Even today, when I hear "Consider and hear me, O Lord my God", I am singing with Mrs. Harring in excellent harmony. Again, I understood that she was hiring me to do housework. I also knew she was a no nonsense person, but different from Mrs. Hart in that she was essentially decent.

Dr. Harring, who'd risen from school teacher to superintendent, was one of the few well paid people in town. And it showed. The typical farmhouse had spacious room on both first and second floor. I was to do house work, but there was an added reason they hired me. Mr. & Mrs. Harring were going on a lengthy visit to relatives in Ontario and they needed a chaperone for their children, Ruth 12, and Lewis 14.

I'd been in their home before, for choir socials and, though not unpleasant, this house tour was different. "While we're away," she said, "would you be able to paint the kitchen and pantry? I have the paint on hand." Though the kitchen was large and the pantry would have to be cleared, I said I liked to paint and would find time when the children were at school.

Care of the basement also awaited and its dimension matched the upper floors – big, square and with a mix of large and small items to clean, move, and return to their places. Hanging from the sturdy rafters was a double row of shelving, which Mrs. Harring said was so placed to hold the eight pies that were baked each week, safe-guarded there, from invading mice!

Upstairs, the large bedroom was used by the parents, with Ruth and Lewis each having their own, and I was given a modest room. I hadn't seen such nice bedrooms since my earliest years when we still had good bed linens, quilts and dressers with matching washstands....

This wasn't my home, but the even-tempered atmosphere of the house created a little glow in me that warmed my bruised spirit. There was something else, too, and that was my eagerness to prove I could do the job and tuck a little money in my empty purse. I would have good room and board and earn really good pay.

Now my years of housework experience came to my rescue. Dinner was to be ready at noon, so whatever else was to do be done, lots of potatoes had to be peeled, mashed, whipped, and piled in a good bowl, only to vanish as though someone had waved a wand over the table. The Harrings were good eaters.

By the time the Harrings left for the trip east, I was at ease with my work. Mrs. was pleased with everything I did, especially the cooking. One odd task was making the piecrust; it had to be rolled 1/8th inch thick; Mr. Harring had had his spleen removed and wasn't to eat any rich food – or, at least, very little.

Like all siblings these two had their disagreements, sometimes erupting into physical battles. Ruth's music lessons and practicing for a Toronto conservatory exam caused Lewis to threaten to shut the piano on her fingers. She responded with strong words and a temper to match. Most of the time I let them go at it, but sometimes I intervened. And they respected me.

Dinner table conversation was adult, interesting and usually intellectual. When supper was over, Ruth often offered to wash dishes, "Because I need to clean my fingernails," she'd say. And I was glad for the help.

Mr. Harring returned home earlier than his wife and, without the watchful eye of his wife, he insisted on eating pie. Within days, he suffered stomach pain and was bedridden. This put a strain on my work, especially when the doctor ordered hot water-bottle treatment. Then another doctor replaced the first and ordered ice-packs! Mr. Harring responded slowly, mostly due to eating properly; when his wife learned of his illness, she returned home.

Ten days to go before the end of my second month, the span for which I'd been hired. Mrs. Harring was pleased that everything she'd asked me to do was done, so I was surprised when she said, "That's fine; but you can be finished tomorrow."

"Tomorrow! Why tomorrow, if I was hired by the month?"

"Because I don't need you anymore," she said, not unkindly, but without feeling.

Once again, I was unemployed and homeless.

BALCARRES HOSPITAL

I found new work, at the Balcarres Hospital for $25 a month. For three and a half months, I answered the telephone and the door, as well as cooked for the dozen or so patients and a staff that included a doctor, three nurses and the male helper. I laundered everything that had to be washed, hung out the wash (with sometimes freezing fingers), ironed the starched uniforms, washed all dishes, pots, pans, slop bowls, pails and floors. When needed, I was also the "run-around-girl" who ran upstairs to do odd jobs while surgery took place in the operating room. Was I tired! I was young and strong but when I dropped onto the couch in a corner of the dining room every night (my 'bedroom') my exhaustion was absolute.

JUNE 21, 1935

I'd been given notice. My job at the hospital was to end June 30th.

A married couple was taking over the operation of the hospital and was going to try to run it themselves. And now what? When I saw an ad in the Regina Leader Post for a full-time housekeeper in Sintaluta, I applied.

While at supper, the phone rang for me. The caller was Harry Jackson, whose ad I'd answered. Mr. Jackson said he'd pay ten dollars a month plus a government grant of five dollars he received because his wife was an invalid. He wanted me to know that this was not an ordinary housekeeping job; his invalid wife required "a lot of care", and "there'll be other duties as well". I told him I was experienced, could handle that, and agreed to be in Sintaluta on July 1.

On June 30th, a friend drove me to Indian Head, from where I'd catch a morning bus to Sintaluta.

I left Balcarres wearing the only shoes I had, my $2.95 Eaton's summers; Bill Mohart, who still resided in Balcarres, and who was not pleased that I had left him, had stolen my only decent pair of Oxfords, along with my little black satin hat. During the time I worked at the hospital, Bill convinced the doctor, who needed every case he could get to cover his costs, that he had appendicitis. I was in the operating room when Bill had the surgery, and saw, along with others present, that there wasn't a thing wrong with that hunk of tissue. Though I'd left him, he remained in my life, always making it his business to know my whereabouts. But his stealing my shoes during the time he'd 'posed' as a patient, did not stop me.

CHAPTER TEN

Sintaluta: "The Hired Help"

Pronounced Sin-ta-lu-ta, its name is derived from the Sioux language; its English meaning is "tail of the fox". Before the CPR made its way across the west, pioneers stopped in this town to refresh their supplies before heading west.

I woke on July 1, 1935, in the only hotel in Indian Head, Saskatchewan, knowing I must get something to eat before boarding a bus to the little village 8 or 9 miles east.

When the hotel clerk handed my bag to the bus driver, he said in a sarcastic manner that embarrassed me, "Yeah, I've got a really big one for you," meaning, the smallest possible bus fare.

No one met me at the bus stop in Sintaluta. I looked up and down the block-long Main Street and in my heart I wished I could run away...anywhere. I'd tied my hair back with a little ribbon bow on top of my head and had on my one decent summer dress, but I knew I must look weary and heart-sore, exactly how I felt. "You looked," Bud Jackson would confirm later, "well, I won't tell you what I thought when I saw you!"

In a store crowded with groceries, hats, hardware and farmers' supplies, I asked the woman behind the counter where Jacksons lived. Her name was Mrs. Black, she was also the United Church organist, and became a friend in the next three years, though I couldn't have imagined it as I observed her frumpy appearance that morning, a dressy hat on her head, as if defying all the jumble of the store surrounding her. "Would you like to sit down?" she asked me kindly; and I knew I looked as wan as I felt.

Worried that someone might be looking for me, I picked

up my only piece of luggage, a small, cheap bag. Someone was walking from the bank at the other end of the street towards me. He approached and, with not a touch of welcome, said he was Bud Jackson and would drive me over to his home. Bud worked at the local bank and boarded at home, a fact I hadn't been told.

The Jackson house was on a rise on the other side of the CPR tracks, an unpainted square building set apart from the barn farther off in a lower area, about a quarter of a mile from town. On the way over, Bud said the local doctor had lent him his car. That was our only conversation.

Shock. Dismay. That's what I felt upon our arrival. Though I'd tended sick people since the age of eleven, nothing could have prepared me. By the one good-sized window in the room, in an arm chair that matched the dining room furniture, and fixed into the chair with some cloth supports, sat Mrs. Jackson.

How can I describe her?

She weighed perhaps 90 pounds and was a caricature of a human being who had suffered from crippling rheumatism since the age of 23. Every part of her was frozen into the shape I saw, including her face, so that her eyes seemed to peer out from an odd angle, and that was because even her neck was not straight. Her thinning hair was combed back in a little bun. In one hand, fixed between two fingers, she held a wooden knitting needle that was topped with a handkerchief, and this she used to wipe her nose or mouth. Her face must have been pretty before the ravages of her illnesses dragged her features out of shape, her nose a bit to one side.

I suppose I took in the awfulness of this in a moment, yet, remembering it now, I feel that I stood stock-still for some few minutes, forcing myself to sound pleasant while, inside, I churned and cried out, Heavens, no! Not this. I can't bear it and I don't want to stay even today.

Mrs. Jackson spoke while I gathered myself: "We have our main meal at noon. Bud will show you the garden and where you'll clean the vegetables at the pump. I know where everything is, so I'll tell you how to get dinner. You can have the upstairs room. Bud, take her bag up." Crippled she was; stupid she was not.

Bud picked up my bag and asked me to follow. We walked through the kitchen and I noted a bedroom off to the left. Up two steps, turn to the right and just a few more stairs and we'd reached the little attic under the roof where I was to sleep and maybe read or write letters. Bud was perfunctory to the point of being unfeeling.

It would have been so good just to lay on the bed and have a nap, but I was expected and needed downstairs. Bud went back to town to return the car; and Mr. Jackson showed me the dugout cellar where some foods could be kept cool. But it was clear from the start that Mrs. Jackson was giving orders, which she did in a rather urgent and poorly articulated voice; because arthritis had affected her mouth, she could not wear dentures. Time after time I was amazed at how she knew every detail of that house, where every jar was stored and what was in it; and it was the same for everything.

From my first hour in that house, it was drudgery, from rising at 6 a.m., to dropping onto my bed at night. I made the bread, butter, pickles, all meals and, at Christmas, the mincemeat. I washed bedding and clothing, scrubbed floors, washed dishes, cleaned and sterilized the cream separator. I gathered eggs, harvested vegetables and washed them at the pump.

But housework was the minor part of my duties; Mrs. Jackson's condition took constant care; just getting her up and putting her to bed was an exercise, since every slight movement caused her pain. With Mr. Jackson's help, I lifted her up in bed to a sitting position, plumping pillows around her so I could get her day started. Later I bathed her, in bed.

On Sundays, Mr. Jackson and I gave her a real bath.

Every morning he and I ate breakfast together and then he'd go out to milk the cow while I struggled to get Mrs. Jackson out of bed and on the makeshift wheelchair. Mr. Jackson had put cheap casters on the four legs of a dining room armchair, and I'd push that cumbersome chair from the bedroom into the front dining/living room.

When Mr. Jackson came in with the milk, it was my job to put it through the separator. That was something new to me and I had to learn how to commence pumping the machine's handle very slowly at first, gradually faster till the spouts showed the separation of milk and cream. Cleaning the separator was a real chore: there were seventeen parts to be washed, scalded and wiped, then put back together.

When meals were ready Mrs. Jackson was fed first; and that, too, was an endurance test. Often she complained that I didn't hold the spoon right, and she judged every morsel that was served. If I was slow to get a spoon of broth to her mouth, she nagged me to "hurry" in that sharp tone of hers. If I had a spoon too soon near her mouth, she could shrink me to a meanness I hated myself for.

One day, a spoonful of chicken soup spilled onto her lap. She was furious and bawled me out. I was almost in tears, but quickly ran to the kitchen while her son angrily told her she didn't deserve someone trying to help her. That didn't make her kinder towards me.

One thing I did demand: that I have time to go to choir practice, and on my first meeting I was given a warm welcome. It was a small church, with a capacity of 150, though a typical winter night gathering was perhaps 25. I was needed for my good soprano, and the compliments were salve to my bruised psyche and warmth to my sodden spirits.

Mr. Jackson also carried a tremendous load and had help with his farm work only intermittently: When the Saskatchewan government gave a grant for farm help in the rich sum of $8 per month, a hired man served; and because Mrs. Jackson relied on total care, the government gave five dollars a month. Mr. Jackson promised he'd give me an extra $2.50 a month, but he never had that much cash. The son, Bud, usually kept his distance.

Crops weren't heavy that year. Mr. Jackson had an ancient steamer that he trusted and even when the younger neighbour on the next section offered to help with threshing and to bring his modern machine over, Mr. Jackson said no, he'd do his own.

The old round oak table in the living room was lengthened to accommodate a crew of men. I was warned that there'd have to be ten loaves of bread every day, enough biscuits to give the workers a substantial morning break, along with jam, cookies and hot tea. All this was in addition to the usual routine involved in looking after Mrs. Jackson.

The first day proved how much extra energy would be required. Mr. Jackson called me at 3 a.m. I came downstairs, took the yeast out of the honey pail that had been set in warm water the night before, and began. In order to have bread for breakfast I had to get up early enough to have a hot fire going by 6:30. By the time the men assembled for breakfast I was ready for them; when they left, it was time to attend to Mrs. Jackson.

The hot biscuits were a chore that kept me running for more wood. It was the same in that house as in every house of that era: Get to manage the great, black wood-eating devil or be doomed in everything you cooked on top of or in the oven.

It was I who had to load the basket to carry the 10 o'clock lunch to the voraciously hungry harvesters out in the middle of the field; and it was I who had to get dinner found, prepared and cooked by noon.

On the very first day of threshing, the old steamer quit. In fact it broke down every day, so that instead of three or four days, the threshers were there until October 2; and me slaving each day from 3 in the morning, till 10 at night. No wonder I developed hives! They broke out in places I'd never ever seen them – around my elbows, between my fingers, even on the soles of my feet. If I dared scratch, an infection set in. The local doctor said my blood was so poor from being run-down, that there was no resistance to infection. I could wear a slipper on my right foot only by removing the instep, as one hive suppurated for over three months.

By this time, I'd had enough. I loathed the whole set-up, the work most of all, but the bullying by Mrs. Jackson was hardest to take. I told Mr. Jackson I'd be leaving. He was alarmed. He knew I was doing my best both around the house and with his wife. His daughter came home that weekend and begged me to stay. The son also stated his case. Under their pressure, I agreed to stay through the winter; as it later proved, it was as big a mistake as I ever made.

No doubt Mrs. Jackson's condition had made her bitter; and no wonder: before she was 23 she had had five miscarriages, and borne twins, but the toll her rheumatism had on her body was the most devastating, and in those days there was no proper treatment for her condition, let alone a cure. The only break in Mrs. Jackson's monotony was a visitor, and one of the townswomen, Mrs. Rally, did call once a month.

When chores were caught up enough after our noon meal, I went to my little room, always dead tired. But in winter the only warmth came if I lifted a bit of carpet that covered the grated register and let heat from the little heater float up. The attic ceiling had frost on every exposed wood and slats.

One winter afternoon, Mrs. Rally visited. At such a time I was to fire up the stove, make tea and serve it with a fresh cake and some canned fruit. I'd made tea for the two ladies and, feeling a need for a rest, went up to my room. As soon as I was out of their hearing, I knew I was being discussed. And sure enough, to my chagrin, I heard Mrs. Jackson referring to me throughout her conversation as 'the help'. How could she? Was there not one atom of mercy left in her disfigured body? By now I knew that there wasn't a kind thought about me. What caused her to hate me? And why should I feel so outraged, when really all I was there for was 'to help'? Still, her attitude stung me to my marrow with a life-long impact. I wanted to grab my old suitcase, stuff my clothing into it, rush downstairs and tell the two women I was leaving. I hated both of them with a white and deadly rage. If I'd been 'just a housemaid', as she implied, could I have accepted the term? It was a demeaning slur.

One Sunday evening, Mr. Forrest, one of the town's better-off merchants, approached me after church and asked if he could have a word with me in private. I stepped aside with him, and he quietly asked me to work at his home. His wife, he said, had been advised by the local doctor to not work anymore. It was like the heavens opening and an angel offering me something warm and sweet. His request meant an easier job and with even a little prestige, since the Forrests were respected citizens. I accepted immediately, but added "I was hired by the month and will have to stay till the end of March."

"I know," he said, "and I wish I could offer you more, but all I can pay you is $6.50; I'll make it more when I can."

Even with a two dollar per month pay cut, this was a godsend, nothing less than what I needed most at that time – to get out of the Jackson household. We agreed we wouldn't talk to anyone else about it and went our separate ways.

As I walked back from church that night, crunching through the snowy road up towards the small, tawdry farm home where I had that tiny space under the attic ceiling, I was in seventh heaven. I kept my secret, not telling the Jacksons until the end of the month, the day before I moved out. I had so few clothes that there was only a small bag and a cardboard box I used for my two best dresses – the dresses I wore to dances.

Of course, I'd met Mrs. Forrest often, at church and other events. I was the town's singer at public, social events, but there was no mistake about my role in their house: once again, I was 'the hired girl'.

Mrs. Forrest gave me her orders in a flat dry voice, and I knew what was expected. "He (she never referred to him by name) will have the stove going and get the kettle boiling. You will make his breakfast and eat it with him. I sleep later, and you'll make my breakfast when I get up." She explained her blood pressure and other physical problems. "The doctor says I'm just to sit a lot, and that's funny because I've worked all my life; but my grandchildren can use lots of sweaters and mitts, and I like to knit."

From the day I started there until the day I left, with the exception of one New Year's morning, Mrs. Forrest never let me sleep in. At 6.30 a.m, from her bed to mine on the opposite side of the wall between us, she called in her low voice, "Jean, it's time to get up. Jean?" Perhaps this judgement is unfair, after all she was the boss and I was the servant; but within a year, I hated that call. It all goes back to a reaction to being ordered by someone older and with a certain amount of power over me.

I dressed quickly, standing over the little register in the floor just above the great black kitchen range that was already warming the kitchen. The kitchen was cozy and inviting. Compared with the small cook stove I'd grown up with, this was a beauty, every part – warming oven, copper reservoir, baking oven – looked stately, almost officious.

But it was an odd house in that it lacked a dining room. There was a small front parlour, roomy enough for one of the overstuffed black leather chairs and a fine piano; but Mr. Forrest chose to put a Quebec heater where ordinarily the dining table would have sat, and this room was where he and she sat most of the time, he in the other large chair, she in a wooden rocker that was always draped with a crocheted shawl. That room had a beautiful mahogany table and over by the window, a china cabinet filled with exquisite pieces of china, crystal and silver. The couch was my domain, plain but pretty with cretonne cover and decorated cushions. In the evenings, when dishes were done and I had this part of the day to myself, I was happy as a clam with some reading material, a book lent by a friend or the one magazine I could afford: *Chatelaine*, at 35 cents a month.

Though we became fond of each other, I addressed them as Mr. and Mrs. They called me Jean from day one. How good it was to show them my talents as a cook and I revelled in it, since it was in stark contrast to my previous job! The piano, however, was the greatest source of pleasure for me and for anyone who visited. I hadn't had a piano since my last year at home, and every time I was within reach of one, I ached to sit down and play. I found some lovely music in the piano bench that had lain untouched since their youngest daughter left home to get married.

One of Mr. Forrest's debtors was Reddy, the alcoholic painter. People weren't hiring him much because everyone was feeling the pinch of what later became a 10-year stretch of depressed income. So Reddy was brought over from his one-room shack and asked to bring samples of wallpaper and paint. Mr. Forrest would have been able to give me a wide smile to show his pleasure, but he was one of those persons who couldn't abide wearing dentures. As a result, he made strange faces when he chewed, clamping his chin up to his nose; and when he smiled, he kept his mouth shut and let his moustache tell you he meant to smile. He was 'smiling' when he said, "Choose any wallpaper you want, Jean; and any paint as well."

My bedroom was larger than any other room in the house and, urged by Mr. Forrest to do what I pleased, I chose to have the walls covered with pink roses climbing up white lattices, and the whole stretch of ceiling made to look like a night of bluest blue with a scattering of silver stars twinkling down on me. My gratitude for such generous consideration was real, and I expressed it warmly. Never once had my Dad papered or painted anything, let alone asked if I had a preference in such matters!

If one looks for a balance in this scene it would be in the rigid routine that both Mr. and Mrs. Forrest observed, developed over a long life of practise. The routines were fixed and followed. He sat in the armchair, she sat in her rocker. He ate breakfast first, and she later. By the time I had the table set, he had emptied the little pan of coal dust from yesterday's fire in the Quebec heater. Mr. Forrest liked people to know that he bought hard coal – more costly than soft coal or wood – to heat it. We sat down; he said a brief Grace, the porridge was eaten or fresh hot toast, with preserves that I was praised for creating. The kitchen was cleared after breakfasts were over.

There was an upstairs routine as well, with time taken to 'workup' the feather mattresses, brush down the narrow carpeted staircase, and pick anything up that lay on the stairs to be stored upstairs; it was one of the good things she taught me: "Don't leave anything laying here and there; put them in their place; be neat!"

Dinners were planned by Mrs. Forrest. Both she and I had a nap after the noontime dinner and washing up, and then I put on a clean dress and walked the block-and-a-half over to one of the two grocery stores for whatever the kitchen needed, except for the roast for Saturday morning. That was Mr. Forrest's job because he liked to go to the butcher and get a special cut of roast to cook in the fine black range. Not only was the rule of the Saturday roast absolute, I was expected to make a cake and a couple of pies as well, since nothing, nothing at all, was to be cooked on Sunday. His boots were also shined on Saturday.

On Sundays, we left for church half an hour early to ensure that their pew was not occupied by anyone else. I was choir leader and waited behind the pews for my singers.

My early schooling was enhanced because of one remarkable woman who inspired appreciation for the beauty of poetry, prose and music. Since McAuley, where I'd learned this from Miss Porter, a church service moves my soul, enabling me to sift through all the rest of daily living and relax. In Sintaluta, while working for Forrest's, that soul-stirring mood cooled the first time they and I walked home from church.

Mrs. Forrest was heavy on her feet and was glad to sit down in her rocking chair. I was hoping to relax when Mr. Forrest walked out to the well, pumped half a dozen pails of water and filled the copper boiler he'd brought in from the shed and set over the hottest plates for Monday morning's wash day. Since he never liked radio and it was Sunday night, I didn't play the piano. Growing up, Sunday night was a time for socialising with piano, other instruments and lots of singing. And thus, of all the routines in the Forrest home, the Sunday evening pre-washday ritual irked me the most.

Still, for a year and a half it was a good way of life. I earned $6.50 a month and, though he never came through with a few extra dollars that he promised, Mr. Forrest did use his business connections to let me order shoes. But, of course, I paid for them.

In their own way, they were good to me. They allowed me to have a birthday party and invite two or three friends. They bragged to guests that I was the best cook in town. They shared in my enjoyment as a performer in singing and acting. When I had my appendix out, they allowed me to go home to recover. Even their daughters brought me a small gift, saying how pleased they were that I took care of their parents. In some ways, I'd never had it so good.

It's difficult to say how he began to bother me because I'd

never regarded his affection for me as anything more than a family kind of admiration. He would eat his breakfast, wipe his heavy moustache, stand up, don a jacket and leave. One morning he put his arm around my waist from behind and drew me close. I didn't respond, nor did I pull away at first. The next day he did the same. Gradually, the hugs got 'squeezy'; and then one day – and I still shrink at the memory – he kissed me on the mouth. Without dentures, his kisses were fleshy and very unpleasant. I was repulsed.

When the kisses seemed to become another ritual, I knew something had to be done. How could I handle this without trouble? Perhaps I had put up with the entire situation and now it was I who needed to point out to him that it was wrong.

"What's wrong with it? I just want you to know how fond of you I've become," he said when I suggested this.

"How do you think *she* would feel about you kissing me?" I asked him.

He seemed unsettled at my remark. My point was difficult for him to argue, and he said he would abide by my feeling and stop his behaviour.

Harassment by Mr. Forrest was unexpected, disturbing and uncomfortable and I know I handled it properly. Since that time there are so many other incidents of that nature – some too difficult to put on paper.

Now, as I write this, I am at an age where harassment by a male will not likely occur again; and it's a strange feeling to be an old female with nary a wink or a flirtatious moment happening. But between then and now, the latter happened again – in Sintaluta; and elsewhere. In the late fall of 1937....

FALLING IN LOVE AGAIN!

Mr. Forrest didn't believe radio was worth having, a relative in Toronto sent *The Telegram* and I allowed myself the *Chatelaine*. And we got the *Regina Leader Post*. Apart from that, my being secretary of the Ladies Aid, conducting the little United Church choir and the Quadrille Club dances on a Friday in the Memorial Hall were the only bits of colour in my day-to-day routine of making meals and cleaning.

In the third year of this routine that I was beginning to inwardly rebel against, came a lovely looking young man, Gordon. Gordon approached me after the church service in the small church where I led the few singers who showed up for choir. We conversed and were quickly interested in each other, but it was after we danced together that our feelings were evident.

The night of the dance I wore an old, navy blue crepe dress Mrs. Forrest had given me. She was short and tubby and I was 5' 4" so I had gathered it into a sort of fit for me and pinned a little lace collar and some red tissue flowers to give it a dress-up look. The dress would have been a failure but for the width of the skirt at the hem and the pleated edging that gave it a nice swirl when stepping out in a dance. I knew I was light-of-foot and had excellent rhythm; and now Gordon complimented me on my dancing. He was good, too. There was no doubt in his mind or mine that we were just meant for each other...and suddenly my life pulsed with a new and needed experience: I was in love with someone manly, handsome; a man who liked poetry and had a personality that swept me off my feet. Oh, it was beautiful!

It snowed gently as we walked home and stopped by the Forrest barn on that New Year's Eve. After a most loving kiss, I made a large "X" in the snow with my foot, pointed down at it and said, "X marks the spot". Gordon seemed surprised and we both laughed. When we entered the back shed off Forrest's home I stopped, put my arms around Gordon and said, "May the Lord bless you and keep you; may he shine his countenance upon you and give you peace." I'll never know why I did that. He accepted my gesture, we went into where Forrests sat by the always red glowing Quebec heater, chatted with them and then he left.

"People are beginning to talk, Jean," Mr. Forrest cautioned after Gordon left. As though I was doing something wrong. "I don't care about people," I retorted. My passion for Gordon was lit and couldn't be turned off; and that is about what I said to Mr. Forrest, weeping as I said it.

Looking back, that romance was the purest and most rewarding of any I've ever experienced – while it lasted. Having said that, I have to correct myself, for I have carried the torch for Gordon all the rest of my life, in spite of knowing that he married and is probably as old and wrinkled as I am now.

After professing his love for me, Gordon moved to Vancouver from where he intended to take the Orion steamship to Australia. When he arrived, he took a job in the mine at Britannia Beach instead. From Vancouver, he wrote pages and pages of the most romantic letters I've ever received, sometimes three per week, with snapshots inside, of himself and the rocky terrain on the West Coast. "Is there a letter for me?" I'd ask the kindly postmaster. "Oh yes, Jean. Here's a big thick one for you," he'd reply.

"I might as well send the entire writing pad!" Gordon wrote in one letter. His letters, in which he continued to profess his love and promises of being together again as soon as possible, sent me winging and I replied in like style. He wrote as though we were going to be married, even though I wasn't yet divorced from Bill Mohart.

Then, without any warning, the letters stopped. I was completely heart-broken, but I didn't feel I could ask his father why I wasn't getting any letters. Instead, I told myself to not let it show too much.

Then my resolve began to be born – something I'd let lie dormant for some time: I would give my notice and leave Forrest's. I was 26 years old and after nearly three years at Forrest's, still earning the same money. But where? I didn't know; all I knew is that I must get away....

The popular music of that day was filled with romantic pathos with lyrics that caused pangs of heartache when listeners like me felt every nuance of those pieces, especially when the vocalist seemed to be singing your song. The unexplained, abrupt end of the romance with Gordon was made worse because I had no answer to "Why? Why did he stop writing?"

A young man, Ronald, had always shown me special attention. His tenor went well with my mezzo soprano. When he was given a piece to practice for the music festival, we met in the small church that was now used only for meetings. Inside was an old pump organ. The Forrest's fine piano would have been much nicer, but Mr. Forrest would have neither approved nor allowed me to bring Ronald there to practice. (When Gordon and I met it was after church or at a dance or at a friend's home.)

With the coming of spring, I could go out after clearing up the supper dishes, walk over to my friend's home and stroll with her along Main Street. It became a ritual through the break-up of winter. Some nights Ronald paired with another town lad whose father let him drive the family car, and we often let them pick us up to drive somewhere just out of town, to talk, laugh about some of the citizens, go back home and, once in a while, stop at my friend's where her mother always welcomed us and served tea and her terrific buns and jam.

Giving a month's notice to the Forrest's, as I had now resolved to do, was going to be harder than anything I'd done in my twenty-six years. For the first time since childhood, I'd enjoyed a comfortable home. My reputation in the town was built through my being their household help and what they allowed me to do in the musical and social life of the church and community at large. I was torn.

Then a Winnipeg couple visited with another friend of

mine and I was asked to play the piano at her home. The guests listened to me sing and suggested I take my talents elsewhere – to Winnipeg. Sure, lots of places to sing there. But Winnipeg! How much money would be necessary to live till I could find a job? They didn't offer any help and saving money wasn't possible on what I was paid; nor did I know a soul who could either lend or give me cash. Still, it was time to move on.

After breakfast with Mr. Forrest one morning, I let him put his arm around me, pulled back a little and said, "I'm really sorry to tell you, but I am going to leave you and Mrs. Forrest, and this is my one-month's notice, so I'll be here until April 1st." He was shocked and said so. "I guess we thought you'd stay with us…" He left to walk to his shop, his countenance troubled, shaking his head with sadness.

When Mrs. Forrest arose later, as usual, I braced myself, and stumbled through giving a month's notice. Now it was done. When I attended the next women's church meeting, a woman with three daughters making their living away from home said, with genuine kindness, "Good for you; I've been hoping you could manage that."

At the same time, Ronald, the young man I sang with, began seeking his fortune elsewhere. A friend told him he could get a job in Trail, BC at $8.00 a day and now he wanted to include me in his plans. To me he was a dear friend, and more; a good person who deserved much better than the small wage he earned looking after the local physician's horse.

For the first time in my life I had made a careful, well thought out and difficult decision, and it gave me a new sense of self assurance. There was a feeling that I had discovered: I could be free to take charge of my life; after three years of being in a comfortable environment, I knew it was time to move on. I was ready to take on the unknown. But I have to admit: The attentiveness of a nice fellow like Ronald perhaps eased some of the hidden hurt I still felt from the bitter and abrupt ceasing of Gordon's fine, heart-warming and caring letters.

Telling me of his hopes to leave town for a better job he heard of, I was surprised that Ronald talked as though I would be with him. It never entered my head. Our friendship was based on being together – quite a lot – for singing together, and I had encouraged him in that regard; but my feelings for him never went beyond that. Besides, he talked of going west and I hoped to go east.

Robbie Burns said for his ear and for all time: "The best laid plans o'mice and men gagn aft agley...." (including women, too).

One evening I was with Ronald and friends. We'd enjoyed the usual singing and dancing, all in good fun. On this night our good-night kiss was warmer, with a touch of passion. This new urgency to live my own life may have tipped the balance that wavered between reason and desire. My restored health, and the hope of new challenges, were heady wine. Not only that, since being on my own in the past three years, I hadn't had any sexual relationship. In the background, silent but more powerful than anything I'd ever known, Mother Nature assumed her role, providing me with a lesson I would never forget. And I let things unfold as they did....

"Don't worry. Nothing will happen," I assured Ronald afterwards; and I really believed that. Twenty-six, with lots of previous sex, I had never once been "caught". My guiding spirit must have been weeping at my utter, wilful turning my back on the care, the genuine concern given me in that moment by Ronald.

Within a few weeks the unthinkable had to be recognised: we had both reacted to impulse, and I, at twenty-six, was 'caught'.

I finished my work on March 31st and my girl friend said her mother wanted me to spend a few days with them. Those were the last few days of one part of my life before my entire world changed.

I had been given a purse of $35 at a little party the church arranged to bid me farewell and Godspeed. The Greyhound bus took me back to Rocanville where my Mother and family made room for me. On April 16th, Mother's birthday, I knew for certain. I was pregnant. Reality began...and it not yet at the finish line.

Months later, I received a letter that Gord had written during this time. The letter, in which he invited me to resume our relationship (he said he'd been ill and hospitalized) had gone to and from the Dead Letter offices in Rocanville and Sintaluta for nearly six months. I replied and told him my news...and there has never been any communication since.

CHAPTER ELEVEN
Kimberley, B.C.

There I was, back with a man who had no sense of decency. How could I? How could I not? I didn't want my child to grow up as a "bastard". Bill Mohart offered to give my child a legitimate name; and more. He promised to do so honourably which, given our past, I might have known was impossible. He did the opposite; he slandered me.

I try not to be sad but I am sad when I look back at the pregnancy. Since my first period, when I was aware of my ability to procreate, I had wanted to be pregnant. To go through this wonderful experience without someone to talk to, and share it with, was the most tragic aspect.

This baby is going to be okay, I told myself; and to the child inside me I said, over and over, "no matter what happens to me, you're going to be treated beautifully."

How did Bill Mohart know I was back in Rocanville with my family and that I was pregnant by a man who was not my husband? Then again, Bill seemed always to find out my whereabouts – even after we divorced, and until the day he died, he tracked and stalked me.

"There's a letter for you," Mother told me one day. "Bill has written to you."

"How does he know where I am?" I asked. There was no answer.

After a month or so of talking with Bill and my parents who suggested I return to him, Bill informed me that Harry & May Redding would be driving from Saskatchewan to their home in Kimberley and "they'll pick you up if you'll meet them in Regina." And so I told mother, "okay I'll go; that'll give my child legitimacy." I should have had both our names changed when we left him, but I had no money back then and so, to this day, that name remains in my life – my son carries it and his children inherited it also. "But I like it," my granddaughter told me, "though I don't you suppose you do," she added. No, I don't. I shudder every time I hear or see it.

I left home in June 1938. From the start, Bill was not nice to me. I talked to my unborn child and sang to him, in private and especially on Friday nights when a group of people met at the home of Mr. Oppenheimer, the music teacher in Kimberley. "Mr. Opie", as we called him, sang well and played good music, too. Not operatic style, but songs like "The Bells of St Mary". I sang and played piano so enthusiastically others worried I might harm the baby; but I took the dance-like movements inside me as a sign that the child approved, even enjoyed the music:

"Oh, the bells of St Mary's, at sweet eventide, shall call me beloved, to come to your side; and down in the valley, the sound of the sea, I know you'll be waiting, yes, waiting for me. …and so my beloved, when red leaves are falling…the love bells…shall ring out for you and for me…. At the door of St. Mary's, I'll wait there for you…."

Another song I sang was: "When you come to the end of a perfect day and you sit alone with your thoughts…do you think, love, at the end of a day, what a perfect day can mean to a tired heart…well this is the end of a perfect day, near the end of a journey too; but it leaves the thought that is big and strong, with a wish that is kind and true, for…the soul …."

And this one, the most popular of Noel Coward's tunes, one that he wrote in a New York taxi while stuck in a traffic jam: "…time may lie heavy between, but what has been is past forgetting, this sweet memory in years will come to me, though my world will go awry, yet my heart will ever lie, just the echo of a sigh – goodbye."

They were love songs, pining songs, and I sang them in part for myself, but more so to my unborn child. I was comforted by music and hoped my baby was, too.

In October, my sister Pat and her husband drove out to Kimberley and brought Betty and Don with them. Betty found work with the school principal's family; and she was a wonderful help to them.

My son was born on January 30, 1939, after a long difficult birth. The doctor visited me on the second day to tell me he didn't know if the baby would make it; he wasn't feeding properly. The baby was exhausted from the long time it took to be born. "But he will live. He has good genes!" I insisted. The doctor shook his head in surprise; but that evening the nurse came to my bedside to tell me, "Your baby took his feeding tonight; he's recovering nicely."

My son, my baby. I named him Richard Allen, after Pat's husband; they had been so good to me. I called him Spencer. No matter if it's universal, motherhood is the greatest of miracles; there is nothing mundane about it.

We returned to the apartment to live with Bill and he continued to treat me poorly. When Vera Sallis, a woman I'd met at the Friday night concerts, offered me her woodshed, Spencer and I moved out of the suite of rooms over Tony Muraka's store where I had lived with Bill Mohart since early summer of 1938. I had kept $100 out of housekeeping money and work, and Vera didn't charge anything for the use of her woodshed and water and toilet use. Perhaps offering me a place to stay eased her heartbreak: She had lost her son when he died, diving into a shallow pool, and was grieving.

It was April 15, 1939. Spencer was three months old and Betty moved in with us to help me. I found work for two young women who paid me $1.50 to do their washing and housework.

Workdays were programmed. I rose at 6, fed and bathed Spencer, then took him to work with me in a cheap ten dollar buggy I'd purchased with money I'd earned doing housework before Spencer's birth. It was a good purchase, with lots of room in the buggy below the mattress for diapers and even groceries. Spencer slept until break time at 9:30 am. After I fed him, he fell asleep again. He repeated this at noon and, after another nap, we went home to have supper with Betty. He was so good and everybody loved having a baby around.

SEPTEMBER 1939

Because my sister Betty will be working for the Levers', I am allowed, with baby Spencer, 6 months old, to live in their house, an improvement on Vera's woodshed. I was working at one of the homes where I did all kinds of work, when the woman had accepted an offer from Mr. Henner to host a dinner where he'd use, display and sell Superhealth Cookwear. Since all the dishes had to be washed, I stayed on and Mr. Henner gave me $1.50.

That year I was very thin. I used to scrub all the horrible old wood floors in Tony Muraka's house that was next door to his store. That must be done on an afternoon when all the clerks slept. Sometimes Betty pitched in, though she was working full time until end of June, when Mrs. Levers and her girls left to visit relatives all summer.

Two hours before dinner I began working with Mr. Henner. He laid out the metal pots and informed me of the menu. I prepared all the food, and set the table as directed by the hostess. I wore a dress I'd bought in Regina, a pique with a little pink stripe and the neat white collar. Mr. Henner and I served the food. I sat and listened to his sales pitch: "These utensils are going to change your way of thinking about food...each lid has a thermometer...is solid...will last a lifetime." He also sold wheat germ, "a new product that ensures a better life, controlls elimination, adds energy and can be put into any food without compromising its taste."

I worked for several more hours after the dinners before returning to my temporary home, completely tired out. Betty would have looked after Spencer. After looking at that beautiful child, my soul rested and I could sleep.

Some sixteen years later I encountered Mr. Henner in a Vancouver restaurant. To my surprise he said he did not remember me at all. Did I bring back memories he would just as soon forget? Though I saw him several times, he never seemed to recognize me.

SPENCER'S FOOT

It was when our family physician was on holiday late that summer that I took Spencer to a senior doctor in Kimberley. Spencer was born with a clubfoot that my doctor had treated in the best way he knew – with a splint and heavy tape. The senior doctor was appalled! He raged and I wept as he told me how terrible this treatment was. "You must get this child to a specialist right away," he said. "And don't let anything stand in the way!" His voice softened as he told me that two of his own children had been born with the same condition

My son Spencer at about six months old, 1939.

for which they'd been successfully treated. He recommended we see a specialist in Calgary immediately.

On October 15, we were off to Calgary, that city known for its friendliness.

CHAPTER TWELVE

Calgary – Brooks

Working for women, gaining secretarial skills and gradually upgrading; that was life in Calgary....

We were met at the train by my parents, who, through the ever-present kindness of Uncle Harry and Aunt Marie and their car, gave us a genuine family welcome. My parents had rented a two room suite for $15 per month in a rooming house and that's where they took us.

1940. Winter in Calgary, my Mother takes Spencer for one of many walks. In front of 639 2nd Ave. NW.

First on the agenda was meeting Dr. Townsend, the specialist. For the next six years, he saw us often and regularly as out-patients at the Red Cross Hospital for children. His compassion for each child and for parents was something we all marvelled at. He was highly regarded and eventually honoured further when a hospital was named after him.

From the start, Spencer was surrounded in Calgary by warm-hearted relatives – cousins, aunts and uncles, and, in particular, the great boon of living with Mother. While I was away from early morning to late at night, she gave him her full care and then some. She made sure that prescribed manipulations to keep his ankle supple were done twice a day. In the bitterest of Calgary winter weather, I took a photo of her with her year old grandson tucked warmly in his go-cart. "This child must have fresh air!" she said. And that was that!

1939

Dear Edna:

Sorry I've taken so long to answer your last letter with the good news that you have a new daughter. Perhaps you'll get a snap of her for your next letter, since we are so far apart I wonder when I'll ever see her – or you. It's been a real change for my 10-month old son and me. Mother and Dad had rented a place for the four of us; and we share an old house in Sunnyside with three other families – and all of us share the same bathroom! So far we are all amicable, and hope it keeps like that.

First I must tell you that the orthopaedic specialist we were referred to is so nice. He and his wife and little baby girl have just moved to this city and my dear son is his first patient. Already I know that we are in good hands, and that this upheaval in our lives is going to fade into the past. Another reason for my tardy correspondence is *because I've been looking for work. My Mom is so helpful. She loves her grandson, too, which takes a real load off my mind. It was really tough in Kimberley when I had to take him with me while I did housework. My employer here is a widower with two children, a son 19 and daughter 11. It's a very nice home but takes a lot of work because I'm now a "housekeeper" and have to keep everything in tiptop condition as well as cook lunch and dinner. If only the son would stop being rude. The girl is spoiled, too. I tell myself that having lost their mother recently makes them the way they are; but they are so demanding. When Mr. McKinn and Earl come home for lunch Earl walks around the house, running his finger on every piece of furniture to see if I've dusted. The fact that I now earn $25.00 a month makes it seem a bit easier. That's 65c per day!*

SEVERAL MONTHS LATER

I'm into a new job, Edna. Mr. McKinn found himself a new wife, who will be taking care of his house. This job also pays $25 a month but the work is much heavier. Mr. Flynn owns a men's clothing store downtown, and the daughter works at Ashdown's in the office. I guess they're OK, but Mrs. Flynn keeps me working from 6.30 a.m. until after I have their dinner dishes put away. By then I am too tired to do anything but drop into bed. Their son attends university in Edmonton, and when he comes home for a weekend – which is often because his girlfriend lives here – he brings his dirty laundry and, in addition, I am to make a week's supply of cookies for him to take back.

1940

Dear Edna:

I got a terrible cold just after Christmas and had to stay home here to recuperate. What's worse, my feet have developed fallen arches. The kindly doctor who takes care of little Spencer told me I'd have to ask the shoemaker who does all the orthopaedic work for the Children's Hospital to figure out how to help me. He has put leather bars under each sole. It's helping, but the pain is bad when I first get up in the morning. It wears off after a couple of hours.

I am thinking of quitting the housekeeper's job at Flynn's. The woman who has the two front rooms here has told me of a couple of people who are looking for help. They need someone who will understand that Mrs. Jones is unwell and needs special care. That would suit me, because my

Sister Pat and I on 8th Ave., Calgary, Summer 1941.

nurse's training would serve.

One of these evenings when I'm home I'll tell you more about the good things that are here, especially having my kind and generous aunt and uncle and family. We go there for Sunday dinners and oh, my, is it ever wonderful. Then music! Music! Music! And we all sing our hearts out. Aunt Marie was a gold and silver medallist when she was younger in both singing and playing the piano.

My Dear Friend Edna:

What a change in my world, your world and now half the people on this old shore: My brother Don, who had a fruitless search for work while riding the rails across Canada, is now in RCAF uniform. He tells us that he has flown over our town, and even buzzed the grain elevators, giving the townsfolk a bit of a thrill. Do the planes also fly over your farm, and do these, the new, strange sounds, cause the animals to run for shelter?

My brother, Don Mathie, RCAF/RAF Britain.

213

The best news I have for you is that Don signed over his subsistence allowance to Mom and Dad and I am borrowing a few dollars from them so I can now go to Garbutt's Secretarial School half a day a week, rather than just the twice-a-week night classes. Of course I still have to keep doing housework. The people I now work for are so different from the people I told you about last year. They are kindly and once in a while give me an extra couple of dollars. That's because Mrs. Jones needs a great deal of care and understanding. She is a bed patient; however it's her brain tumour that makes her difficult: she hates everything, so I have to coax her to eat. Good thing I'm experienced; besides I feel fortunate to be allowed to work half days there, something I asked for so I could attend school. My typing and shorthand are coming along....

1942

Dear Pal of my once happy schooldays: Hey look at! Typewriters are great, though certainly less personal than handwriting. Hope you don't mind. I'm experimenting by using my new skill on you. Sorry for the mistakes. We have to be able to do 35 words a minute before they'll recommend us for a job....

SPENCER

When Spencer was in his fifth year, a new and improved treatment for clubfoot was invented by two New York doctors – the Dennis Brown splint. Today, that is applied to newborns while bones are softer and correction takes only a short period of time. Spencer's treatment had consisted of casts and splints. Casts were done at the hospital, removed there as well. I have always had strong arms and legs and carrying this chubby lad was 'old hat' for me, so we would board the creaky street car, make a transfer, all the time enjoying the ride. Alas, he sensed our hospital destination three blocks in advance and, knowing what was to come, cried out loudly and woefully. Other streetcar riders glared at me but with compassion for Spencer!

It was an uphill walk from streetcar stop to hospital, with no let-up from Spencer. Once we arrived, and he was among all the other children there on "Outpatient Day", he settled down. But when a cast was to be removed and we both knew it would hurt, we had a standard brief dialogue. "Hold my hand, Mummy, and I won't cry." "I'm holding your hand, dear, and I won't cry either." We both cried.

Should a child's self-assertiveness be curbed? I wondered about that as Spencer grew and became more active. One day, I received a visit from the neighbour, a mother of two little girls. "We bought such good toys for the children and your son dropped them, one by one, down the sewer at the street corner," she reported.

"Why did you do it, Spencer?" I asked, during a sit-down discussion. "Because they sounded nice when they hit the water," he answered.

Another time a man visited our home and confronted me, his fist clenched in anger. "Your kids gotta keep outa my garden. They're digging things up and eating them, too." Spencer and his friends crowded around the man, curious. "We didn't have any vegetables," they insisted, with dirt-black mouths and all of them reeking of onions.

Another day I rushed down the street to use the phone in the bakery. "Should I give Spencer something to make him vomit?" I asked the doctor. "The neighbour on the other side of the street sent her daughter to tell me that Spencer had eaten some of the tar they were using on a roof job." "Not to worry, Jean. If it bothers him, he'll throw it up."

Dear Edna: It is so good to hear from you and your growing family. I remember how lovely it was to visit you: the beauty of your farm and the many springs that gave such good water; most of all, the garden you planted that gave bountiful crops, and oh, that cream, on porridge and fruit! Do the pigs still get loose and find their way onto the train tracks? The first time I visited you a few pigs had been run over on the tracks, and their greasy carcasses derailed the train!

Here I am, so far from your home where the only noise comes from the passing train or the squealing of the pigs, or the neighing of those big beautiful horses. And now, you'll have two youngsters to round out each day. The sounds I hear from the street here are very different: the screeching of the street-cars as they grind to a stop just at our corner. It's funny, Edna, how quickly I've got used to living in a city. The secretarial school is downtown, that makes it handy for me to meet my cousins who work near the school. They know everything about this town and that's help for me, being a greenhorn.

Great news! I've got a paying job in a busy office. My uncle is manager of the Workmen's Compensation Board for southern Alberta and requires help through the summer when his secretarial staff are on holidays. I was so excited when he said I was to work for him and when I protested, "…but I only have 35 words a minute", he replied, "Never mind. I use the Dictaphone mostly." Now, Edna, all my years of growing up helping in Dad's store are proving helpful. The WCB work means handling customers at the counter, being knowledgeable about cash and of course, lots of typing. On my first day Miss Mitchell said, "It's noon. We quit now for an hour…." I was so used to working hard every morning that I said, "But I haven't done any work!" She laughed and said, "What you've been doing is work!"

216

LIVING ON THE CHICKEN FARM

It was our great fortune to be recipients of Uncle Harry and Aunt Marie Hill's warmth, generosity and good humour. Uncle Harry had spent his earliest years on a farm, and had memories of a good life spent close to nature, with farmyard animals and fowl as part of everyday life. Decades afterwards, he wanted to add to his day-to-day routine as Manager of the Southern Alberta Workmen's Compensation Board and decided to rent a small farm on the outskirts of Calgary. The barn could hold several hundred chickens; an attached shed was good for storage of food and farm tools. The neat one-storey cottage had electricity and running water.

"Jean," he said to me one Sunday when we were enjoying one of Aunt Marie's memorable meals, "there's that empty house on the chicken farm; we thought you and Spencer and your parents might like to live there."

Would we ever! With my uncle's offer we'd now share better accommodations. Our own background was helpful, too, since we'd lived on the prairie within proximity of livestock.

At this time, Calgary was bursting at the seams with Army and Air Force personnel. There were jobs a-plenty and with my newly acquired skills I applied and was accepted at No. 2 Wireless & Air Gunnery Training depot, where the Commonwealth Training plan trained students from every part of the Commonwealth: Great Britain, Scotland, Australia, New Zealand.

We moved from the city to the quiet area of Nose Creek, just a mile below the airport. Brewster's Bus passed the farm gate; however I decided to buy a bicycle which I learned, at great peril, to master through downtown Calgary traffic and over the rough knobby terrain farther out where gopher holes abounded.

Every evening Uncle Harry and Aunt Marie drove out to collect the day's produce. Dad and Mother fed the chickens and gathered eggs; Aunt Marie and Mother usually cleaned and stacked the eggs in crates. The men mixed the rationed feed and cleaned the roosts.

The excitable chickens were difficult to count in a large flock, but soon there was no denying that their numbers were decreasing. Strewn feathers were clear evidence that an enemy lurked nearby; not a gopher, a badger! Help came when mother's visiting brother took up a shovel, determined to catch the badger; and the battle began. The badger's ability to tunnel was baffling. Night after night, the digging continued, farther and deeper until, finally, after he'd devoured more chickens than we could afford to lose, the badger was caught and killed!

For a young boy, life on the farm was one endless adventure. Reading was an important part of our life and money was always found to buy good books, especially for Spencer. We encouraged him to research all manner of things; and he did. Since moving to the farm, we'd added a bull calf whom we named Ferdinand from the then popular song; "Ferdie" for short. It shouldn't have come as a surprise that when Ferdie the bull was to be emasculated, Spencer

Spencer and me on the chicken farm.

researched the procedure. And insisted that he and his cousin Larry wouldn't miss the operation.

That summer, Mother and I repeatedly noticed and complained about a heavy, unpleasant odour by the front door. "Oh," said Spencer, "it must be from where I hid Ferdie's operation." He saved worms, too, in the far reaches of the kitchen table's drawer so that no one but he knew where they were until my fingers found the gummy mess.

One day, while Mother hung wash on the line, a train passed. A man stood on a platform outside the dining car, waving. Could it be? Yes, she told me that night; "it was Bill Mohart; he must have got a job on the train as a baker!" Somehow, he always managed to discover my whereabouts.

Spencer and I shared lots of honest-to-goodness fun during the 'chicken farm days'; and Spencer enjoyed teasing me. After cycling home after work and having supper with family, it was time to gather the eggs, always wary of cluckers – those dear mother hens determined to hatch a brood.

"Oh, Mom," Spencer said with surprise, "there's a nest up in the loft."

"Are you sure?"

"Yes. She's hiding her eggs I think."

"O.K., I'll climb the ladder and look." At the top, I gently felt the straw. "No nest. No eggs," I'd call down, only to hear his chuckle and realize I'd walked right into his little trick.

Calgary's Nose Creek hills are easy to access; when snow-covered, they were just right for sledding. Off we went on Sunday mornings, each carrying a makeshift toboggan – a piece of metal or some strong cardboard. Time and again, when we reached the top, Spencer invited me to share his 'slider'. "Is this for real this time or are you kidding me?" I'd ask. "Of course," he assured me, feigning innocence. "C'm on, Mom. I won't dump you. I promise." With a shove and a whoosh, we pushed off, sliding faster and faster. As we neared the bottom, he stuck his foot out, and off we tumbled! "You rascal, you dumped me again!"

The candour of childhood is sometimes like a drink of cool fresh water to adults. Like any child, Spencer simply said it like it was. One day, we were invited to tea at Mrs. Hogan's, the owner of a Secretarial School I attended after completing my work at the No. 2 Wireless & Air Gunnery Training depot. Mother invited Spencer, then six years old, to join in the conversation. "Spencer, how do you like living on a farm?" He said he did; then added, "...like the day when they operated on Ferdie and took his testicles out." Mrs. Hogan seemed at a loss for words, while Mother, without taking a breath, looked at me and said, "Please pass the sugar, Jean." "More tea?" asked Mrs. Hogan.

On another occasion I took Spencer with me to watch Noel Coward's "In Which We Serve". The theatre was crowded so Spencer sat on my knee. When the British

Singing with the United Church choir, Brooks, Alberta.

submarine crew on the movie screen was besieged by the enemy, the audience's excitement grew. "Kill the buggers!" yelled Spencer. All heads turned, and I tried desperately to hide behind Spencer and under the wide brim of my hat.

From Chickens To Brooks, Alberta

At thirty-three, life had shown me that it couldn't be laid out like a fine architect's plan with success following. Spencer was now six years old, had started school while we were on the chicken farm; and his report card said he was doing well. Knowing the chicken farm didn't have much of a future, and needing a breather from our living arrangements – father and I were having too many disagreements – I began looking for work elsewhere. I thought it would be good for both of us to locate in a town not too far from Calgary, our good friends and relatives; and thus responded to an ad in the paper for work in Brooks, Alberta, that read: "Pleasant working conditions, adequate salary, with housekeeping arrangements supplied (optional)." I was invited to meet with the manager of the Eastern Irrigation District, hired, and began working as stenographer on September 1, 1945.

I have often said that Mother and I threw the ball of life back and forth. When she needed my help during her illness I was able to give it; and now she came to the rescue in caring for Spencer, who loved her then and as long as she lived.

The train left the outskirts of the city and streaked onto the sweeping prairie, dry with stiff sparse grasses struggling for life on the edge of the CPR right-of-way. The contrast of comfort and security with family on the chicken farm with the town ahead with all its unknowns shook my composure. Had I made the right decision? The steady rhythm of the train's wheels comforted. Yes; it was time to move on.

My year in Brooks, Alberta, was a real rollercoaster. At first, I worked as a steno for Wes Crooks, Engineer for the EID; and I lived upstairs, sharing the kitchen and sitting room with the President's secretary. That arrangement quickly became unpleasant, our disagreements having to do with male callers. For a short time she entertained her amour in her bedroom, while I and my friend sat in the sitting room, with the door locked always, because German Prisoners Of War, like the men we dated, were "Out of Bounds anywhere outside their designated housing."

And then my roommate had me fired. I left Mr. Brunsden's office and walked up the lane to where my boss Wes Crook and his wife Alta, lived. Alta and I shed tears, Wes was extremely embarrassed; but he didn't dare oppose the President.

I applied at a Real Estate and Insurance office and was hired on a monthly basis. This was a low point in my life. I had to find a new place to live, and by now Spencer lived with me again. A kind couple allowed us to live, temporarily, in space inside a vacant store. Next, I rented a cabin in a little resort, but when tourist season began we were forced to move – this time into a vacant trailer behind a home.

My new employer was not a nice man though his family had a good reputation. After completing a PhD in

Kurt Postey, a German POW I fell for.

agriculture, he had married a young woman from a wealthy family in Winnipeg. Outwardly, they appeared happily married; then one day, without a word to anyone, she vanished, returning to her family. Soon, he acquired the reputation of a man of many casual romantic liaisons. That was obvious to me as soon as I was in his office. His business partner, a retired farmer with a strong clientele, was genuinely kind and helped me understand the insurance business. I was desperate to get out of an intolerable workaday situation as well our lodgings.

With the war's end in 1945 my life and every one else's changed. My parents had sold their few remaining household goods and, at my brother's behest, moved to Vancouver, B.C. My mother was keenly aware of our difficult situation. She urged me to come to Vancouver; inside her letter was a full page of ads for dozens of jobs. "If you move here, you, Spencer, Dad and I will find a home together, and I will be able to help in Spencer's life." What a boon! I gave notice, both in the insurance office and with a temporary job I'd acquired with Ducks Unlimited.

My beloved sister Betty shown here in her graduation photo from nursing school at Holy Cross Hospital, Calgary in 1945.

Spencer and I bussed to Kimberley, where Pat and Allen were also pulling up stakes to move to Vancouver. They had offered to take Spencer with them; and he could stay with my sister Rene in Burnaby until I arrived. He was in good hands.

I returned to Brooks and completed my commitments; then left October 31 for Calgary. Oh, how I needed the break from my short but painful Brooks experience! I gave myself the opportunity to breathe free and happier by staying with Aunt Marie for a week. She surprised me in discussions, particularly those about women's lives; she had astonishing candour and insight. Then good Uncle Harry and Aunt Marie drove me to the CPR station one November morning and I headed into a brand new sphere of my life.

CHAPTER THIRTEEN

A Burnaby Home & Union Work in Vancouver

The train rattled rhythmically, winding its way amid the wonderful scenery of the foothills of Calgary, then Banff, Cranbrook, the Kootenays, Hell's Gate, down to the Fraser Valley and finally the Lower Mainland and Vancouver. At one point, I went to the space between cars for a change of air, and we passed a group of our Japanese citizens who were now prisoners in their own country. I waved and smiled; they returned my gesture: victims of something they were caught up in, not having caused....

NOVEMBER 9, 1946

After a pleasant journey, the CPR train arrived in Coquitlam at 9 pm. My older sister and her husband met me; he knew the area and had requested I disembark there rather than downtown where there was more traffic. They drove an older car and my arrival was after dark.

Rene and I hadn't seen each other for several years, but we greeted one another with a sisterly kiss. Rene hadn't told Spencer I would be there the next morning and I will never forget walking into the bedroom where he slept: my lad, my dear, dear son. How my heart banged as I waited for him to wake up and realize I was there! "Mother!" he said, and we clung to each other briefly. We were to stay in Rene and Jim Fraser's home until the end of March 1947.

My sister had four children who kept her very busy; and although Jim worked in a New Westminster sawmill, they struggled to make ends meet. The IWA's first dramatic full-scale strike had a devastating effect on their and many other workers' households, and Jim was a dyed-in-the-wool Union man. I didn't want to be an extra burden; that meant finding a job soon.

Rene and Jim's home was in Burnaby so, when I found work, transportation was vital. Vancouver public transport was vastly different from my experience in Calgary where the rickety street car took me to the city limits and Brewster's bus or my bicycle took me to the gate of the chicken farm where Dad, Mother, Spencer and I had lived. Vancouver was a new and rougher working world. Here, I'd learn to get into a queue, keep both feet on the ground and hang tough till I was inside the interurban train.

I quickly adjusted. In less than a month I easily jostled for a place among more experienced travellers. Only once did an accident happen. On that occasion we were halfway between Vancouver and my stop at Fraser Arms in Burnaby, and, as usual, we who still had a distance to travel were half asleep. "Wake up! Wake up! We're going to have an accident!" the conductor shouted. The woman across the aisle screamed and fainted, while I panicked! Where WERE my shoes? I had only one pair and couldn't go to work without shoes. I dropped to my knees to look under the seats and then: Bang! Jolt! The train moaned and halted. The cars behind the operator's had uncoupled; the couplings bent and ground noisily when we caught up and reattached. I located my shoes under the front seat, pulled my skirt over my knees and smiled when a conductor came by to say that a Greyhound bus would deliver us home.

FINDING WORK

My first office job was brief. Dr. Lorne Woods and I had met on friendly terms when I worked part-time for Ducks Unlimited in Brooks, Alberta and he was there on a duck hunt. I said I was moving to Vancouver and he said to pay him a visit, an offer that gave small comfort when I went into the city a few days after our arrival. Rene guided me to the Medical Building.

Dr. Woods' nurse questioned me, seemed pleased with my nursing background and assured me I'd have no difficulty in finding work. I spoke briefly with the cordial Doctor, who told me he knew of other opportunities for work in the same building, and made an appointment for me to meet a couple who owned a fish-packing business. They, too, gave me some valuable hints. I also met a man who planned to open his own brokerage; he asked if I could wait several weeks for work. How could I possibly do that? I needed to contribute financially sooner than that. After the interviews Rene and I went to Woodward's; I felt a sense of happiness as we walked into that grand store. Things will work out, I told myself.

The following day Dr. Woods' nurse phoned. She was to have her bunions removed and would be off work for at least a month. "Do you think you could handle my job temporarily?" Perfect! I could get to know downtown Vancouver and continue my search for permanent work.

Doctor Woods was a highly skilled specialist, with a province-wide clientele. It seemed we should have no difficulty in agreeing to pay that equalled the salary of his regular nurse; but it took a few discussions until we came to an agreement.

Working for Dr. Woods was different from anything I'd ever done. It was good that I'd had some hospital experience because, with only a smattering of advice, I was immediately made receptionist and asked to ensure that Dr. Woods' instruments were sterilized. I worked regular office hours, Monday to Friday, and Saturday morning; and kept his office and personal books.

The work went well. Meanwhile, I kept reading the classified ads and found one in need of a steno. The words "interesting work" appealed to me.

I called the office of the United Steelworkers of America and arranged for an interview. Meeting Eileen Tallman Sufrin was a fortuitous stroke of fate. Small and attractive, with a lovely warm voice, she conducted a business-like interview. Yes, I assured her, I could type, keep books, had worked among men; and yes, my background at home and past places of employment had sensitized me to working with people. Moreover, my maternal grandfather organized the Conservative party when Sir Charles Tupper ventured into Manitoba in the early 1900s.

"Well!" Eileen said, "that was something in those days. Are you interested in politics?"

"Yes, I am," I responded, "but not as a Conservative." Something made me add, "I lived in Saskatchewan during the Great Depression, and I'm only sorry that I couldn't have been there last year when the people voted for a welcome change."

It seemed no more than ten minutes later that, on mutual agreement, I was hired as steno-bookkeeper for two unions just starting out – the United Packinghouse Workers of America (UPWA) and Retail, Wholesale and Department Store Union of America (RWDSU). Toronto was headquarters for both unions and their directors, Eileen told me, were Fred Dowling (UPWA) and Norman Twist (RWDSU). Then she gave me the picture of the era that was being born for unorganized workers in and around Vancouver.

No other person could have helped me as Eileen did. Her personality was matched by a fine intellect and belief in the cause; and she became my mentor; if not, I would never have 'stayed the course'. Trade unionists aren't so different from other groups; it is when their members become paid staff that their mettle is tried, weighed in the balance of what's good and true and worth giving one's best for the good of the movement. In that arena, the old sayings 'you separate the boys from the men' or 'the wheat from the chaff' come true; and I had to learn all about that yet, the hard way, for, ever since childhood, I'd wanted heroes. It took some time for me to understand that the union movement, this new but powerful part of Canadian life, was done by inexperienced and unskilled humans, driven mainly by a raw zeal for the cause. Eileen knew all that from having been an active part of the volatile CCF Youth and more; she had organized bank employees, who were immediately moved to another area; but her main success was in winning certification in the John Inglis manufacturing plant for hundreds of workers. (A superb organizer, Eileen Sufrin was the first woman to win a strike for women workers. She relates it in her splendid book "The Eaton Drive".) And that's why she had been seconded from the Toronto based United Steelworkers of America to take charge of the Vancouver office and the political situation developing in BC. By the time we met and became friends, she'd been in B.C. for a few years and had already made a name for herself and the Steelworkers Union, as well as ensuring the election of CCF candidates.

905 DOMINION BUILDING

Monday, December 10, 1946. The Interurban left Fraser Arms station, arriving in Vancouver one-half hour later. I left the former B.C. Electric building at Main and Hastings and walked to the Dominion building, at the corner of Hastings and Cambie. The fourteen-storey building was easily identified by its strong yellow colour and the neat, dark blue dome at the top. It was owned by a Mr. Cohen. The main floor was occupied by the bank, its counters and offices; and, below that, a Honeydew Restaurant served tenants and the passing crowd.

Whatever other fears I had, on this day I had a job with a promise of pay: $100 per month, i.e. $50 from UPWA and $50 from RWDSU. BC Electric fare was 15 cents per ride or a month of tickets for $12.50 and, if I could afford it, the Greyhound bus was 25 cents per trip to Burnaby. I'd brought a lunch with me as well as a little cash for coffee and some money to buy meat down the street in Woodward's store at Abbott and Hastings.

In the suite that was now my workplace, the various union members were welcomed by two office secretaries (a kinder title for the workhorse stenos). Each had her desk and an Underwood typewriter. There was a bank of filing cabinets, one for each of the three Unions. The small room off the right held the Gestetner (a manual copier), shelving for ink and paper, as well as stationery and record books. My entry into this new world was like being shoved into a whirlpool

Working at the Gestetner for the Vancouver Labour Council, a task I spent countless hours doing in my years as secretary.

without any sense of how to come up for air. I was unschooled and completely ignorant about trade unions. What was I getting into?

Almost as soon as I was familiar with the setup of our office at 905 in the (now Toronto) Dominion Building, Eileen explained that there was a union for office workers – Office & Professional Workers of Canada (OPWOC), and I would be their newest member with monthly dues of $1.50. That was a jolt, since my salary would amount to only $100 a month.

Eileen also showed me how to keep books for each of the two unions. She gave me a small petty cash fund for each union, and cautioned me to "be careful to keep a running balance." There were no check-offs of union membership dues back then, hence all monies were brought to the office by Shop Stewards who approached each worker to collect the dues. And not every worker was pleased when approached by a shop steward who, if not tough when he started the job, quickly became so. Little Louie Shaw, from Packinghouse, was the shop steward at the time. "I'm awfully sorry about the state of the money," he'd say as he handed over the dues from the guys on the killing floor, the bills badly crumpled, some dirty with blood. (We eventually offered a six-week series of lectures, with guest speakers to educate employees about unionism. The popularity of the event was heart-warming; guys wanted to learn about how to be a good shop steward; and to gain an understanding of politics & labour; and how to think on your feet. Local unions paid for a dinner held in a fine restaurant – Purdy's, on Georgia & Granville was the first one – in its private backroom. The good thing was there was lots of discussion.)

Each union chose a local, active member to be its local spokesperson, forwarded the name to Head Office in Toronto and waited for confirmation. Joe Brown got the job for UPWA. Since the Steelworkers footed the bill for RWDSU (at that time without any members), National Director

Charlie Millard picked a member of the Vancouver Steelworkers, Harold Jones, to have the Rep's job. A couple of years previous, Jones expected to have the Steel Rep's job but when Millard sorted things out in Vancouver he chose someone of quite different mien: Dirk Bear, a big, stolid and ponderous male. To the end of his days, Jones never forgot that slight. Now, sharing a smaller office than Bear's, the two new business agents had to work out schedules and all other details, including sharing one secretary. Each National Director paid the local Rep as well as $50 per month for their shared steno.

There couldn't have been a wider mix of personalities in that small office space. Dirk Bear treated all others as underlings. "Dirk has no equals," noted one prominent member. "You are either above him, and he will kowtow to you; or you are below him and he'll wipe his feet on you." That's how Dirk treated his subordinate Ted Austin: "Here's ten cents for the meter on my car. Run down and do it," he ordered.

Brown (UPWA) was a personality of different shades, like the old Scottish saying, 'neither fish, flesh nor good red herring'. In my first year I rather liked him. His attractive wife invited the office staff to their home a couple of times for a pleasant social evening; but by the end of my second year he became involved with one of the female union members, bragging about how they enjoyed "lying together on a big, hot rock".

My newness to the job, and a keen desire to please, put me at a disadvantage when I was asked to work overtime, without pay. Eileen had signed me up in OPWOC, but the Agreement didn't hold water in a union office in its formative stages. I calculated that I put in at least a full month's time without being recompensed. Naively confused regarding my own personal needs, I actually allowed my ticket to the famous Russian Army Chorus to go unused, and worked overtime instead, compiling a special leaflet the entire evening instead of attending the concert! Brown wasn't ever intentionally unkind, but his butcher trade may have tended to make him rude in language and manners. He had a tough, new kind of occupation, one that could result in many changes to him in both his personal and business relations.

Harold Jones (RWDSU) couldn't be described without mixing his personal life with any other part of him because he kept those aspects volatile until he died at age 37 of lung cancer. His wife instructed the clergy who delivered his funeral eulogy to warn all listeners against living the kind of life Harold had exemplified: womanizing, drinking, smoking, strong ribald language that he enjoyed using, particularly when describing union/company negotiations. He bragged constantly about the entire scope of his life-encompassing exploits. Even my couple of years in the Commonwealth Air Training Headquarters office seemed, in retrospect, simple and juvenile compared to the fast moving sophistication I was now a part of. But it didn't take long to figure out how each Rep (Union Representative) rated on the office 'totem pole' – Steel was on top, Packinghouse on the bottom, and Retail in the middle.

Steel was there first; its head office in Toronto had the first National Director – Charlie Millard. Steel was definitely the

Our very first home in Burnaby where Mother, Father, Spencer and I lived 1947-50.

most powerful, the most highly regarded; it gave its employees benefits such as pensions, unheard of in anything other than some of the better corporations.

The Packinghouse Workers were the 'poor relations'. Their National Director, Fred Dowling, simply said, "Get office space, pay the cheapest rent you can find, I'll pay your salary at a starting rate, and give you $50 a months toward a stenographer." In fairness to him, when he visited Vancouver to check on progress or otherwise, he slept in his day clothing on a bench in the Steelworkers Hall, in the Lee Building at Broadway and Main.

Retail, Wholesale & Department Store began with the same statistics. Their National Director, Norm Twist, was a different sort, however; he stayed at The Vancouver Hotel, looked natty and was cheerful in his business dealings. We were shocked several years later when financial discrepancies caused his sudden disappearance from the Canadian union scene.

Every colour, hue and shade of the rainbow was reflected in the personalities of each of the five paid union persons working in Suite 205 when I became one of the staff in 1946. It was exciting to learn a new vocabulary and assimilate this new atmosphere with its myriad of office procedures and techniques, but at the end of each day, I was terribly tired.

It was a time of survival in all aspects of life. Not only was I learning a new job, I was responsible for clothing and feeding my son and me, my cost of transportation from Burnaby to Vancouver, and dealing with building a new home at 2104 Windsor Street, Burnaby. While I was in Alberta, I'd received a war bond as a gift from a brief romantic interest. With help from sister Rene's husband, Jim Fraser, and my $50, Dad and I purchased a fine lot. We – meaning Mother, Father, Spencer and me – occupied the unfinished home in April 1947. I was the only one with a job and this was frustrating, especially since Dad thought he should have bacon for breakfast, meat in a lunch sandwich, and meat and potatoes for supper, a habit he'd begun in Brandon where he frequented Mrs. Shank's Cured Meats & Sausages. I'd buy what I thought was enough meat for two or three days from Woodward's Meat Department, then arrive home, hungry after a long day's work, expecting, and needing, a hearty meal, only to find most everything eaten. Once, Dad invited sister Pat's in-laws for dinner. "Where's my supper? Is it warming?" I asked when I came in. They kind of laughed, and Dad joked, "Too bad; we ate it." Throughout this time, our kitchen was pretty bare; and I resented that Dad didn't understand as well as his refusal to change his habits. For a while, he worked in the kitchen of a supper club on the corner lot of Sperling & Kingsway. He'd come home thrilled by small cooking tricks he'd picked up from the chef, like using baking powder to make batter stick. The job lasted only briefly…my dad talked too much.

When things were rough, and they were in those years, I reminded myself that I had made the decision to find work that held interest and promise of growth, then shrugged off all discomforts and gave it all I could.

DearEdna:

Hello you, there in Manitoba! Greetings from British Columbia and the Wild West City of Vancouver! I know. It's a long time since you've had a letter. By the new address, "VANCOUVER", you'll be surprised. So am I. When Mother and Dad left the prairies and moved in with Don and his wife in Vancouver, they invited Spencer and me to move west, too…with Mother's promise, "I'll help you with Spencer and he'll have a home to come to after school!" How could I resist?

Though we are living in Burnaby, my new job takes me to downtown Vancouver. This is a quite a change, Edna, and that's putting it mildly. I ride the BC Electric interurban train to and from the city. When the train bumps along its wobbly rails with its crowds of home-goers, my day's work catches up with me: my eyes burn from all-day artificial light, and my feet and ankles are sore and a bit swollen, but after the train has stopped at a few stations I can usually find a seat. Off come my shoes, up go my feet onto the foot rail and I doze off, knowing that when the conductor yells, "Fraser Arms!" I'll wake up in time to grab my purse and shoes, to rush to get off in nothing flat.

Everything in my life has changed, Edna. Before moving to BC my work and after-work hours were less hurried, with a simpler routine. Now, it seems, at every turn I'm but one of many hundreds competing for time and space.

I still pack a lunch, but on payday I treat myself to a hot bacon and mushroom sandwich in the Honeydew, for 35 cents. If I have time, I hurry down a block to the lovely Woodward's store. Their grocery department in the basement is something else! If I don't have time, I go across the road to Victory Square, put a newspaper on the grass, eat my lunch and lie down in the sunshine for ten minutes, knowing my body-clock will wake me up.

Everything about my job is new to me. The two unions I work for are just starting up...the atmosphere in our office...is business-like but friendly enough. I do like the woman, Eileen, who hired me...(she) is helpful...very kind...(and I) hope it works out well.

Mother and Dad and I have put every cent into building a little house. The snapshot I'm enclosing helps, but it can't show you the beautiful trees in our backyard, which provide my son and his friends with a handy and marvellous place to play.

I am looking for a choir somewhere so that I can do some singing, and through a friend of my sister's who now gives me a perm, I'm promised that I can join a group. Hurray! I sure need something like that.

You and I have come through terrific changes in our personal lives, Edna, and right now I am trying to keep up with the change in location and the emptiness in my heart at the break-up of an affair. You and I have always been able to tell each other things we couldn't, or wouldn't, tell others, even our Mothers! But when I wrote to you about being secretary to the Engineer for the EID in Brooks I left out meeting one of the Prisoners-of-War who were there. The POWs had offered their services to Canada, not wanting to sit around a camp day after day. That helped the labour shortage. My hospitable boss and his wife invited me to their home, where I played and sang "Roses of Picardy" on most visits. They also invited the POW officers, even at the risk of some citizen's displeasure. It was in their home I met Kurt. We had a beautiful love affair, meeting under some difficulties, except for the kindness and understanding of my boss and wife.

When the war ended, Kurt had no choice but to go back to Germany. We will keep in touch. I don't feel inclined to go there, and this move to a new province, a new job and completely different set of circumstances, has helped this jarring transition. This letter is just for you. You know only too well how the heart can ache. Having a friend to talk to about my love-life does give some ease. All this is so far from the kind of days at your farm. Your four children keep you busy and, I hope, happy.

I had come to work at 905 Dominion that Monday morning to sit at my desk which faced the other stenographer's. I opened a thick letter, tucked with folded, handwritten pages. The letter was simply addressed to Jean Mohart. I recognized the writing as Pete Smith's but the contents surprised me: Pete was in love with me, and declared this poetically, pleadingly.

"Oh, oh, oh," I uttered softly as I read. My co-worker looked at me questioningly. "I can't tell you who this is from, Marie," I said. A stiff, strong person, she didn't ask questions.

Pete's next office appearance was one late afternoon. He'd phoned and invited me to meet him after work in the Honeydew Restaurant. We met, walked down to the CPR depot and stood at the wrought iron fence overlooking the tracks below. "Your letter surprised me," I said, "actually, it shook me. You're a happily married man."

"Yes," he said, "it seems that way. But I love you more deeply than I've ever loved anyone."

"That cannot be."

"Yes, Jean. I've thought about this for a long time. I see you everywhere; in the moon, in the stars...in all my thoughts. I can't go to sleep without thinking of you. I love you. I love you!"

I stood there; listening to something I wanted yet didn't want to hear because I knew, instinctively, that this was a bad situation. "Let's go home," I suggested.

We left the CPR station and walked to the BC Electric tram station, both he and I saying very little now. He may have had a sense of relief at relieving his pent up feelings; but my mind was in turmoil. We'd had such fun on Saturdays in the Steelworkers' office when the off-duty working stiffs came into the office to talk unions; and Pete was a far left political thinker.

I'd been very lonely since arriving in BC, lonely not only for male companionship but for genuinely human feelings. When we parted, he kissed me fervently.

On the interurban, practically empty at that time of night, I wanted to talk to someone. That wasn't possible, nor would I be able to talk to my Mother. We had lived in little prairie towns where gossip made life less dull, though it sometimes ruined its victim; and one type of someone's troubles that was a source of weird pleasure was when a marriage break-up was news, with "the other woman" getting the worst of it.

Never before had I encountered anything like this dilemma; that was why my first reaction was to shy away. I had met his wife, a nice person whom I didn't want to hurt, especially since she and Pete were considered by all who knew them as 'happily married' (though Pete confessed to me at one point that he'd married his wife only to acquire a Father; he'd been orphaned very young).

In the months that followed, Pete's charm and persuasiveness turned my life around, though I found him to be unusually jealous. My mother and my sister were not pleased, but they were forbearing. They had given more than ordinary love and support for me during the harsh years following my first marriage and separations. They wanted me to be happy.

A year later...and the romance with Pete remained alive, but with uneasiness in my heart. He'd given me a diamond ring but it wasn't to be worn in public. He came over on Saturday nights, and I am ashamed now as I recall how we coaxed my mother to go visit my brother and his wife just so we could have a few hours alone. (During this time, Dad had either returned to Rocanville or was out at Pat's farm). On special holidays like Christmas or New Year's, Pete spent time first with his family and afterwards came to where I lived. But we carried on.

"I'm on a learning curve" wasn't a popular expression in 1947; however, the phrase aptly describes a new phase of my working life. Besides endless typing union contracts in a parlance still new to me, my ears were still getting attuned to the language of the Union Reps whose conversations were so interesting that I often wanted to stop typing and listen. There was continual excitement when a strike loomed; at such times my job required a bit of artistic ability. Leaflets must be designed, with a clear, yet succinctly worded message expressing the union's point of view; and "we need it right now!" There was much overtime, at regular pay, for in 1947 there was no 'time-and-a-half'.

Only months into my out-of-the-ordinary job, Eileen asked me to join the Negotiating Committee for the Office Workers Union; and my "learning curve" leapt right off the page! Fortunately, Eileen's experience and expertise was second to none. It was her demeanour when we met with the employer that created the proper atmosphere: pleasant yet businesslike, with obvious respect for her adversary. "Know your contract," she advised me and the other member of our committee; and that advice proved helpful when we were to meet with a local Co-op firm where a contract was up for renewal. A date for meeting was agreed. I studied that contract from A-Z, hoping to listen more than speak.

The first negotiating meeting took place in the manager's office. The entire discussion was in good order with each party speaking in quiet but business-like tones. We arranged to meet again to tie up all the loose ends and sign the contract. I had listened with some trepidation to the male staff describing some rough and loud encounters, finding the OPWOC negotiating civilized by comparison. (It was a few years later when I was on the committee to meet with men from the IWA on contract negotiations and by then my own attitude had steadied down, since I had grown more experienced in the distinctly different world of unionism.)

On another occasion, two of us were to meet with the President of B.C. Federation of Labour and its Secretary Treasurer. Uppermost in negotiations, Local 8 members asked us to win a wage increase. My colleague worked in a downtown union office and since I was across the street from her we discussed how we would make our case. We agreed to meet in the IWA regional office. We knew each of these men and they knew both of us. It was understood that this wasn't to be a friendly chat; they and we were meeting strictly on a business level.

We put our proposal on the table and waited.

The secretary treasurer kept one finger on the proposal and then, looking hard at us, declared, "You girls look like you think you're on the gravy train!" "Not at all," we responded, surprised, but with serious certainty. "Just look at comparative wages."

Another rather loud declaration followed. "You girls think you're good enough to get the same as the guys on the green chain!"

"We aren't discussing the IWA rates on the green chain," my colleague reminded them. "We represent women who have skills and experience in our positions...every one of us works hard, with plenty of overtime to do the job as our classification asks!"

The president, a less bombastic man, looked at the proposals. "Don't you know," he asked with seriousness, "that we are scraping the bottom of the barrel? We don't know where you think this kind of money is coming from."

We listened with straight faces, responded as sagely as we could. Acquainted daily with all matters they referred to, including their financial ability to meet our proposal, we and they huffed and puffed for a few more minutes, signed the contract as presented, shook hands and bid them Goodnight. We waited till they were out of earshot before we looked at each other; and agreed that it was a good session, "with entertainment thrown in".

It's recognized that office workers are the most difficult to organize. They are somewhat secluded from the blue-collar workers, who can organize in large numbers without an overseer looking over their shoulders. Regarded by the blue-collar worker as more or less elitist, office workers didn't get moral support from the other side of the office walls. If the Office & Technical Workers union could count on support from the industrial workers in the same plant, that was great; but if not, our cause could be lost.

One morning our little picket of women office employees stood outside the gates of a plant where many blue-collar workers were employed, hoping that the sanctity of the picket line would be observed. Everyone there, from plant and office, knew the bitterness of that situation, how the certification was challenged, how much was at stake for the union members, and how we needed to take this stand. When the plant workers arrived it seemed that they would respect our picket line. We held our pickets high and sang "Solidarity Forever" as loud as we could. It wasn't convincing; the plant workers walked right through and to work. We lost three times: with our union brothers, with plant management and most of all, with the people who had the guts to take their case to that end.

By the time I left my position at Regional office No. 1 IWA, Local 8 Office and Professional Workers had been dissolved in the formation of Office and Technical Employees Union, Local 15. Our members never went on strike, though some negotiations were hard won, however, classifications were well written and wages improved. Pensions were talked about, since they were granted to all male staff; but, in spite of stiff bargaining, in 1971, when I departed, women were not granted pensions.

Burnaby was a good place to live in 1947-1949. Though I worked in Vancouver and travel time cut my time at home short, we enjoyed the little home on Windsor Street. It would have been better if my wages had improved or if my Dad had found steady work; nonetheless my diary records birthday parties, many invitees to dinner that included Jack and Margaret Webster and their small family who had recently arrived in Canada, with scant resources. Spencer got a second-hand bike when a friend offered it at an affordable price; and he was becoming quite a responsible lad, expected to keep the wood box filled and to share chores with my dad. Neighbours trusted Spencer enough to hire him to walk their two handsome well-bred Sealyham dogs. His allowance was never going to make him rich, but he was careful, only over-spending because he was generous with friends and his cousins.

Since birth, Spencer had known changes. By the time he was seven he may have preferred it otherwise, but his way of accepting discomfort, and even pain, amazed those around him, particularly the specialist who treated him for his first seven years. When he was in hospital for a tonsillectomy he suggested to the other sick children that it would be easier for them if they didn't cry because then "it wouldn't hurt so much." By the time I joined him and my parents, sisters and families in Burnaby, he had made a name for himself as a scrapper – if the need arose. He was proving to himself that he was able to maintain his own persona in spite of being on his own. But these two brief separations were very trying for him and for me. The answer was to create a home that we knew to be ours, giving the deep sense of security that is necessary to all of us: humans and animals alike.

Until July 1, 1950 we had our own home on a street where Spencer met and made friends. We had good times, taking a street car on a Sunday afternoon into the city for all the wonders one could want — at English Bay, or the CPR station where the startling bronze statue of a soldier being carried heavenward by an angel elicited a question by Spencer to me about when and if such things really happened. After a hearty picnic lunch, we found a place for Mother to sit while we went on a walk of discovery. When it came time to go home Spencer didn't want to be coaxed away from the tank where an octopus was having his dinner, skilfully snatching the unwary bait and swallowing it whole. Such natural drama drew us back there often.

Because he had no siblings, Spencer sometimes invited a friend along. That gave Mother and me a little time to relax and enjoy an outing. My job at the union office occasionally hosted family picnics for employees. What a grand change it was to travel on the CPR ferry, where the dining room tables were set with white linen cloths, fine china and silver cutlery! On one such trip the boat hit a wharf and tables went crashing; and how exciting for Spencer and his friend! The boys were not just sailing, they were would-be explorers having a whale of a time....

Most parents prefer to tell kids that it's a pretty good world, and encourage them to trust people they meet and associate with. We caution as well: "Watch out for the mean kid"; or "Better keep your distance from the bully," and "stay close to your friends if you sense trouble." Spencer had a calm, kindly, optimistic personality. One day both grandparents were away, visiting old friends, leaving Spencer to fend for his self. He was advised that it would be OK to have other kids visit, but to never leave anyone unsupervised in the house.

A slightly older boy, known as 'the wise guy', had joined the familiar Windsor Street gang. On the day Spencer was home alone, he asked to see Spence's treasurer: some tiny, valuable gold ingots a friend had given me in Kimberley (and which I, in turn, gave to Spencer for his birthday). "How did the day go?" I asked him that evening. "Fine," he said. "Grandma left lots for me to eat; and I made a fire for my supper." Good for him, I thought.

A few days later, he came to me and, with a look of disbelief, said, "My ten-dollar bill and the ingots are missing." "Was there any time when you left a friend or friends alone in the house?" I asked. He thought for a moment, then said, "Only for a couple of minutes when I brought some wood in."

I don't know who felt worse, me or the lad's foster mother when I confronted her with my suspicions that the boy in her care was a thief. "Oh dear," she said sadly, "I had hoped so much that this wouldn't happen." Then we talked to the boy; he denied everything.

"Of course it was him," the manager of the little store down on Kingsway said when we spoke. "He came in here that night and spent ten dollars on candy." Our only option was to ask for police help; in short order, they took care of the boy with "a history of convictions."

B.C. TRADE UNION POLITICS 1947 - 1948

"Politics," said a well known figure in the CCF, "is the art of the possible." Sounds nice, orderly and simple. Not in British Columbia when two groups of union members engaged in a power-struggle. B.C. Communists, the 'red block', waged war on their opponents, the 'white block', starting their battle with Local union members of the IWA. Harold Pritchett, then President of both the IWA and the B.C. Federation of Labour (it covered all unions for B.C.), was also chief organizer for the Communist Party of B.C. Tensions mounted, turning member against member and family against family. The B.C. labour movement has never seen anything to compare with the battle, the wins and losses that, day after day, made front page news.

Already maintaining a majority of delegates to meetings of Vancouver Labour Council and the B.C. Federation of Labour, union members in what was labelled 'the white bloc' knew there would be no change without intense field work, tenacity and the absolute necessity to find appointees to both important labour bodies who would have the background, trust and zeal to stick with the coming squabble – thick and thin. Two were chosen, both United Packinghouse union members: Jim Bury from Burns Packing plant and George Home from Bissinger Hide.

None of the working people I knew back then had cars, nor could they afford taxis. To ensure a successful campaign meant visiting every prospective, 'safe' voter – after a day's work, travelling by public transportation. Expenses were kept to a bare minimum, with no extras allowed. After fierce campaigning by both sides, when elections took place, the Vancouver Labour Council and the B.C. Federation each won by one vote. The White Bloc was in control.

It may be that union members today will not hear of this or even read about it. They might even say, "So what!" or "Ho hum!" If so, that is their loss precisely because what we are today was forged by what happened at that October 1948 meeting at 339 West Pender Street, Vancouver, humorously dubbed by some as The Kremlin. Other labour historians have written about the turmoil that followed, so I will record only how my job changed at that time.

LEAVING THE DOMINION BUILDING

In my two years at 905 my work was noticed and approved with some appreciation for my efforts above and beyond nine-to-five o'clock. Now I was invited to talk with the Vancouver Labour Council and the B. C. Federation: would I consider working for both? Would I do the work of two stenos for the pay of one while the crisis in finances remained? I said "yes".

What brought this about? The strife rocking the B.C. Federation of Labour had caused the bank to freeze its financial assets. Now, the newly elected officials asked for the cooperation of the Vancouver Labour Council (it constituted bodies for New Westminster & Vancouver and included the two unions I had been working for). The Federation had to bring the B.C. trade unionists back into believing in cooperation and George Home, a real career man, planned for a convention in February 1950.

Upon reflection, I wanted a change. With Eileen's departure, which had happened before the vote, the workplace atmosphere was without the peculiar warmth she gave. (The union directors in Toronto had decided that it was time to take on the great Eaton Empire, and their choice was to call Eileen back to head this gargantuan effort. This was a stunning loss to B.C. unionists in the confrontation between the White Block and the Red Bloc; but she had given thorough direction and was able to leave a keen, well organized section.) The Steel Rep never created friendly cooperation in me. In fact, one day, when he stopped by my desk, he insulted me terribly. On my desk lay a list I'd made out at the request of his kindly Russian father who said he could find me building materials for the house my parents and I were constructing. His generous offer was welcomed – after the war, nails and other construction items were at a premium. "What's this?" asked the Steel Rep. He picked up the list.

"Your father offered to get these things for me." I said, with embarrassment. "My father doesn't know what he's doing!" he responded. With that, he tore up the piece of paper. He wasn't aware of my hot blush and, of course, I didn't tell his father what his son said.

As for the two other Union Reps, there was no need to consider either as I made my decision. I was tired of the dynamics they caused in the office; one was very rude and the other told constant tales of his crude romantics, repeating them with every new group of members.

Offices can be dreary places without a touch of humour, but certain jokes are titillating only in a vaudeville show. I never heard my dad tell a dirty joke, nor had I heard such crude stories in any previous office, though some of my naiveté had been burned off during my employment at #2 Wireless Air Gunnery in Calgary during the war years. In today's world, there would be charges of sexual harassment. When one of the Reps stood near my desk and declared, "No girl is a part of the office furniture until she has been screwed to the desk," I was not amused. Did he mean me? "Haw, haw," the other Rep bawled, with no reaction from the third, more sober one.

Two years later, this atmosphere had grown intolerable and I was ready for a change. I accepted the job offer and moved to the Holden Building.

THE HOLDEN BUILDING

"My father," the building's heir and manageress, Mrs. Winbigler, liked to recount, "arrived in Vancouver with 75 cents in his overalls and worked as a common labourer for many years before he erected this fine building." She was rightly proud; in its earlier days, The Holden Building was something to brag about. It was constructed with fine wood and splendid marble throughout, and there was a wide, elegant staircase with wrought iron balustrades. The now dated washrooms must have been the envy of other building owners. The building had housed Vancouver's first city council offices – back then, a most suitable locale for meetings.

Miss Holden, now Mrs. Winbigler, had married a doctor when both were a little past middle-age. She was a large woman who could have passed for Winston Churchill's sister; but she dressed well and her hats were consistently custom-made of fine quality felt, with a wide, turned up brim. We often chatted when I paid our rent or when we met in the hallway.

Alas, our friendly relations were sorely tried one day as I

passed by her office and noted the cleaning staff lined up in front of her desk. "Why, why, why did you sign a union card?" she asked them loudly. "You didn't have to do anything like that."

I stood, just out of sight, transfixed.

"Well, we would like to have better working conditions," one worker said nervously. "You only have to tell me!" she said. Her tone had become coaxing.

"...and the pay isn't very good here either," the fellow went on.

"Look," said Mrs. Winbigler, "I'll give you anything you want if you'll just tear up your Union cards!" Apparently she wasn't aware that this statement would be used when the employees took their case to the Labour Relations Board – which they did, and won their case, keeping their jobs and their union memberships.

Room 214 Holden was an inside room with no outside light, its fluorescent light burning every hour into our often overworked eyes and spirits. My new job was difficult and demanding as both bosses wanted their work done as soon as a meeting was over. "Have you got the Minutes of Council Meeting typed and printed?" Jim Bury, a socialist to the core, asked often. Many times I came close to replying sarcastically. He knew I worked hard to satisfy everyone!

The method of producing a record in those days, compared with today, was medieval. From shorthand notes, and Jim's illegible writing, I transferred Minutes to the special sheets for the hand-operated Gestetner. The printed pages were then spread out on the boardroom table and stapled together. Sometimes fellows off work came in, saw how busy I was answering the phone and the counter service, and they'd help out. It was plain we needed extra office help.

Unionized, we sent out a call, and Ethel was hired. Her typing skills were very good, she caught on quickly to all the kafuffle that was part of the day's work, and she was highly sociable with an ebullient sense of humour, just what we needed. But oh, Ethel's sense of neatness in her person and her desk were something else. Time and again, when her desk was piled high from one end to the other and things fell off while her cigarette hung from the right side of her mouth, she would laugh at the mess and then George Home would say, tersely, "Clean up that desk!"

Having moved to the Holden Building meant being much closer to the BC Electric, which was a gain in time, but with a complete change in the local scene. The building's neighbourhood was unique. The street was just coming to life when I hurried from the tram station to the office. At one hotel, a number of 'all-nighters' sloped against the wall, mumbling to one another. The rooming house always had a couple of 'winos' lounging or recovering outside; and things picked up even more at the White Lunch and beyond, where the pawn shop proprietor removed the metal grillwork off the door and windows. But personal safety was not an issue; no one bothered me.

By noon, the streets were alive; and hungry workers stood in line outside "Only Fish", an eatery a few doors down from the Holden Building. My wages and responsibilities didn't allow for restaurant eating, but if someone treated me, or I got a bonus for overtime work, I ate there, too; or at a tiny place in Woodward's parking lot where a burger with extra bacon and a fried egg cost 35 cents!

My daily routine was to eat my home-made lunch in the room used by Vancouver Labour Council three floors up, where an enterprising chap sold home-made soup and sandwiches for 25 cents, coffee for a dime and a cookie for a nickel. The room had only three small tables, but this was the place to meet other unionists from the nearby B.C. Fed & Labour Council office.

Another landmark in the Holden Building neighbourhood was the once great theatre, 'The Empress'; in its glory days, well-known stars from all over performed two shows a day and on the weekend. Much of its lustre was gone, but the theatre was a favourite for lumber workers, in town for a few days, looking for ways to forget the camps where their underwear hung to dry in the same room as their bunks, and where meals were so poor that, on occasion, the chef was chased off the premises with threats of vengeance!

My work was most often overtime, leaving Spencer with time on his hands if we had planned to shop at Woodward's at day's end. "If you're going work till after five, why don't I go see a show at the theatre up the street?" he asked one day. He was only eleven but already had opinions of his own. "Fine," I said. "Here's enough money for a ticket and some candy. Just come straight here when the show's out."

We were on the tram, on our way home to Burnaby, when he roused me from my meandering, work-related thoughts. As if musing aloud, he said, "That was the strangest show I've ever been to. I had a good seat not too far from the stage, but when the show began, all these guys rushed up from the back and told me to move. But I kept my seat. Then those women came out and danced. Mom, I really don't think they were wearing anything on top, but those guys were hollering and jumping up and down so much I couldn't get a good look. Do you think they were really naked?"

"Where on earth were you?" I asked, now wide-awake.

"I went up to the Empress Theatre like you said; and it's funny, they didn't want to give me a ticket at first." Both Mother and son were educated on the Holden Building neighbourhood that day!

POLITICS AND UNION WORK

I was introduced to politics at an early age; and it remains in my blood. Mother took me to meetings; we caught rides to hear a candidate speaking in Moosomin – Rocanville was considered 'second class', so everything went on in Moosomin,

251

which was on the main railway line. I remember being asked to sing at one rally, belting out: "John Henry was a little baby, sittin' on his mammy's knee...."

During the CCF campaign in 1933, I was a scrutineer at the polling station, which was held in the same hall as the dances. A scrutineer guards that each person's vote is in and accepted. It was a provincial election and one of the nominees was the conservative Dr. Munroe, at whose nominating meeting I had sung. Now I watched 94-year-old Grandma Strong, the community's matriarch, being led into the hall. "How are you?" I greeted her loudly; she was very hard-of-hearing. She was escorted into a booth, the conversation inside broadcast for all. "Grandma Strong, you wanted to vote for Dr. Munroe?" shouted her escort. "Oh, it's a lovely day," she answered. "Grandma Strong, you wanted to vote for Dr. Munroe!" "I'm quite well, thank you."

In the years where I was employed with unions, requests came for help in a political campaign and, unless an urgent matter required the union's full attention, we accepted. Memories of those times still trigger a surge of pleasure: we are engaged in battle, for a good cause; we have energy to burn, the pulse increasing as the fighters' adrenalin floods the system. It was as natural as breathing for me to share work with the union and the political arena.

It didn't matter that we didn't have the same kind of money as our opponents; we asked for donations – a desk and chair, office supplies, an old sofa, a table for someone to sit, take a breath and chat with a co-worker, a space with a bathroom, and donations of money – fifty cents or fifty dollars, whatever donors could spare. In one campaign in Vancouver our funds totalled only $4000, a pittance compared to the well-oiled opposition who reported many times that.

The outside of the building that housed Vancouver East headquarters in the 1950s wasn't impressive either, in fact, compared to the shops along the street, it was a bit dowdy.

The entrance was just a plain, worn door and the windows didn't entice, unless you were a loyal, hard-working booster. Sometimes a good, printed sign announcing a special event was posted, but most times even the sign was modest, done by hand, and simply informing passers-by that a 'good speaker' would address the next meeting, entrance fee by donation only. But the sign announcing "The Send-off for our Members of the Legislature!" meant something important.

I don't remember if it cost $1.50 for such events, but I do recall that tickets were sold out every year. MLAs from Vancouver and up-country were treated like heroes that evening. Who catered to a crowd at those popular events? The women of Vancouver East CCF, of course, and what a fine dinner they served! I recall one event when I arrived late, met with the noise of loud, happy voices of friends greeting one another, the frowzy old hall filled with tantalizing aromas of roast beef and gravy, with apple pie for dessert. "For heaven's sake, help me with this card table; we've run out of tables for the mob," a robust, red-faced woman friend said. Those women knew how to handle any emergency.

My after-dinner job at those meetings was to mount the stage and, with Gwen Dowding's accompaniment, lead the crowd in a rousing sing-song, often ending with Ernie Winch's favourite, "Keep right on to the end of the road...." Each MLA gave a short speech that caused yelps of "Hurrah!" and applause. A senior, sometimes former MLA like Gretchen Steeves, would conclude the evening by promising one hundred per cent support for the Members while in Victoria. What I remember most about those annual meetings is how every person there, MLA and supporter alike, left with a keen sense of gladness to be involved in working together for the cause we held dear.

Outside of those meetings, campaign managers earned their salt! They kept the faithful in good spirits, prodded the candidate to, "Go out and knock on doors. Right now. Every day!" all the while worried about how to run an election platform on the goodwill and generosity of members and supporters. Volunteers are appreciated for their generosity and their endurance, especially in door-to-door canvassing in unfriendly territory. That's what makes a political campaign so fascinating, so involving; whether it's a win or lose, it's a learning experience for party and candidate alike.

In my collection of papers, I found this note that I had posted for my fellow volunteers; and which Tom Berger, then NDP MLA for Burrard riding and later a judge, responded to.

August 25, 1966

TO ALL AND SUNDRY:

I have just come in to work and found – for the umpteenth time – that a stencil which I cut and ran a few hundred copies – has to be changed.

The IWA is donating so much in supplies to this riding and many others that they now have to curtail this generous 'never mind counting anything' attitude.

THEREFORE, from now on I will cut a stencil and run it ONLY WHEN FINALLY INITIALLED BY THE WRITER.

There is no need to continue what is already far too much waste.

Jean

OK OK O.K,

Mea culpa. Meal culpa.

Please forgive me Jean.

Tom

In a recent national poll Tommy Douglas was rated Canada's No. 1 citizen. We in the New Democratic Party are enormously proud of him, and some of us have been fortunate to have known him well and worked for him. My particular personal memory of him is when we stood before a crowd and sang together. I often composed parodies to old, well-known tunes to kick-start a meeting. If Tommy was present, he picked it up and sang with feeling and in a good tenor voice, before going on to give one of his great speeches. In everything he did he taught us so much with his

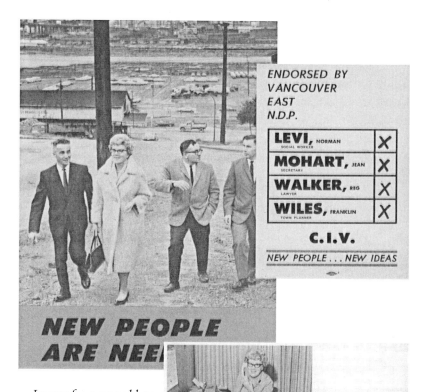

Images from pamphlets on my political involvement running for Vancouver City Council, 1966.

Mrs. Jean Mohart, private secretary to the I.W.A. regional president, is known to many for her work in the founding of the Memorial Society, the non-profit funeral services society which she heads. Mrs. Mohart, 54, is a grandmother, active in the Unitarian Church.

unmatchable humanitarian persona. Our hearts were sore when a vicious campaign by the Liberals unseated him; but his dignified response gave us new courage. He used the stirring quote from Dryden's poem of 1702 to bring us to our feet, cheering both him and ourselves on:

"Fight on, fight on, my merry men, I am little wounded, but not slain.

I'll just lay down and bleed a while, and then rise up and fight again."

Changing Homes: From Windsor to 2227 Pine St.

In the Spring of 1950, I knew my relationship with Pete couldn't continue with our respective living arrangements. Perhaps, I thought, if I took a room somewhere on my own, he'll make up his mind about me. "If he can't make up his mind in a year, it doesn't look good," a good friend's husband advised me. How right he was!

I found an ad for a room that cost $33 per month and went to see it. My wages were only $120 per month and with that I had to purchase groceries and all other necessities for Mother, Dad, Spencer and myself. But I had to force Pete to make a decision! I didn't know then, that to think that way was with clouded vision; and only Pete could make up his own mind.

With Pete's help, I moved to a room. He seemed unhappy that night, but said he was getting a cold.

A few nights of going to that miserable room – where the toilet held a chamber pot encrusted with old urine – made me unhappy enough to phone Mattison's, our Burnaby neighbour, and ask to speak to Mother. "How are things?" I asked. "Fine," she replied. "How's Spence?" "Just fine." "I'd like to come home tonight," I said. "That's alright," she said.

I took a streetcar, then the interurban, glad to just see my eleven year old son. He wasn't excited to see me. The shocker that knocked sense into my head was when I suggested to

Spencer that he might like to come with me to the room I had and he replied, "I'll stay here with Grandma." I said no more. Even though the room took a lump of my much needed money, it cost me that sum to know that, whatever Pete was in my life, nothing compared with how I loved my son and wanted him to want to be with me. I would sell the house and find a better place where the both of us could live.

In the Holden Building office of the Vancouver Labour Council and B.C. Federation of Labour we had many visitors, not all from Unions. Darwin Charlton, a life-long member of the NDP (his father was one of the first organizers of the CCF party in BC in the early 1930s) often dropped in after visiting the 3rd floor CCF offices. Hearing that I was looking for rooms in Vancouver, and knowing my circumstances, he suggested I contact his sister. He stayed at her home when he came to the city for a change from his home in the Interior.

"What kind of space does she have?" I asked, perhaps with some fear, for now I had to pay a monthly rent from my salary of $35 a week. We'd sold the Burnaby home to a mail courier; and since he and his wife and two children existed on the pittance that Canada Post paid, and I was desperate to get the house off my hands, I agreed to a $40 monthly payment on the price of $4000.00.

I arranged to visit Darwin's sister after work. The bus service was excellent. From 214, the Holden Building, on East Hastings Street to 2227 Pine Street, it took less than 15 minutes. Inside the front door on the right was the ice-box. While she showed me in, the landlady revealed that she had three sons and that her husband was a tugboat operator. Upstairs were two bedrooms, but only one was for rent – with room for a double bed and a 3-drawer dresser. The room had one window (out of which Spencer would find himself hanging during a game with one of the sons).

Where was our 'living' room? Down the hall we passed the only bathroom for the family and Spencer and me. The rear room was ours. In one corner stood a two-burner gas kitchen stove, and opposite it was a cupboard for all kitchen needs. A small wood table and a couch completed the furnishings. There was no washing machine, but, said Mrs. Bennett, "There's a laundry a couple of blocks over from Granville where I take my washing." So, I'd have to buy a tin washtub to keep ourselves clean, and carry bedding and towels up the street when necessary.

My spirits sank. I felt utterly lonely. I was tired, too, from doing the hard work of two stenos; and it didn't help that my landlady spoke in a plaintive tone.

"It'll be $28.50 per month for rent, including the cost of the gas used," she informed me at the end of our 'tour'. I knew little about Vancouver rental prices and assumed this was fair.

On July 1st, after three years of living in the first house I owned, Spencer and I had a new address: 2227 Pine Street, Vancouver.

Later that day Pete Smith came over to help. He brought with him a gift: a fine carving knife, saying I'd need this for my cooking. "You need a new table, too, Jean," he noted. That was obvious. We shopped for one the next Saturday. I paid $10.00 for it – a lot of money then.

I write these words in 2005, in my office, that table beside me, its edges crowded with memories: there's me, sitting alone, writing letters; then again, talking with Betty and Dr. Leonard Marsh, and laughing with the entire unbelievable wrath they brought wherever they were. And yes, sitting at the table with Pete Smith who, when we shopped for the table, said, in a voice as clear today as back then, "Get a good one, Jean." Too bad I didn't follow that principle in other relationships!

Our suite furnished, Spencer and I settled into the new neighbourhood near the Alexandra Neighbourhood House. It was a great place where Spencer and other children played outdoor and indoor games. One afternoon, I heard Spencer's footsteps on the stairs and sounds as if he was in great pain. I tied a towel around my wet head and ran to meet him. His head was bruised and one shin was gashed and bleeding. "The same guy that stole my money; he and his gang beat me up," he told me. Wet head or not, we marched right over there.

"Five against one!" I stormed at the boys when we found them. They smiled and began tossing a small ball to each other. "Hey, boy, don't you think Spencer's a nice kind of kid?" said one; and then, "Oh my, did Spencer go home and tell his Momma that somebody kicked him? Oh, gee! Ain't that too bad, now. Aren't we sorry for him."

I knew my raging would lead nowhere, so I telephoned the police. The officer who took the complaint thought we should know that "the kid's family lives somewhere under the bridge...they're a bad lot, with police records...his mother and sisters also...." Our second encounter of that kind was also the last; and occasionally we've wondered about that lad's future.

That summer, 1951, Spencer received a brand new bicycle from Pete. Asked what he wanted for good school marks he said, "A whole watermelon." We both liked Pete, and hoped and believed the relationship would develop into a permanent one. That is another part of thinking with your heart, and how often didn't Mother say, with a grin, "Thinking? Well, you know what THOUGHT did! Stuck a feather in the manure pile and THOUGHT it would grow!!"

CHAPTER FOURTEEN

Vancouver – Toronto – Cloverdale – Vancouver

Perhaps if I were in a confessing mood I'd say that I wonder how much overtime my Guardian Angel puts in.

TOWN MEETING IN CANADA – AUGUST 24, 1951

For several years the radio station CJOR ran a weekly Friday night public meeting called "Town Meeting in Canada". Arthur Helps, who Dr. Marsh jokingly referred to as 'Arthur Hinders', was the show's moderator. The show opened with the sound of a bell ringing and a voice, like some town crier, calling out "Town Meeting in Canada". I was invited to be on the show when the topic was "Should Married Women be discouraged from seeking employment?" The show began and we four panellists were introduced as follows:

W. J. Trainor, barrister; BSc University of B. C.

Mrs. Jean Mohart, Office Secretary, BC Federation of Labour CLC

Mrs. F. Boughton, Radio chairman of the BC Teachers' Federation

Robert MacDonald, barrister; 5 years with the RCA

Mrs. Boughton was very careful to say that it was "better for a woman to stay home and take care of her children" without ever actually saying she shouldn't go to work. What she did say was that working mothers couldn't be good parents and didn't do justice to their children and family. At that point, I blew up a bit and said, "Look! I have a child and

261

I don't think it's making that big of a difference between my son and me." Afterwards, my boss told me to not get so personal in these public discussions.

That was hard for me to do, because not only was it personal, I spoke for hundreds of women like myself; working women employed, for example, in the needles trade which had the worst contracts of all. And the Burns Packing House

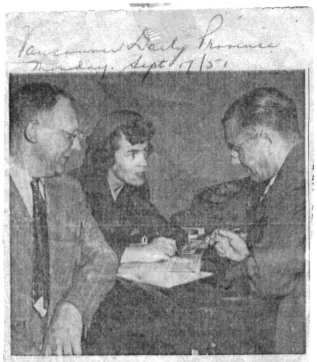

Newspaper clipping from the Vancouver Daily Province, Sept. 17, 1951. The caption says: FIRST DELEGATE: to register Sunday for the Canadian Congress of Labor convention at Hotel Vancouver was Harry Chappell, railroad union head. He gets necessary help from Joseph James, chairman of the credentials committee, and Jean Mohart, Vancouver Labor Council worker.

where, one day, the administrators decided to examine every woman's purse and found one woman had twenty-eight eggs in her purse! And why was she stealing eggs? Because she wasn't paid enough to buy them. Unionization had just begun; some women worked for seventy-four cents an hour. I knew from my work, from typing the list, that, in one industry, there were 400 classifications of workers; and that meant if the foreman didn't like you, he or she might say, "I'm changing your work category into another classification"; and with that, a worker might get ten cents less per hour. If she protested, a worker might be assigned to a lower-paid classification. A lot depended if you were in cahoots with foremen or foreladies. And the union movement put forth a recommendation to reduce the number of classifications. (The category that most confused me when I typed them up was "pissler". "What's that?" I asked one of the guys. "You ought to be able to figure that one out," he answered. "Remember the Burns' Meat motto, 'we use every bit of the meat'?" A pissler therefore, excised the animal's 'pissing' organ. With that, I was laughingly reminded never to eat Pork 'N Beans which used that bit of meat. Cannery workers also offered precautions about a certain brand of canned raspberries that were stored, for later canning, in barrels known to be home also to mice.)

Yes, my heart was with the workers, especially women, who worked, too often, under awful conditions. The Town Hall was my first opportunity to speak publicly on that issue, and secondly, to give an opinion as a single Mom. Except for my little blow-up, our discussion was amicable.

The genteel topic in 1951 is no longer relevant. The world has changed materially and socially. My solace comes from a Grade III reader: Great oaks from little acorns grow.

FORD BUILDING TENANTS 1951-1952

There was one tenant in the Ford building nearby known

to many women; and his service was a well known secret. Only once did I enter his waiting room, with a friend.

Sally and I shared an interest in unionism, politics, the arts and good food. Like me, Sally was the sole income earner for her family of four. Now she was pregnant. She cried as she told me about the difficult decision she and her disabled husband had made.

An appointment was made with the Ford Building physician and I accompanied her. He handed her an East Hastings address and a bottle containing a few ounces of brown liquid, which he told her to take and, "if nothing happens", to see him again. He stressed confidentiality.

Sally spent the night with me. The next day, I returned from work to find her wan and very tired. We talked quietly and not a lot about the matter. She said she had never sat in such a dreary room, "filled with hopelessness and fear; and no one talked." The procedure happened in a back room, performed by two people in professional white garb.

My 'suite' was in a house with only one bathroom, shared with a four member family downstairs. My friend used the toilet and I followed. What I saw caused alarm: she had expelled the catheter; without it, the procedure would not complete; and worse, the $200 that had taken a year to save (for an 'emergency') was out the window.

"Phone the house you were at and tell them," I advised Sally, which she did. "Too bad, but there's nothing more we can do," they told her. I was appalled. "Phone them again," I insisted, "and tell them you are coming back and expect to have this procedure done properly. If they still refuse, tell them you'll be accompanied by the police."

The plan worked. Afterwards, my friend returned to her home, not far from Vancouver. Two nights later, the abortion was effected; and she haemorrhaged profusely. Her doctor, who'd been sympathetic to her plight, but unwilling to provide the abortion and risk losing his license, didn't need to be told what was happening. She went into surgery immediately. The abortion resulted in a terrible infection; and her life was held in the balance twice more before she was well enough to be discharged from the hospital.

UNION WORK 1951

My personal life in that year seemed to have found smoother sailing. My salary had improved a little, my son and I were in a better suite, he was doing well at school, my parents had moved out to the Cloverdale farm where my sister, husband and three boys lived, a boon for us since there is nothing nicer for a city dweller than having the warmth of a family visit coupled with the special goodness that comes from fresh, country air. But now, there were to be changes in the relative comfort I'd been enjoying.

The Canadian Labour Congress Ottawa office broke from years of tradition when it decided to hold its annual convention in Vancouver. The 'white block' was now in control of Vancouver Labour Council and though there were still a few camps where I.W.A. 'Red bloc' members clung to power, to all intents and purposes, 'all was quiet on the western front'. The changes of fortunes since I began working for the B.C. Federation in 1948 to now were striking; the Moose Hall was cheap but adequate, hardly to be compared with the trappings of Hotel Vancouver, which, in this case, was paid for by the Canadian Labour Congress. Everyone pitched in to make it a success.

The Steelworkers' union was about to embark on a Time and Wage Study. National Director Charlie Millard chose Dirk Bear to be front and centre of this new venture, while Dirk was allowed to choose a man to work with him. To our surprise, he chose Pete Smith, one of his stalwarts in Vancouver, to move east and work with him. With that, my own future was involved. My little barge was heading for choppy waters.

"That means I'll be moving to Toronto," Pete told me, a little shocked, though also pleased. We sat quietly, counting the delegates' fees, wondering about our own future.

Pete left for Toronto by car the last week in October, with my promise that Spencer and I would join him later. Pete's job would take tedious hours of learning and then develop into a heavy routine that meant travelling to the widely scattered Steel plants in Ontario. It wasn't easy for me to give notice that I'd be leaving my job; the Federation's annual convention would be held in early February and would require extra planning, entailing the usual overload of stenographic work. My family, Mother especially, was not at all pleased, wondering if I would go to Toronto when it wasn't clear if my fiancé (he had given me a ring!) was free to marry. "Your divorce; has it been settled?" Mother asked Pete when he phoned one day. "Yes!" he said, "it's all settled."

My amour wrote beautiful letters after he arrived in Toronto. He implored me, almost daily, to join him. "You can't really mean it," said my bosses and others, including family, who hoped we wouldn't move to Toronto. What to do? The move would be a radical change for me and for my young son. Spencer was to enter his thirteenth year, a crucial time in his young life; and it wasn't good to disrupt him in mid-year. Our three years in Burnaby had been our only period where we felt settled. In Burnaby we'd been close to Deer Lake, where Spencer loved the natural life that excited him so that, when he came rushing home on a Sunday afternoon, he begged me to return to the lake because there were "the biggest frogs you'd ever see." Now, our Pine Street digs allowed him to walk to Kitsilano and swim any time, any day. But the prospect of becoming a threesome-family, I believed, would ease the rocky change of location. And so, believing that 'love conquers all', and in Pete's professed love and promise to marry me, I packed and we moved to Toronto.

We arrived on February 12, 1952. After a week in a hotel I

found a suite of rooms out in the east end in a duplex near Kew Beach. When the kindly woman upstairs asked a lot of questions I felt uncomfortable; when she asked if we were married I said "Yes", forgetting that my trunk lay on the outside patio with my name in large letters; and I knew she'd seen it. It wasn't easy for my son, who was asked about parents, but again, Spencer's ability to accommodate amazed me. I remained less certain. This romance was still not a sure thing: the fellow wasn't divorced, as I had been led to believe; and worse....

Women, we're told, are more intuitive than men. Under ordinary circumstances that's fine; it's when one's senses are clouded by caring that intuition is thwarted. And that's how it was for me; the proverbial 'cloud no bigger than a man's hand' shaded my eyes. Something was amiss, had been since the day we arrived in Toronto and Pete had seemed distracted; but I couldn't put a finger on it. Not yet.

Meanwhile, the three of us created a lovely Sunday routine: while I made Sunday dinner, Spencer and Pete took a long walk. Sunday dinner was special to me since my earliest childhood when Dad cooked the roast and a friend or visitors joined us. Sundays concluded with a seven o'clock church service where we sang hymns to mark the day's end: "The day Thou gavest, Lord, is ended" or "Now the day is over...."

It was a Sunday when my intuition cleared abruptly. How beautiful it was to be wakened by my son who brought me a plate of pancakes, walking ever-so-carefully to avoid tipping the syrup swamped plate! That afternoon, Spencer and Pete prepared to leave for their routine walk. "Would you mind dropping this suit off at the cleaner's tomorrow on your way to work?" Pete asked. He had to leave early and, since my office was nearby the cleaner's, I readily agreed. "You might see if I've cleaned out all the pockets," he added; and they were off.

When dinner was underway, I put his suit by my coat to

remind me, and then looked through the pockets. Inside was a typewritten letter, signed by a woman who begged him to "continue with perhaps less of those torrid moments". The words shattered my world. I had fallen into a neat trap!

How did I speak to him sanely when he returned from their walk? "This letter," I said, holding it up. "Tell me honestly; are you having an affair?" His smile had the edge of a smirk. "Oh, you read it. Well, no; but *she's* pushing it."

What a mean, cowardly response! Then, suddenly, I remembered a party we'd attended at *her* home. While I'd been playing piano for a songster, Pete had vanished. He loved singing; so where was he? In another room, with the hostess! It hadn't registered at the time, but now it all made sense. I'd moved to Toronto to make a new life; instead it collapsed, piece by piece. I'd ignored my intuition and clung instead to my hopeful naïveté, which kept me going – until that Sunday afternoon.

Hindsight is perfect. For the next few months life was difficult. Spencer and I moved to a small two room suite on an upper floor where the heat was torrid, day and all night. Toronto had its hottest summer in one hundred and ten years. My son and I longed for Vancouver and the Kitsilano beaches where he could swim all day for free; here, not only did he have to pay bus fare to travel many miles to a pool, he had to pay for a swim!

Like every dark cloud, there was a silver lining. Every Sunday my old friend, Eileen Sufrin, invited us to dinner. When a vacancy occurred in her office, I was hired to work there. Pete kept in touch, but for all intents and purposes we were on our own.

Then a visit to a doctor forced a decision. The doctor recommended a hospital test, a biopsy of the small lumps in my right breast.

I took stock. Wallis Simpson, wife of the Duke of Windsor, entitled her memoir, "The Heart Has Its Reasons".

In the autumn of 1952, my head said, Get a grip, Jean. You and this guy are never going to make it; but my sad heart wanted to renew what had begun with sweet hopes and dreams. Then came more news that helped me make a decision: Pete's wife had sold their house in Vancouver and would be in Toronto soon. The hard truth was that Pete wanted me out of the way. He wanted his share of their estate and perhaps even a reunion! My intuition told me this; and now I listened. We would move back and I'd have the hospital test in BC.

No doubt about it, Pete was relieved. To ease our trip back, he paid for a compartment on the train, no doubt in part to assuage his own guilt.

From time to time, I heard that Pete and his wife were divorced. Several years later, a woman I didn't know, burst into my office, asked if I was Jean Mohart, and then told me she was going to sue Pete Smith for "breach of promise". He'd promised to marry her, too!

Certain severance came when Pete contacted me several years later during a Vancouver work assignment. "I'd like to see the new offices of the IWA; I heard some fine woods were used in the construction," he told me over the phone. I consented to meet him. As I showed him through the building, he showed more interest in me than the tour; when his odd visit ended, he said, "You know, Jean, you were the only one I ever loved."

My reply? I broke into song, softly, but clearly: "Put it on the ground; spread it all around; and it will make your flowers bloom!" (Years later, when my husband Frank and I drove home from a union party for an old friend, Frank expressed worry that seeing Pete at that event would upset our relationship. "Not to worry," I assured him. "He did me a favour." And I meant that, was absolutely certain that Pete's philandering, though hurtful, had saved me from a fate worse than death.)

CLOVERDALE

How fortunate are those who have a family like mine!

Spencer and I arrived in British Columbia on August 3, 1952 to the warm, loving greeting of my sister Pat and her husband. They insisted we bunk with them in Cloverdale until we were settled and more secure.

Within days of inhaling the sweet air of the Fraser Valley, Pat and I visited the Municipal Hall in Cloverdale where her husband was employed. The Secretary Treasurer greeted us, adding that he had a problem because one of his stenos had moved away. "I'm unemployed," I said. "How about hiring me?" It took less than five minutes to make a deal.

It felt natural to be in a small town again. At first Spencer and I lived in two rented rooms above the Clova Theatre, sharing space with two young chaps who were easy to get along with, even when they or we plugged in too many gadgets at once and our power cut out – usually at supper time. Spencer and I had a standing joke when he went to the theatre below us: "Don't get lost trying to find your way home after the show," I'd say. "I'll try not to," he'd reply.

One day we were standing together, making supper, and I turned to speak to Spencer. Suddenly, I was aware that I was looking up. It was a turning point for us both as we realized, for the first time, that he had grown taller than me. We

The 'wee' house in Cloverdale, 1952-53.

looked at one another quizzically and he said, with a grin, "Well, I wonder who's boss in this house now?"

In the office at the Cloverdale municipal hall, I heard all the local news with generous dollops of gossip tossed in. That's how I heard about Mrs. Collishaw's small house coming available October 1st. A home, however modest! No matter that it had been a stable, then a garage and finally a house that had never been painted. No matter that it cowered in comparison to the wonderful old barn to one side of it and the big yellow house at the front of the lot.

We moved with the help of my brother-in-law, and that evening I happily cooked supper – a favourite of Bangers & Mash, with vegetables and a dessert. Spencer sat at the table, waiting for dinner. "Mother, I'm so tired of moving," he said. "I know dear, I hope we can settle down for a longer spell now," I said optimistically.

I was broke, however Eaton's trusted me and I purchased a sofa-bed and chair. Mother's sewing added nice cushions, curtains and a space for hanging jackets. We painted the walls and a kind carpenter at the office built us a bookcase. Home, sweet sweet home!

We also found a warm welcome at the United church – just in time for me to sing a solo of "Thanks be to God" for the Thanksgiving service. What a wonderful way to heal my sorely bent heart! The young United Church minister and his wife were fine musicians; and the choir was led by a leader of ability, with the right personality to draw out the best in us.

On weekends, Spencer and I visited Pat's farm where we partook in home-cooked meals and the warmth of being in the family circle. If I had planned this move, I couldn't have done better than our next two years in Cloverdale. Back then, Cloverdale was a small town with a laid-back image; people greeted each other on the street whether friends or not. After Toronto's hubbub, shopping in Cloverdale was relaxed. The rotund English butcher chatted with you while he served you

– just like it was in my childhood. And it was the same in the drug store, grocery and hardware store, and in the restaurants.

Why didn't I return to Vancouver? Too much to remind me of the four and a half years devoted to loving Pete; and it was time to get him out of my system! Living in Cloverdale did just that. Here, I met new people every day, was a secretary to the municipal engineer – a lovely man with a delightful sense of humour. I had helpful co-workers and belonged to a union. Salaries could be improved; and there was a challenge for me to sink my teeth into. Good! I enjoyed union talks.

Friends from Vancouver visited frequently; and if I took a weekend to visit them, the Greyhound bus was comfortable and cheap. The most rewarding Saturday afternoon visits were at the home of Dr. Leonard & Betty Marsh. (Dr. Marsh, an economist, was commissioned by Prime Minister Mackenzie King to devise a new manifest for the federal government's plan to create new social benefits.)

"I'm happy; I don't want any more changes for the time being," I said when asked about my life.

RADICAL SURGERY!

Our telephone jangled just after New Year's Day. The receptionist for my doctor, whom I'd visited the week before, said, "You are to be in the Royal Columbia Hospital January 15th for a D&C and a biopsy." She provided further details.

Our four months in Cloverdale had given me enough time to work with the union to secure medical insurance at work, its cost covered in part by the individual. I remember looking at that item and wondering how best to budget for it and then, at the last moment, deciding to write the cheque. My Guardian Angel was at work again!

The first evening in the hospital was spent chatting with

roommates. Supper that night was ham and escalloped potatoes and I ate with relish. I brushed off complaints with, "We must eat if we are to get better."

Hospitals didn't discharge patients as quickly back then; I was there almost a week. Up, feeling fine, dressed to go home, I waited for the doctor to discharge me. He was late, maybe called elsewhere, I thought. When he arrived, he yanked the curtains around my bed, sat down and blurted out, "I have bad news for you. It's cancer." Dear God, I thought; I'm being gypped! "You're not in my hands now," he continued. "You must be at the Cancer Institute tomorrow morning at 8."

"No, Dr. Frinton," I said quietly. "I must go home first; I need to tell my son and my family, and then I'll face whatever comes."

He understood and that was helpful. He admitted how difficult it was for him to deliver this news, said he'd be in touch with the Cancer Institute and keep me informed from now on.

I arrived at UBC's Health Center the next cold morning. I was ushered into a room to undress and wait for an examination. All around me were glass cases of instruments. Having worked in a hospital this didn't bother me; waiting for an hour did. I was chilly and finally called an attendant. Had I been forgotten? Apparently not. Within five minutes, five doctors entered and, without a word, each of them gave me an internal exam. They headed for the door. I sat up. "I've waited for some time in this room," I said, waving my hand to indicate its contents. "And you can't walk out without telling me something."

They stopped and the senior doctor spoke. "Mrs. Mohart is right. She should be told something." Then he spoke directly to me. "Dr. Hardy will talk to you in her office as soon as you're dressed."

Dr. Hardy was a tall, kindly person. She asked me to sit in the chair near her desk. "We feel you must have treatment immediately," she said, "but I'm afraid you're going to lose all your reproductive organs." We talked only a few minutes longer. I would get word very soon that the next surgery would be done in the Royal Columbian, where there was a fine physician. My brother-in-law and I went home, picked my son up from school and went on to the farm.

Three weeks later, Dr. F. Kinsey performed a coninization, a sort of stop-gap for the time being. It was a painful, bloody operation which I again recovered from on my sister's farm for a week. I was glad to get back into our little home and build up my strength for the final surgery. Radiation had been discussed, but the decision was for surgery.

My major concern other than for myself was my son. "You'd better not have cancer," he'd said one day after hearing classmates discuss cancer. With that, we had a heart-to-heart, and I explained as best I could, the physiology of our bodies and the medical treatment I'd have. From then on, we took matters as calmly as we could, speaking without unnecessary drama.

In the last week of March, Pat and Mother accompanied me to the hospital. I was to have a radical, extreme surgery. Mother wept as I was admitted; Pat comforted her. "I'm certain the outcome will be okay," I said. "Remember, there'll be no scars on my face, only on my tummy."

Recovery took much longer. My job was being held for me but according to the union contract, my pay stopped December 31st.

Family, friends and neighbours gave me moral support and more; my usual recuperative powers performed well. Both my son and I stayed at Pat and Allen's farmhouse until I could walk. The abdominal stitches wouldn't allow me to stand up, but if I remained bent over, I could manage using a bicycle.

There was a lovely stream on the farm where the young lads spotted a nice-sized steelhead. The only way to catch it was to jump in and grab it; one day, Spencer did just that. He came in dripping and cold, with bright red cheeks. Less than a week later, he had a high fever and severe pain in his joints. Rheumatic fever! That year cortisone was already available, and it cost $35.00 a week. My pay was $40.00 a week and Hospital Insurance $1.00 per day. Without further elaboration, let me say only that ten years later my books showed a credit balance. Most importantly, both us of recovered, though he had a slight heart murmur for a time.

Let no one ever criticize small-town life! People in and just outside of Cloverdale overwhelmed us with their kindnesses. A tap on the door before we were up meant there was a gift of fresh vegetables or fruit, bread, cookies, cakes and heavenly home-made buns, jars of canned fruit and jams – all with their good wishes attached. It really was 'manna from heaven'. The friend who babysat the minister's small children was moved to tell me that the children included us in their good-night prayer. Living in Cloverdale then was an amazing bonus. We couldn't have had it better!

In August, while holidaying, I was invited to consider working for the Steelworkers' Union. The salary would allow me a better lifestyle; and it was tempting! Spencer was now in high school and Vancouver held many attractions for me such as a music and theatre. Best of all, our two years in Cloverdale had eased the heartache, my sadness and sorrow after the Toronto fiasco. I was back on an even keel.

CITY SLICKERS AGAIN

It's September, 1954 and we're back in the big town, certainly more lively and exciting than Cloverdale. We were pleased to be back; Spencer attended King Edward School and I worked at the Steelworkers' office on West Broadway. Spencer soon had a friend to pal around with and I became involved in the interests and activities of previous times: politics, the theatre, investigating eateries and shopping, in big and small stores. A former friend asked if I'd like to attend a service in the Unitarian church one Sunday morning, and this resulted in another turning point in my life – spiritually and philosophically.

Unitarianism appealed to me for the way it opened my mind to a wider intellectual and spiritual search. Discussion abounded, (Unitarians enjoy exploratory discourse); and sacred music was interspersed with music from great composers. A Youth group offered opportunities for fun and serious thinking, particularly at a summer camp, held at Seabeck, on the Hood Canal in Washington. I, too, found the sessions at Seabeck enriching with little time for fun. One of the preachers was a handsome young minister, Robert Fulgam, who later wrote the book, "All I ever needed to know, I learned in kindergarten".

It was hard to believe that just a couple of years previous my life hung in the balance. In conversation with my Creator (with whom I maintain a constant connection) the present is good and the future looks bright. Thanks be to God.

One of the union men came in to the office once a month to do the books for his Local. An industrious fellow, he chatted with me about the home improvements he did himself. Home! For years I'd been without, and my longing for 'home' ran deep. "If you really want a home, Jean," he told me when I shared that desire with him, "there's a nice little house on our street that's for sale. If you want it, we'll lend you the down payment at a low interest." The sound in my ears was my heart pounding. Want it? How could I refuse the deal he offered?

Feb 22 – Farm 1955

Dear Jean & Spencer:

A beautiful morning. Could I be of any use to you in moving? Let me know & I'll be there or if you need a man Dad no doubt would be glad to help.

We had a letter from Betty & they're fine & she is busy with Easter Music & has a solo. Bryn sent me a Valentine he made himself and the printing is exceptionally good.

Pat is expecting Vivian Service this afternoon & yesterday received no less than two invitations to Stanly parties, the first one from Mrs. Khun Jr.

I want to catch the mail lady. So good Bye; the mail lady has just called so I'll run over to the corner and catch her coming down the hill.

Love, mom

We moved in on February 5, 1955. The previous owner left it in fine condition, with one exception: the sawdust for the big range in the kitchen was too damp to burn; but that was a minor flaw. Made up for by the hot water heating system her engineer husband had built, one that gave us the best and unbeatable comfort. When we converted to gas, the repairman stared at the tidy little unit. "Is it OK?" I asked, alarmed. "Yes," said the man, smiling; "but it's all made upside-down, and I've never seen anything like it."

Mortgages are beastly things; but I had no option. It meant cutting costs in other ways, but the house became a heavenly place for my Mother, son and myself. A good CCF friend with carpentry skills helped out. After the sawdust was hauled away, there were parties downstairs and up; and I hosted dinner and overnight guests. A good friend, Dorothy Livesay, loaned me her piano when she went to England for a year's study. Could it get any better?

Cervantes, one of the world's greatest ever, wrote about 'tilting at Windmills'. Don Quixote did that, but the difference between him and me was he always had a devoted servant who understood the wild imaginings of his master. When a man 17 years my junior pursued me with ardour, it would have been wiser to thank him and look in another direction. He was a psychology student at the University, and seemed to be constantly analyzing my son and me. But his lively conversation, his enjoyment of music and his dancing – and the pleasure he took of my company – surprised me. When his schooling ended, he left, abruptly, without apology and returned to his Toronto home. And I got my feet on the ground again. Another lesson learned.

May 30, 1955

Dear Jean:
I have just cut a beautiful blossom of a scarlet of a tuberous begonia Mrs. Drew gave me and there is another flower and two buds. All the same beautiful red and exactly like velvet.

You mentioned about me doing some sewing for you, blouses you said. Does that mean for me to bring in the sewing machine? I quite expect Don and family might be out next Sun. June 5th as they haven't been out since Mother's day and I could get the machine that far and perhaps one of these parcel deliveries would pick it up as I know Don isn't anxious to make the trip into Vancouver. So let me know what's on your mind.

Pat & Allan have gone over to Carrie's…. So the house is very quiet.

I am making over one of Mrs. White's dresses, it is a dress suit, I turned it – am putting on a white silk collar, the coat or beret from Melvina never arrived and as work has resumed on the house I thot it (better) to hang on to the dollars. I may not go in with Don Sunday but come a day or so later. Would you still like Dad to do some digging? I think this is all if I think of any thing I'll add it tomorrow.

Tuesday 9:30 a.m. Well, here's tomorrow, washing started, nothing of particular interest, had a good night's rest. So ready for the day.

The mail lady surprises us by being early.

Oh. Vivian Service had a little daughter Thurs and as far as I know – all is well.

Love to Spencer & yourself, mom

MATHIE – Dec. 20, 1955. Gordon Alexander Mathie, of 19243 Campbell River Road, Cloverdale B.C., age 72 years. Survived by his loving wife; 1 son, Charles (Don) in Burnaby; 4 daughters, Mrs. J (Rene) Fraser, Burnaby; Mrs. Jean Mozart (sic), Vancouver; Mrs. A. (Pat) Richards, Cloverdale; Mrs. W (Betty) Wells, Kimberely, BC; 2 brothers and 3 sisters. Deceased was a pioneer of Brandon and a member of Brandon Association. Funeral service from Thursday Dec 22 at 2 p.m. from Chapel Hill Funeral Parlour, 15274 Victoria Ave., White Rock, to Hazelmere Cemetery. Rev R. Warne and Bev W Collings officiating.

In March 1958, I was ready for a fresh challenge and submitted my resignation to the Steelworkers' boss. The provincial legislature was in session, needed another steno and so, with Mother taking over at my home, I worked in Victoria until the end of the session, and then returned to Vancouver, finding employment again, albeit briefly, with a Marriage Bureau.

CHAPTER FIFTEEN
Looking for Romance

This is a story about a man and a woman; make of it what you want.

The Man: Single, born in Montreal, he lives in Vancouver where he rents a one bedroom suite on Denman, furnished with the basic necessities, purchased, on credit, from Eaton's.

The Woman: Born in a small Prairie town, she now lives in a small home in Vancouver, newly employed in a Marriage Bureau. Married in 1932, she finally received a divorce in 1951 from a man she tried to live with five times.

THE MAN AND WOMAN MEET

When The Woman meets The Man in 1958 she is hungry for romance. Even welcomes the idea of marriage, believing it will provide a fuller, more enjoyable life with, hopefully, some financial support.

The relationship begins when he walks into the Marriage Bureau office where she works. Anyone with two cents worth of brains would have seen through this guy by the second meeting. Did she need a mate that badly? Later, she will wonder about that.

It is a Saturday night. The manager has left the business dealings to her and another year-long staff member, Mary.

The Woman enjoys this new job with its interesting clients – over one hundred and fifty men and women registered; every one of them hoping to make a happy liaison – not one though, as willing to risk as The Woman who stands now, behind her desk, offering her hand to The Man who had made an appointment. He looks like he's been in business, she thinks, sizing him up quickly. A bit portly, but not unpleasant. From his easy, seemingly relaxed, answers to her questions, she determines that he is a man who's "been around".

The interview is chatty. This is nice, she thinks. When she asks him to look at the list of potential women he abruptly says, "I'd like to know you." Very nice, she thinks.

With no other clients to see, The Woman tells Mary she's shutting her office. Mary, who recently found a man she will soon wed, nods, winks and says, "Have a good evening."

It is their first date and, like a couple of youngsters, The Man and The Woman head down Granville Street, ready for adventure.

Neither has a car so they walk – walk and talk. Conversation flows easily. He is different from the more down-to-earth men of the IWA office staff, the males in her church congregation and the long-time political/union guests. He is, she thinks, a sophisticated gent.

They saunter along Granville for a few blocks. Not wanting to go to his apartment, she suggests they go to her home.

It is an early May evening when they take the bus to her modest home on Turner Street where she has lived for three years. It is the first home of her own and she loves its neatness and the trees on the lot: a fruit-bearing pear tree, a flowering laburnum and an old but still vigorous black cherry. The Man has no doubt been in grander homes, and knows her home for what it is: a tiny one and one-half storey bungalow in Vancouver's low-income area.

The Woman makes tea; and The Man sits on the chesterfield, commenting on several things he likes in the room, particularly the piano; and makes flattering remarks when she says, "Yes, I play; and I sing, too."

When the teapot is drained and every cookie eaten, they discuss diverse likes and personal ideas. He listens with an eagerness that she has never before experienced with a man.

He is a raconteur, a man-of-the-world, one who turns any phrase with casual and intelligent ease. He talks about his past with slightly concealed bravado and she finds the conversation leading to, well, yes, leading to...this.

He leans towards her and gives her a gentle kiss. They move closer and closer with The Man repeating things like, "...and we will go to that place and this one and oh, we will have such wonderful times...."

Still sitting close as could be on the sofa, The Woman catches her breath at the picture he envisions for "us". The wonderful things "we" will do "together".

In a state of bemused bewilderment at the course of their meeting, and in innocence unbelievable considering her background, she says, a bit shakily, "Do you mean we'll be married?" To which he replies, "We'll do anything you want, my dear."

She collects herself and asks, "When?"

"It's whatever you say, my dear," says The Man.

At three in the morning, he parts with kisses and promises of, "I'll call you tomorrow."

For The Woman, this is the culmination of a long time of wishing and hoping. Being swept off her feet makes it more glamorous.

The morning after, though it's Sunday, not a workday, she phones her Manager.

"How did things go last night?" Mary asks.

"I arranged a marriage!" replies The Woman, in a barely controlled voice.

"Oh. Whose?"

"My own!" crows The Woman. "My own!"

Mary doesn't hide her astonishment; she asks many questions, not well satisfied with the bubbly reportage, though later, she will be compassionate.

Sunday afternoon The Man returns to The Woman's home. It is, she thinks, the happiest Sunday in a long time.

She has phoned her sister in Cloverdale who says they will drive in to meet The Man later that day. Her brother is not so pleased and says, "time will prove whether you're right or not."

"Not with this guy," she assures him. "I know him well enough already."

The cracks, of course, quickly appear, recognized by The Woman's sister and Mother, but denied by The Woman for months to come.

The Man soon moves into her home. Long-time friends are astounded. When introduced to The Man and asked for their opinion, they give him fair marks.

The Woman is happy; immersed in the experience. Her first wedding wasn't pretty; she will make this one as nice as she can afford. She plans every detail, discusses it enthusiastically with The Man who is easy to work with on anything....

When he calls her at her office to say that the two suits he'd ordered have arrived – a fine black serge and a good tweed – and he can't pick them up because "I'm broke temporarily", she gives him the necessary cash. When they select a wedding ring, he quietly says, "sorry, but I don't have any money today." She pays the jeweller.

June 26, 1958. The wedding is nice. Her dress was designed for her by a noted Vancouver designer. And she wore a sweet little pink chiffon hat with a custom title on it: "Ask Me". Very charming. They are married in her church by the minister she's known for the past three years. He must have wondered, as she did, why the groom took his vows so nervously and that he smelled of whisky.

A reception with all relatives and close friends follows, but as they leave the church, rather than travelling in her sister and brother-in-law's car as planned, The Man has ordered a taxi and practically throws The Woman into it – as if leaving the scene of a crime. Their honeymoon could have been a wake-up sign.

They drive to the U.S. border. She waits in the car while he goes inside. "We can't proceed," he tells her. She won't remember the reason he gives. But later, she guesses he faked a conversation with the customs officer. The Man always seems fearful around officials or police officers. Once, after seeing a road block ahead, they drove miles off the main roads to get to her sister's house.

But now, here she is, still in her honeymoon finery, as they drive down the road to her sister's where they soon leave because her sister has clothes sorted all over the kitchen floor for the next morning's wash day.

They drive up to Penticton, visit friends and soon head back to Vancouver. That is The Man and The Woman's romantic honeymoon.

They settle down and The Man's complaints about his job begin. "If you simply can't stand it, perhaps you should find

Above left: Marrying 'The Man', 1958.
Right: The photo of 'The Man' I found along with an article titled
"I Like Being a Bum" a few years after he wandered off, he is on the left.

285

another job," The Woman says understandingly. The boss's son, The Man tells her, got the promotion The Man wanted, something The Woman later doesn't believe. "Has The Man served time?" someone asks, while another comments, "The Man has too many trades and can do too many things; it's a little suspicious, don't you think?"

In July 1958, The Woman receives a telephone call from the large Vancouver Local, asking her to work in their office. They are doing a huge mail-out and need extra help. It couldn't have come at a better time; The Man has quit his job, and The Woman has been at loose ends since her temporary work in Victoria and brief time at the Marriage Bureau.

The Vancouver Local office is in the same building as the IWA Regional District #1, so it is like "old home week" for The Woman who is now surrounded by her union friends. When Joe Morris, President of Region #1 asks her to be his personal secretary, she accepts enthusiastically. Joe Morris, who was instrumental in the hard-won battle to save the union from Communist control, is a legend in his time. "You gotta roll with the punches," he tells The Woman often.

With The Woman hard at work again, the newlyweds have an income. She asks a businessman church member if he could find The Man work. He can. It lasts three weeks. Then, he works at a car auction; that lasts only a few months. Meanwhile, he renovates their kitchen and porch and finds odd jobs such as mending furniture and minor household renovations. "I could find good work if I had a car," he says repeatedly. They make a deal, with The Woman's signature guaranteeing payment.

The Woman's mother often lives with her, but now, the mother's ability to get along with just about anyone is tested to the limit. The Man stays mostly at home, sitting around, reading and eating. But The Woman is prepared to accept The Man and, if possible, help him to make a living for himself and be of some support to her.

One night, when The Woman's mother is away, two burly, well-dressed men ring the doorbell. The man explains the detectives "are searching for someone on this street who is apparently concocting drugs." The Woman serves tea and cookies and after a brief, friendly chat in which she and The Man vouch for each neighbour's trustworthiness, the two men leave.

What conversation actually took place between The Man and the officers before she entered the room, The Woman will never know. In time, she comes to believe that they were indeed policemen, but checking on The Man, perhaps knowing, already then, who he was.

After the visit, The Man stops looking for work. By Spring, 1959 there is definite 'low' in the relationship. The Man and The Woman see very little of each other; she leaves for work early and often works overtime; when she comes home, she makes dinner, eats and rests, is in bed by ten o'clock. They sleep in separate beds.

One night she wakens, startled, and sits up quickly. "Oh, it's you!" she says, seeing him.

It is three a.m. This has become his pattern and on this night she reacts strongly. "This can't go on much longer. You are never going to get a job sitting at home and reading half the night; and it's not going to go on much longer!"

The Man doesn't reply. The Woman goes back to sleep.

The next day her son calls her at work to catch a ride home. It's windy and rainy.

"It's funny The Man didn't call me today," she says on the drive home.

"Didn't he phone you?" her son asks. "He said he would when I stopped in at the house about 11 o'clock. He said he was leaving for a job in Kelowna. His suitcase was so full there was stuff spilling out of it."

The Woman knows there is no job in Kelowna – or anywhere.

When they arrive home, she discovers that all of The Man's clothes are gone!

"I never liked that man," her sister admits to her later that evening.

When smoking in an office was still allowed, and The Woman had worked in an office where the Board Room was often dense with cigarette smoke, she sometimes opened the windows on the lane for relief. Each window had a transom that opened from the top and, depending on a person's height, could be reached and opened only if one stood on the window sill. Wanting to clear the air one day, The Woman did just that when, suddenly, the larger pane tilted outward. She clung to the upper sill, calling for help until two co-workers rushed in to help her down. "You know, Jean," said one, "all those old men below who are always looking through the bins for something to eat would have found you, and they would have said, '*White men crazy. She good for another ten years.*'"

NOVEMBER 1959

A letter addressed to The Man arrives in The Woman's mail. The return address is a Toronto law firm. "We are the agents for our client, Jane Doe, whom you married in January 1957," states the letter, and then goes on to say, "Since you were already married…" Already married! The date cited is eighteen months prior to The Man's marriage to The Woman in Vancouver!

And now The Woman knows the truth. She married someone who already had two wives! A polygamist who, in each case, left his partner with debts of his making.

A few years later The Woman notices a photo in the *Vancouver Sun* of a man on a park bench. "I like being a bum" says the caption. It is The Man under a different name.

After legal counsel, The Woman decides not to prosecute. The marriage is null and void. She resumes her previous name and pays the car debt. Her job is certain; she carries on.

CHAPTER SIXTEEN

Another Address;
Another Avocation!

I had no idea that my interest in this new venture (Memorial Society) would involve me so thoroughly, proving as time went on to be most valuable as a learning process, both for myself and for the hundreds of thousands of individuals who became members in the Society, knowing their personal wishes would be respected and carried out to the letter, and with reasonable costs.

APRIL 1963

2139 Turner Street had been a fine place to live since February 1955 and I would have stayed there for several years if the houses across the street weren't being bought and knocked down to make room for an extension of Templeton High school. "Will that improve or lessen the value of my

Vancouver home on West 13th that I turned into a 'boarding house'.

home?" I asked the insurance agent where I worked. "Properties adjacent to high schools will lose value," he said.

A friend who had recently become a real estate salesperson was eager to make a sale, and with her help, I began looking at properties in the area of Broadway and McDonald Street. A house on West 13th Avenue caught my eye, and I arranged for a loan with my friends at the Credit Union. On April 12th, 1963, I had a new address.

I had a bad cold and was utterly exhausted. Once again, Mother came to my rescue, working hard so we could move in. My hairdresser sent a bouquet of spring flowers and on moving day my entire family showed up.

"Look out for Allen!" I screamed, afraid my brother-in-law would be crushed by the piano. Moving it into the small vestibule was quite a challenge; it had to be tipped on its side and poor Allen somehow ended up pinned against the wall in behind the piano! By four o'clock my belongings were in the house, and all that remained was to arrange them.

To help pay off the new mortgage, I hoped to supply 'Room & Board' for three, perhaps four students from nearby UBC. But first I had to freshen up my new home. The previous owner left behind an incomplete renovation that needed immediate attention. The IWA office hours were 9:00 a.m. to 4:30 p.m., leaving me time after work to paint the kitchen cabinets and dining room area, purchase beds and bedding, dishes and a few kitchen utensils. At 79, Mother remained enthusiastic and energetic, and she and I did Trojan work on that house.

SUMMER OF 1963

What a busy time! In addition to the move and work on the house, my daily planner was almost full. Negotiations between the IWA and Forest Industrial Relations kept on thru the summer, typewriters and Gestetner doing overtime. Vancouver's Unitarian church had planned an Open House for their new facility on 49th & Oak; the celebration included a play by Christopher Fry, "Boy with", in which I had a part; that meant three or four rehearsals a week.

One night a heavy pain in my right arm kept me awake. It's from painting, I told myself, hoping it would go away. It worsened, and when it traveled from one spot to another, I saw my doctor. He examined me, and asked, "What are those sores across your back?" He summoned me into his office where he removed a book off the shelf. "Sit beside me," he said, "and read this; I think you're intelligent enough to understand."

"Shingles," I read, "the same virus as chicken pox, herpes." With that, he prescribed medication, as well as plenty of relaxation and rest.

I didn't miss a day at the IWA office, but painting took a sudden stop and I missed a rehearsal or two. It was Mother's care that saw me through. Every morning, at 6 am, she stood at my bedside, one of the four large pills I was to take daily in her hand, along with a cup of hot milk to wash it down. I remember that when I was very young and in bed with a chest cold I wanted Mother to rub my chest with her rough, warm hands.

During the day, Mother continued to work on the house, to ready it for boarders.

THE BOARDING HOUSE

Growing up in the Prairies, every town had one or more 'boarding houses', usually maintained by women who needed money due to loss of income following the death of the man of the house. Generally speaking, boarders were won or lost on the culinary skills of the housekeeper; and sometimes a woman's cooking brought in teachers and the young fellows clerking at the local bank. Sunday, Monday, Tuesday...meals had to be ready and on the table at regular hours, beds changed, linens changed, clothing washed, hung out, brought in, moistened and rolled up, ready for the sad irons; and not all homes had an indoor toilet.

My 13th Avenue home had the modern conveniences that a city provided, but I couldn't afford a new washing machine, so the *Beatty* Mother and I had bought in Calgary at $5.00 per month had to suffice. It was the same machine that cost me three months of Night School at Garbutt's Business College in Calgary as I couldn't afford to make payments for the machine as well as pay tuition; and Garbutt's refused to defer that fee. The machine came with two tubs – one for washing, one for rinsing – and a bench for the tubs. (Earlier, when I was doing housekeeping for a living, there wasn't a wringer; even sheets were wrung by hand. My hands and arms became so strong that I could swing a bucket of water in each without spilling one drop. Then came manual wringers with handles, to be followed by electric machines and wringers, and woe betide the fingers that were caught while the towel was being wrung through!)

The previous owner of the house had allowed the extra long clothesline that went from the back door to the lane to

Susan, a boarder and I making music together at my W. 13th Ave. home.

rust and the stove required a new element. Once again my carpenter friend helped out, commenting as he did that, "I can't believe what I'm paying for lumber; those guys in the IWA are making prices go sky high!"

One of my older women friends had told me that previous to retiring she'd operated a boarding house with a difference: it was a cooperative. My long experience since I was eleven entailed cooking and cleaning house, so why not try that? Bed and board would be supplied, with residents assisting in dishwashing, making their beds and generally being helpful. I took in a young couple, a male and a female, from Washington. He wanted post-grad studies; she was to begin a course in psychology. "Would you be willing to participate with me in some aspects of housekeeping at a lower cost of board?" I asked. "Sure," they answered. They would help with dishes after our dinner, keep the bedroom neat and leave the living room to me after supper. Fine. Soon after, I visited a friend on Vancouver Island; on my return my boarders had drawn up a four page letter with their idea of 'cooperating'. By their accounting I owed them money! We tried to settle something between us, but negotiations came to an abrupt halt when the young woman suddenly vanished. We found her, but her disappearance became a daily occurrence. The worst was yet to come. She would take all the bedclothes, pull them over her and hide in a corner; and once, when I was alone in the kitchen looking in the fridge, she crept up behind me and said strange things. At my insistence the young man made an appointment for her with a UBC doctor who recommended she return home as soon as possible and be put into care because, "She is in a very dark cloud." They left; and my cooperative housing went down the drain. Back to Plan A.

Two students, both young men from Vancouver Island, moved into the upstairs space. Mother helped served breakfast and dinner, and she became their surrogate Grandma with her fresh-from-the-oven cookies. Brian, who had a head of thick curly red hair, was punctual and kept himself respectably clean and tidy, while the other, Jeff, resembled a 'nobody's child' – his hair was unkempt, he wore old shirts and slacks, mismatched socks and had holes in the soles of his shoes. And he was always late; and that included paying his rent.

Not long and a third fellow joined us. The YMCA sent over Tony, a handsome fellow who'd asked for "something homelike". Since Mother was back at Pat's farm, the downstairs bedroom was available. It was pleasant, with a good window overlooking the beautiful tree-lined street; and it was next to the bathroom. When I interviewed Tony he said he liked to start the day with a good breakfast, would not be home for lunch, but would enjoy dinner. We quickly came to an agreement. I lost track of the other two students, but Tony and I have maintained a friendship to this day. He and I still laugh about those breakfasts that included three slices of toast, bacon, two eggs and three cups of tea, the latter, to the astonishment of Jeff, poured by Tony with the teapot held 'way above the cup. The humorous conversations brought a great sound of laughter to that house. Those were good times.

I grew fond of the people with whom I shared my home, and was saddened when they left and vanished: Bill, a two year long boarder who was lonesome, thoughtful, and entertaining; Sheila, the woman whose mate tried to murder her; Susan, who simply walked away from her husband and children…it still puzzles me that our sharing that time was just that. Or did they simply wish to forget the reason they spent time with me?

THE MEMORIAL SOCIETY

There I was, not quite thirteen years of age, seated in the choir loft. The funeral in McAuley on that day was for a fine old man who deserved more than usual respect. That meant the entire population, farmers and townsfolk alike, would put aside all other duties, shake the dust off their blue serge suits and black dresses, choose a few flowers from the yard and, scrubbed or shaved clean as a whistle, head to the Presbyterian church.

The deceased wasn't Presbyterian, but there was no Anglican church and that mattered little, for people in McAuley came together in a mixed congregation often and for many community events. An Anglican priest from Elkhorn would conduct the service. The organist was granted a half-day off from school to pump the organ. The familiar hymns, like "Forever with the Lord" or "Jesus, Lover of my Soul" could be sung with or without enough hymnbooks. The family had one special request: would someone sing a solo? And that's where I came in. I knew the song well and was not nervous.

The choir space was a couple of steps above the pews which meant that my gaze fell just above the coffin, onto the faces of the congregation. As I waited for the readings, the eulogy and hymns to end, I was curious about one thing: my best friend's mother told her that Mr. Barker died of gangrene. I'd never heard of that illness. Did it mean he'd turned green?

When the coffin was opened I tried to satisfy my curiosity, but wasn't able to see any sign of green on his exposed face and hands. As the mourners filed past the coffin, there was a shriek from a former friend and neighbour: the undertaker had neglected to close the deceased's lower jaw, leaving him open-mouthed! It was a good thing I didn't have to sing again.

From the church, everyone followed the family to the cemetery, the coffin securely bound to a Democrat, a double buggy. In a time like that, all of us, children and older citizens, were like one family, and everyone went back into town where the stores, barbershop, post office and blacksmith shops were back in business. The Ladies Aid served tea at the manse, since there was no kitchen in the church. Afterwards, it was time to socialize and for Edna and me to scan the black felt toppers of those who could afford them. Mr. Gibson's Christie Stiff bowler looked as good as new. We also rated the women's hats and neat black dresses.

Customs varied within congregations, but most funerals stuck to routine. In one town it was understood that a respected elder always led mourners in the farewell walk past the opened coffin. It was only proper to wait until Grandma Dibble paused, laid a hand on the forehead of the body, nodded her head ever so slightly and walked on. When Grandma Dibble had satisfied herself that the cold body in

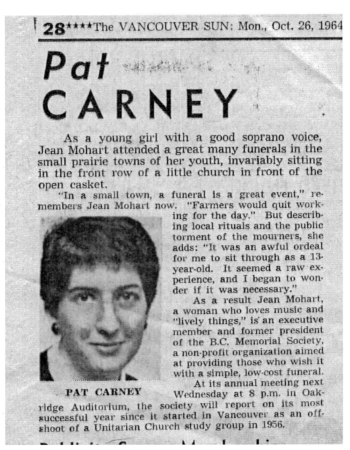

Pat CARNEY

As a young girl with a good soprano voice, Jean Mohart attended a great many funerals in the small prairie towns of her youth, invariably sitting in the front row of a little church in front of the open casket.

"In a small town, a funeral is a great event," remembers Jean Mohart now. "Farmers would quit working for the day." But describing local rituals and the public torment of the mourners, she adds: "It was an awful ordeal for me to sit through as a 13-year-old. It seemed a raw experience, and I began to wonder if it was necessary."

As a result Jean Mohart, a woman who loves music and "lively things," is an executive member and former president of the B.C. Memorial Society, a non-profit organization aimed at providing those who wish it with a simple, low-cost funeral.

At its annual meeting next Wednesday at 8 p.m. in Oakridge Auditorium, the society will report on its most successful year since it started in Vancouver as an offshoot of a Unitarian Church study group in 1956.

PAT CARNEY

Pat Carney, then journalist for the Vancouver Sun, wrote about my involvement with the Memorial Society.

296

the coffin was indeed dead, we assembled to file past and that concluded the funeral services at the church.

With time, funeral practices changed, not so much in small towns as in cities. As in the United States, undertakers gradually created a large and lucrative industry. The undertaker became a 'Funeral Director', subtly conveying the idea that family members or friends ought to leave 'directing' the funeral services to them. In earlier times, women washed the body and prepared it for burial, men dug the grave and the funeral was held in a church. The new, developing funeral industry with its treatment of the body: facial cosmetics, embalming, a Cadillac hearse and limousine for mourners caught on and soon, funeral prices sky-rocketed.

In Seattle, Washington a group of people realized the need for a more modest and sensitive approach. They formed the People's Memorial Society which immediately gained public support. In Vancouver, BC Members of the Unitarian Church Social Action Committee consulted with the U.S. group to gain some first-hand knowledge in dealing with the delicate subject of death and dying. Complaints from the public and clergy about customs and costs had given the Social Action Committee sufficient reason to call a public meeting. It was held on October 12, 1956 at 7:30 p.m. in the Unitarian Church at 12th Avenue and Granville. I was invited to attend and asked to bring interested union members, since the matter for discussion had wide appeal to working people. The Memorial Society of BC was in business.

PROMOTING THE MEMORIAL SOCIETY

Good news travels fast. But has there ever been a better method of spreading news than by word of mouth? The Memorial Society had good news; in fact it was very good news! "Do you really mean that, with your help, we can make our own funeral arrangements?" we were asked time and again.

From the start, I believed, absolutely, in the objectives of the Society. Naturally the topic required a sensitive and intelligent approach, but it was the realism in our mandate that held wide appeal, and Vancouver's two daily newspapers provided a jump-start with well written editorials and articles. Radio and television interviews took place, sometimes more than once a week. Telephone calls, letters and requests on the street gave us solid support. It was high time for an even more strategic promotion that would satisfy the public's eagerness to know more about the Memorial Society of British Columbia. The Board elected me to be their Public Relations officer. For 18 years I lived and breathed the Memorial Society, going across Canada in three separate tours, setting up societies in each city, meeting people who wanted to do something different and fighting for those who, even with the documented wish-list of the deceased in hand, were asked by funeral directors, "Are you sure this is what your aunt would want to do?" Or, as in my case, when, posing as a customer, I visited a Funeral Home and, after showing me all the coffins, from least to most expensive, the Undertaker stopped before the latter, placed his hand gently over mine, and said, "Wouldn't you like to see your Daddy in this one?"

Giving credit where it's due, my parents' obvious pleasure in meeting and dealing with people got me off to a fine start. Customers didn't come to Mathie's Grocery merely to shop, they looked forward to a genuinely friendly greeting, such as "Hello, Mrs. Clarke, how nice to see you. Do sit down for a minute." While Mrs. Clarke – or whoever the customer happened to be – eased her feet, Dad filled her order and chatted or told a corny joke. Mrs. Clarke left the store happier than when she came in.

That was the way most people felt after listening to a radio program, when Chuck Davis and I often worked together, or perhaps caught the prime time "Seven O'clock" television show. Public meetings were equally satisfying to listeners, for we were telling people what they wanted to hear – that every person could take charge of funeral planning, in advance; including costs – a radical change.

By the time I was elected to Public Relations I knew the persons who brought the Society into being as well as the members of the Board of Directors. They knew me, too, through my various public roles: I was an officer of the Office & Professional Workers Union, Local 15; actively involved in political and social reform; and a Sunday school teacher at the Unitarian church. I had decades of experience, including an awareness that in any job, paid or otherwise, being sensitive towards others was critical (I've never known anyone who demonstrated that more clearly than my mother). Finally, I had a deep sense of the rightness in the Society's mandate – and to this date it holds to the original principles.

When the Society's Board of Directors and I met we developed a bond that boded well for us and our membership. But no one serves a public institution without some critical comment, so it was not surprising that the undertakers expressed disapproval and opposition to the Memorial Society. Our mandate was perceived as an attack; and, truth

In Chicago, promoting the Memorial Society, 1966,

be told, we openly criticized them.

"Why don't you just shut up and mind your own business!" an irate undertaker remarked after one of my speeches in a Canadian city.

Although he had tradition on his side, I replied "I will not be shut up. And 'minding my business' is exactly what I'm advocating!"

Not only did we have to re-educate the public to simplicity, we had to correct rumours about the Memorial Society such as: "They stack bodies in garages"; "they sell bodies"; "they only allow cremation"; and many more.

The flip-side was more pleasant. During an interview at the CBC one evening a man called from Nanaimo: "I enjoyed what you said very much. I like what you are doing. More power to you!"

My cause is just because my heart is pure, I remembered Sir Galahad's words.

As most promotional work took place in the evening, my employment at the Regional office of the International Woodworkers did not interfere with the Memorial Society demands. Only brief interviews were conducted in my office and, fortunately, my employer was sympathetic to my involvement which I promoted in our Union's paper.

THE WESTERN CANADIAN LUMBER WORKER
MAY, 1965

ANSWER: TO THE HIGH COST OF DEATH

By Jean Mohart, Public Relations Director, of the Memorial Society of BC

To an IWA member it's as simple as ABC: you call a meeting, you decide what you'll go for, elect a negotiation committee, submit your demands to the other side and then stick with the bargaining until you've achieved the best deal possible. It happens in other spheres, too.

In November 1956, about 50 people found themselves sitting in a meeting because they felt enough public support could be found to tackle a specific problem: the high cost of dying and a reduction of some of the overdone trappings foisted upon grief-stricken survivors. They were a cross-section of the public – several trade unionists, some office-workers and some from manufacturing plants; an accountant, a few housewives, ministers, an architect, a personnel man, a social worker, a couple of teachers.

Certain of the soundness of their idea, they applied to the Registrar of Societies, set up an executive and began looking for members who would work to develop the organization.

Constitution

Members weren't too hard to find; but very soon the group knew their most difficult task was to secure cooperation from an undertaker who would work with the Directors as directed by the newly-executed constitution: "To 'Promote, through education and otherwise, dignity and simplicity in funeral rites'" and "To 'Assist in planning in advance of death for the disposition of members' remains, and for Memorial services.'"

Much persuasion, after many futile interviews, finally secured a minimum price on the four basic services we required. These four basic services form the crux of our work; they cover necessary items in the simplest possible manner. Strict instructions from our members were to transact business only with an undertaker who would agree to the following:

1. Pick up remains

2. Registration of death and one death certificate

3. Minimum cost coffin

4. Transportation of remains to crematorium or cemetery.

Arrangements for a Memorial Service were left for the member to state on the Designation Form provided by the Society.

Search

It was an exhausting search to find such an undertaker. The conventional "Funeral Director" offers quite a number of services with a price which does not show a break-down of costs. Our members insisted they wanted no shampooing, face-powder, skin tinting, embalming (which entails horrors too gruesome to describe), fancy lining in coffins, extra pillows (stuffed with old newspaper cuttings), 'slumber' rooms or any of the totally unnecessary primping ad nauseum. Until 1960 we were tolerated by three firms, but their obvious reluctance to do business with us slowed our work. We realized that until we could work with someone more cooperative we were going to wander in the wilderness of a modern dilemma.

Watching a television program that featured our Society, Bill Backstad, an undertaker, caught the idea.

A continuing battle against a large, vested interest is something we have learned to cope with. Misrepresentations are circulated in the hope of prejudicing the public against us. During the most recent session of the provincial legislature the undertakers sought to have legislation enacted which would compel the odious practise of embalming. They *sought the power to create themselves as a judicial body which could grant or withhold license to embalm, to revoke that license or make regulations as they saw fit, to penalize a violator $25.00 a day (payable to their Board), in short, to legislate Memorial Societies out of existence. Bob Strachan's keen perception and nimble legislative talent prevented enactment of this insidious and undemocratic Act.*

Qualifications

To join the Memorial Society is simple. An individual membership is $5.00, for a family (two or more persons) it is $10.00.

THE MEMORIAL SOCIETY: OFFICE AND UNDERTAKER

Like the old radio program, in which the police says flatly, "Just the facts, Ma'm!" I will attempt to do simply that.

As said, when the Memorial Society began promoting its alternative funeral services, Bill Backstad responded. I had never heard of him when he contacted me, "to talk". We met at The Neptune in New Westminster and after a few pleasantries he expressed "serious interest" in the Memorial Society. His wish was to attend a Board meeting where he would propose to serve as the Society's undertaker. He observed that when overcome with the loss of a loved one, people 'went overboard' on expenses or just followed whatever suggestion was made by the undertaker. More often than not the services rendered were designed to emphasize rather than diminish grief, and some practises were positively repugnant....

Our long lunch was a mostly one-sided conversation; he was fluent and, from what I gathered, experienced in sales. At one point, he referred to himself as "a hustler", a classification of work I knew nothing about, except from the movies.

Backstad talked all the way back to my office. I said I would let him know if and when the Board would allow him to make his proposals.

Since the Society was established, three funeral homes in Vancouver provided services at fairly reasonable rates; but members reported dissatisfaction. There were times when a client had to insist on getting what was requested, and was pressured to change, or alter, the signed and witnessed form provided by the Memorial Society. And thus, we accepted Bill's proposal and referred our members to "First Memorial Services Limited", which he and his wife Phyllis founded on the North Shore in 1961.

The Society's executive and Board of Directors were all volunteers, and we were doing well, but when membership

The low cost of dying in B.C. doesn't delight everyone

The topic of low-cost funerals has B.C. undertakers burying one another under a war of words and the provincial government considering an inquiry into the funeral industry.

At the centre of a bitter dispute is the Memorial Society of British Columbia, which has done away with traditional opulence, cut funeral costs in half and grown to 40,000 members. Its funerals, handled under contract by First Memorial Services of North Vancouver, usually involve cremation and eliminate the need for embalming, cosmetology and expensive caskets.

First Memorial's president Doug Foreman says his firm is the fastest-growing in the province, and possibly in Canada. Foreman says he arranges 15 per cent of all funerals in B.C. — an average of five a day — and claims the reason for the high cost of conventional ceremonies is that many traditional-style funeral directors do not have enough business.

Established funeral directors in Vancouver make no secret of their animosity toward both the Memorial Society and Foreman's firm. They say they too can provide low-cost funerals but one spokesman likens them to a "disposal service" and claims most people don't want them.

"It's like the difference between dining out and drive-in hamburgers," says Irene Howard, secretary of the Funeral Services Association, which represents about 80 per cent of funeral directors in the province. Association president Curly Goheen, of Penticton, says it welcomes the suggestion of a royal inquiry commission, advanced by B.C. New Democratic leader Dave Barrett.

The association says it has nothing to hide, but asks that any investigation include the activities of the Memorial Society and any funeral clubs or similar organizations operating in the province.

The recent furore over funerals began when the association placed advertisements in local newspapers warning the public to beware of organizations canvassing to arrange funerals, and pointing out that pre-arranged funerals are illegal in B.C. unless approved by the Public Utilities Commission. Next thing, Doug Foreman's First Memorial Services, which operates under PUC approval, found itself being investigated by the RCMP on an anonymous complaint under B.C.'s Pre-Arranged Funerals Act.

The Memorial Society's Jean Mohart says expensive funerals are an outrage.

Clipping from an article about the Memorial Society from 'The Canadian Magazine', July 10, 1971.

zoomed to several thousand it was time to hire a stenographer. Mrs. Phyllis Backstad, wife of Bill, the undertaker serving the Society, offered her services at a modest rate of pay. It appeared to be a satisfactory arrangement, since she was already assisting the Society in processing memberships.

After careful research and negotiation The Society made a contract with the Backstad's firm (1965) to provide the four basic services to our members for $100.00. Not long and The Memorial Society of BC became the third largest on the continent.

OCTOBER 17, 1968

At a BC Memorial Society meeting, I received the following tribute. "I don't suppose there is any way the membership can repay you for your efforts. Thank the Good Lord that there are people like you capable of enormous self-sacrifice and we thank you for all you've done." Five hundred people attending the Society's annual meeting rose to their feet and gave me a standing ovation. The membership of the B.C. Memorial Society was now 18,000.

CONFLICTS ARISE

Credit must be given to Backstad for the sheer guts it took to be the 'rogue' undertaker. The funeral industry treated him with contempt and made his job as difficult and unpleasant as possible; but nothing could hold back the astounding growth of the Memorial Society which, of course, meant the same degree of financial reward for him. I appeared constantly in daily newspaper, radio and television. Once, when I felt we should wait a few days between news briefs, Backstad called me and asked me to do an interview, flattering me with his comment that "with each interview another 1,000 memberships are received."

In November 1971 the Memorial Society asked me to consider the position of Executive Director, with salary. Up to then I had never received any compensation for my work, only my expenses were covered. If I accepted, I'd have to leave my other job.

At this time, I'd put in over fourteen years with the IWA as personal secretary to two top notch presidents, Joe Morris, Jack Moore and then Jack Munro (The first time I heard Jack speak at a regional convention, I told him, "You are going to be president someday, Jack." Time has proved it to be so). After careful consideration, and with some regret, I resigned as secretary to the president of Region #1, IWA. And suddenly, everything changed!

> *February 2, 1972*
>
> *Dear Jean:*
>
> *Just a note to congratulate you on your new post.*
>
> *The work you have done for the society on a part-time basis has been outstanding. Now that you're full-time, the only people who have to worry are the funeral directors' lobby and Jack Moore – whatever is he going to do replace you?*
>
> *Best wishes,*
>
> *Tom Berger*

The title 'Executive Director' meant that I was entrusted with the overall work of keeping the Society's affairs in good shape. It was really a continuation of what I had been doing since I became Public Relations. Leslie Oades remained the Society's treasurer, doing work that became more and more onerous. He had a day-job and did the Society's books in the evening, sometimes working all weekend to catch up. More and more often, members asked that we please move the office to downtown Vancouver, less wearing to travel to than First Memorial Services in North Vancouver. Most Board members were residents of Vancouver, and all but Mr. Backstad agreed to the more advantageous location. Office and meeting space was rented in the Toronto Dominion building, however only the day-to-day office work was carried on there because Backstad kept all the Designation Forms and other data at their location in North Vancouver. When the Memorial Society and First Memorial Service had signed a contract in 1965 wherein Backstad was sole undertaker, none of the Board members had any reason to suspect that any of the Society's rights would be over run or usurped by the undertaker.

Within a couple of years of that signed agreement, the volume of business for First Memorial allowed for a notable increase in staff in both office and undertaking services; and from other areas in the province people were asking for First Memorial's services. Our Society kept in touch with other Memorial Societies both in Canada and the United States where the same stories of success were reported.

The Society's only income came from a $10.00 membership and its finances were causing me to ponder on my own future. I was working more hours than I had ever worked because I wanted to insure that public relations as well as the office were kept up and running. My mother was living at my home at that time and cautioned me to cut some of the time I was putting in. She was right, and I knew that, but I also felt that the Society's future lay, in part at least, with me and my ability to keep running. Fortunately or otherwise, forces beyond my own planning were at work.

From 1964 to 1971, the Backstads and I had worked well together. They frequently invited me to have dinner at their home, and I reciprocated. When the new location, with its offices, undertaking rooms and crematorium opened, I gave a congratulatory speech. But by early 1973, Backstad's truculence needed attention. At that time, the Society's president was a man whom I had known for years, a quiet spoken person with years of office procedure. One day he telephoned me to say that he was highly annoyed – Backstad had refused to allow the Society to have its own records. "You are letting him dangle you and the Society as if we were on a string," I said. My response annoyed the President further, and he conveyed this to me. Our discussion became heated and I blurted out, "I wonder who's running the Society?!" The president then declared I was suspended for speaking to him like that. A few days later we met, I with a lawyer, and my suspension was lifted; but there was no way back to peaceful relations.

From the start, the Backstads had been allowed to attend all Board meetings. Now we were caught in a mess of our own making. A few nights after my run-in with the President, a special meeting was called during which both Backstads denounced me. I have a taped record of that meeting. "Jean's all wrong," Phyllis said. In a voice crackling with rage, Bill referred to me as "so stupid she can't even make a speech without confusing people". I wanted to defend myself, but an inner voice said it would be better to say nothing; every accusation was untrue and mean-natured. The president's gentlemanly response restored some sense of reality, and other Board members refuted the attack on me.

I had made a fatal error: In recommending that the Society consider contracting undertakers in outlying area that they work with the Society, I overlooked the matter of money! Backstad had threatened to sue the Society more than once, and I had only myself to blame.

A week later, the Motion I put to the Board, "that the Society discuss the possibility as requested by undertakers wanting to sign contracts with the Society", was defeated; the president had to break the tie. I resigned. I did not want to carry on with any rancour between the Society and the

Backstads. When the newspapers, radio and television asked me to tell my side of the story, I declined. A public row would only confuse the Society's members, and I did not wish to jeopardize the trust our members had in the Memorial Society.

APRIL 14, 1977

The following is an excerpt of a letter from Tom Deachman, praising my efforts to help establish the Memorial Society across Canada. "Jean...you and I have had our differences from time to time, but I always felt you were one of the truly great motivating forces in this country. I admire you for the leadership you have given so many movements. Our history is studded with the names of some great, great women activists and I hope someday you will be recognized for the many contributions you have made, because you are one of them."

1986

Hindsight is 20/20. In a speech I delivered to the BC Memorial Society in 1986, I said, "...It's so easy to look back and think if I had done this – or had not done that.... This is a human trait, and I am not different from others in that regard." I went on to recall a question I'd once been asked during an interview: "Do you think the success of what you are promoting is due to you and your efforts or is because it is 'an idea whose time has come'?" My reply was quick, easy and honest: "What the Memorial Society stands for is successful because it is an idea whose time has come...and even now – my espousal of the principles enunciated in the Society's constitution continues and will be a part of my life, as long as I live."

CHAPTER SEVENTEEN
Frank & Jean

There is a lot of Frank's life I was not privy to, so why then, if he kept so much of himself and his life to himself only, write about him at all? It's simple; because ever since 1927, when I was fifteen years of age, and living in Rocanville, he's been part of my life. When Frank left Rocanville to attend Normal School, I fully expected we'd resume our relationship upon his return and that we'd eventually marry. And we did; only not until later in life.

FRANK B. SCOTT

"Frank was a complex man," his sister Marjorie told me recently. And she was right; he was. His early years, before I knew him, were formative and solidified certain aspects of his personality. To understand Frank, one has to consider the big picture – from start to finish. He is a firstborn child, a beautiful baby; perfect, thinks his Mother. Though followed by two sisters, it is Frank who always comes first in his mother's eyes; and this is obvious to all. When five-year-old Frank does something naughty like urinate up and down the walls of the outdoor toilet, his mother tries hard not to smile as she tells him, "You shouldn't do that." He knows she is amused, not angry; and it is like that in whatever he does – just a word of disapproval, then a pat on the head and a gentle, "Now go along and play and be a good boy." At bedtime, she cuddles Frank and sings him a Scottish lullaby; then, after a kiss, leaves his room whispering, "Sleep tight, dear laddie."

When Frank is nine, his mother explains that she must travel a long way on the train because she is going to have an operation in the city. She will soon be back home, feeling better; and she will write to him while she's away. "Now be a good boy, Frank," she says, "and promise you'll be nice to your sisters and not tease them." He promises that, and, "Yes, I won't forget to practice piano."

He misses his mother. She was fussy about being clean and always made sure he ate his porridge; but most of all he misses the way she sang as she worked around the house, lovely lilting songs like "Duncan Gray". "Ha, ha!" she'd laugh in the middle of the song, then continue to sing "...The wooin' o' it". Now, no one sing to him at bedtime. Still, he tries to be brave, as he promised.

Frank practices piano and when he attends his lesson the following week, Mrs. Porter praises him and tells him how pleased his mother will be when she hears that he is ready for another music lesson book. When he returns home after the lesson he is surprised to find family friends seated in the living room, all of them weeping. "What's happened? Why are you here?" he asks. "Oh, poor Mrs. Scott," says one; and another, "Oh, Francis, it's your Mother; she's gone." "Oh, those poor little girls; those dear little girls," the women moan. What about me? Frank thinks. Only Mr. Barrett puts an arm around Frank, but every part of the young boy feels like stone. Bewildered and shocked, he goes to his bedroom upstairs, quite alone; more alone that he has ever felt. Not even his Dad is there, he is with his Mother in the city.

When Mr. Scott comes home he invites Frank into the parlour. It's easy to tell that Father is upset; and they sit quietly, until Father tells him "something terrible and unexpected happened at the hospital. Mother died from a kind of poisoning. She is now in heaven. Her body will be brought to the house before supper time." When it is delivered and she is placed in the coffin, Frank's father takes him into the parlour again. The blinds are drawn and the doors closed. Together, they look at his mother's still, dear form. "Look at her, Frank," his father says in a grief-thickened voice. "It's all we now have." It is a scant but unforgettable moment.

Prairie winters are cruel, frost settles deep into the earth. For three days and three nights a bonfire is kept going to thaw the ground so a grave can be dug, while at home nothing is the same: people come and go, bring flowers and food at all hours of the day. Then Frank's Mother's cousin arrives from Scotland, and preparations are made for the funeral that will always be referred to as "the saddest day ever for that town." The girls, age seven and five, are considered too young to attend the funeral service, but young Frank agrees to accompany his father.

The entire community and all around mourn the loss of a woman known for her charm and warm, Scottish personality. She carried out the first bridal shower; indeed, gave parties for every occasion, and what wonderful parties they were! But above all, like Frank, they remember her sweet singing – at home, at church, or a concert.

Although the weather is at its coldest, the church is overflowing; afterwards everyone follows the cortege to the cemetery just a mile out of town. Frank stands beside his father, neither of them speaking; Mrs. Scott's death and her funeral like a bad dream, unreal in every aspect. He looks up to see the preacher's hand pick up a piece of frozen earth. He hears the preacher chant, "Ashes to ashes, dust to dust..." He sees the preacher's clenched hand rise, fall and empty, hears the frozen clod's THUD as it hits and splinters on the coffin. The sound jolts young Frank with a force he has never felt, its cruelty – that it was tossed onto the container which held his mother – like a double blow. Something inside him is struck in that moment, too; and stays frozen. He may have heard sobbing, but all he remembers in years to come is his tight throat and how it felt like a fist was pounding his chest. Overnight, young Frank is old, groping to find a measure of composure in his topsy-turvy world. Perhaps if someone had taken him aside and helped him deal with his grief, things might have been different; but, of course, one can only speculate. From that time on Frank B Scott is unable to laugh.

Home life, for the next six years, includes a series of "housekeepers"; and then, in 1925, his father remarries. The relationship between Frank and the new mistress of the household gets off to a poor start when Frank, a lad of sixteen, tinkers on the piano and his step-mother says, "That is my piano." On another occasion, when he slumps onto the chesterfield and rests his foot on a cushion, she says, "That is my chesterfield." He never touches the piano again; and stays off the chesterfield. The other members of the family aren't always happy, either; but for Frank and the step-mother it is nothing more than an armed truce with flare-ups. She phones his father at the store one day when Frank walks across the just-waxed floor. Waxing floors is really hard work, but Frank doesn't know about that....

Remembering Frank Scott & Jean Mathie when we first 'went steady'.

It was in the context of this dynamic that I entered Frank's life for the first time, a young, wild romantic teenager who believed, euphorically, in a Hollywood movie version of love, that is, boy meets girl, girl chases boy, boy is coy, girl plays hard to get, they fall in love, get married and live happily ever after. Frank was a bit slow on the uptake, but with plenty of encouragement he caught the idea; and soon, Frank Scott, the serious young fellow, and I, vivacious Jean Mathie, were going steady.

The above may have a hint of flippancy about it, but I loved Frank Scott with all my heart. As recorded elsewhere, he was part of the elite Scott family in a strata-conscious Rocanville, while I was part of a family without any traditional aura. Nor did my father belong to any of the long established, respected men's organizations; he was a mere clerk, then a small store owner; and Mother was too ill and had no will to be socially involved. That left me on my own to carve out a personal reputation, a necessary component in that little town that wasn't even on the main highway but had a quota of unwritten standards for every man, woman or child within its boundaries.

So it was that when Frank finished the course for teachers in Regina that I waited anxiously for him to come over to our house and resume our romance. It was late, after nine o'clock, when he knocked on the back door and we sat down with our feet on the oven door to begin picking up where we'd left off. "It took you a long time to get here," I said, after a fervent kiss and hug. With quiet seriousness he said, "If you knew what I've been doing, you could be surprised I'm here at all."

"What's happened? Is it something wrong in your family?"

He looked at me – and Frank had lovely blue eyes – then explained: "My Dad had a talk with me tonight." That was natural, I supposed, since he'd been away from home for almost a year and was now embarked on a professional career.

"No, it was about me, and about us."

"Did he ask you to stop seeing me?" I asked, now concerned.

"He started by talking about my being on my own...responsibility...building a reputation; and then he spoke about you and me."

"Is he against us continuing to be together?"

"He led into the argument that I shouldn't be going steady with anyone for a time; finally saying as a warning 'Don't let yourself get involved.'" (That, I surmised, was perhaps based on all too frequent local 'shotgun weddings', which were not in the Scott book of etiquette.) "He finished by saying, 'Besides, I don't like her old man!'"

And that was that. Frank's eyes turned elsewhere; and our paths took different directions...

I was sitting in my office in 1960 when, without warning, I heard a familiar whistle, one I hadn't heard since the spring of 1930 – the first line of "When Whippoorwills call...." I stopped what I was doing, and realized I was trembling. Where was he? Sounded so close. I looked up and there he stood, just outside my office door. I knew he'd married in 1937.

"Are you alone?" I asked.

"No, my wife's in the Ladies Room."

She joined us momentarily and that settled me down. They sat across from my desk, and I was glad they weren't any closer. Frank and I chatted about Rocanville and its present goings-on until, suddenly, his wife interrupted with, "I should leave you and Frank to talk by yourselves."

"There is nothing remaining in my former relationship with Frank," I said, firmly, after three more such interruptions, "and I would rather you didn't mention it." End of that; visit over.

My life was full of travel in 1970, organizing Memorial Society chapters in cities from Vancouver to Halifax. In August I caught a plane in Ottawa and disembarked in

Winnipeg, where, to my surprise, I saw Frank Scott walking toward me. "What are *you* doing here? And where is the Society member?" I asked bluntly.

"I saw your photo in the Free Press, so I phoned the Society and asked if I could meet you. Dr. Brown was rather busy and relieved to not have to take more time off work."

I was tired and displeased with this unexpected encounter, but accepted the ride to my hotel. I thanked Frank and ended our meeting as quickly as I could, with, "I have important engagements all day and this evening."

"You're tired, Jean," he said understandingly and left. "I'll see you tomorrow afternoon, at your meeting."

That evening, I returned from my dinner meeting with members of the Manitoba legislature and was about to step into the elevator when Frank, who'd been waiting in the rotunda, rushed up to me. "Please Jeannie; just let me talk to you," he pleaded. He refused to accept that I was too tired and persisted.

"OK, Frank, but just 10 minutes."

Upstairs, I gave him the only chair in my room while I sat on the edge of the bed. He liked to twit me afterwards that I treated him with such cold, business-like words. "Frank Scott," I said sternly, "you broke my heart a long time ago. I want you to know that there is no warmth in any feeling for you now. That romance is dead and there isn't even a spark in the cinder."

He persisted further, requesting more of my time.

"No, Frank…. And after I speak tomorrow evening I am going home."

I relented a little and had lunch with him the next day. It was polite, not unfriendly. That was all, and when my sister asked me about meeting him and how I would sum it up, I said that we were in "different worlds" than when we were young, fond of each other and together most of the time.

I didn't see him again until the following year.

I was home that afternoon in 1971 when there was a knock at the door. Mother had phoned my office to inform me that our houseguest, Mrs. Richards, Pat's mother-in-law, had fallen from the chesterfield chair and Mother couldn't get her up. I ran from neighbour to neighbour until I found one who would help me put her to bed. "I don't know why the Lord lets me live," Mrs. Richards said repeatedly until, finally, I told her that her remark was an insult to God, "since the decision isn't yours anyway."

When I opened the door, it was Frank Scott who stood there. Truth be told, Frank did not cause a quiver in me at that time. A lesson to remember from that incident is that we never know what currents continue to run deep inside, alive, though unseen and unfelt – until woken. Frank knew me; and knew how to stir the waters.

I called my sister Pat to ask if I could bring him out to her home in the Cloverdale area, since she knew him from our Rocanville days. Back then, when we'd courted and Frank bought me a cheap diamond ring from the Regina Woolworth's store, I was like every female of those days, and particularly in that small prairie town – certain we'd marry. But this was now and I heard Pat say, "Sure, come visit us." While we were there, Pat asked if I planned to attend the July 1st Saskatchewan 'Homecoming' in Rocanville. I hadn't thought about it.

"I intend to be there," Frank said. He was in Vancouver on a business trip and would be going to Victoria for a few days before heading back to Winnipeg, but hoped to be in Rocanville on July 1st to take in the festivities.

Life, you Traitor, I wanted to cry out; and in the next split second there's only one truthful remark to be made: I was sinking rapidly into a fairytale romance – without resistance.

For a couple of years the only male attraction in my life had been a pleasant chap from Tacoma, Washington. We dined and danced, most often going out as a foursome with other friends. He was a pilot, with his own plane and sometimes he flew to Vancouver; and we wrote letters, a nice way of getting acquainted. That relationship was developing – until the excitement around 'Homecoming'....

On the drive from Cloverdale back to my home, the conversation Frank and I had was easy. "Did you know that so-and-so is now a High School Principal?" and "Did you hear that our old friend George is now the Director of Music in Assinaboia?" It was enjoyable, home-town talk. We said Goodbye and he leaned toward me, giving me a nice, quick kiss. I smiled at him, glad to be home.

Plans were soon made for the trip. I'd share the cost and, along with my younger sister Betty, travel with Pat & Allen in their motor home. Allen was born and grew up in Moosomin, only 20 miles from Rocanville so he and Pat could take in festivities in both towns. Celebrations would be from July 1–4.

The cockles in my heart simmered in the nights prior to our June 28th departure. From the moment we turned onto the highway, I was light-headed at the thought of meeting friends from my youth and reliving also, the recent meeting with Frank Scott.

It was a great trip until the thick, sticky Regina gumbo slowed us down; but aside from that, it was easy travelling, and we arrived safely in Rocanville, each of us filled with our own unique memories as we joined a gathering in the small room off the ice rink where one of my old admirers asked if I'd have supper with him. Pleased at the invitation, I accepted.

We were just ready to leave when Frank Scott rushed in. "I've driven all day, I'm starved. Let's go down to the restaurant, Jean." With that, he took me by the elbow, swung me toward him and kissed me; and the simmer in my heart turned into a sizzle.

"Same old thing. That Frank Scott again," my dinner date said with a shrug. He was right; it was déjà vu all over again. But of course, some things had changed.

Now, Frank was an insurance salesman, driving a gold Cadillac; and what an impression that made! My life, too, had undergone radical changes, yet here we were, Frank and Jean – in a state of starry-eyed bliss.

That night, a group of old friends met in one of the fine old homes. After trading stories about the intervening years, we did what we used to do so well: we sang song after song that we still knew by heart. Even without a sheet of music, I played those songs as if I was eighteen.

At evening's end, Frank asked if I knew the song, "Chloe...if you're near or far, I gotta go where you are..." Afterwards, I accepted his offer to drive me to my motel where we exchanged warm embraces...and I followed my dearest heart's longings.

He left for Winnipeg the next day; and the letter he sent from there touched me. It included years of regret for his unkempt handling of his life; and his hope for the future. In that letter he portrayed himself as he never could at other times; perhaps it was written more as an act of conscience.

Frank had brought himself back from a long spate of personal difficulties. He had been a member of Alcoholics Anonymous (AA) since 1956 and had never once fallen off the wagon; and he had, with sheer hard work, reconstituted his working life and was now proud to be associated with the International Order of Foresters, promoting life insurance with sickness benefits. At the Reunion, Frank had looked well, was sure of himself and very handsome. With surprising suddenness he was, to me, the former boyfriend, only now it was better. He made no bones about it; he cared deeply about me and wanted our relationship to come alive again.

Frank's plan was to move from Winnipeg to Vancouver, with hopes of resuming the kind of successful career he had built in Winnipeg. Frank wrote a few letters (on his business paper) and telephoned. When I asked how to contact him he said he was using a pay phone; and when he arrived in Vancouver that was the same practice, in spite of his telling me that "they" were renting a suite in the Edmonds area. Anyone with a good sense of what's real and what isn't would have assumed immediately that he was being devious. I suspected this and wanted to contact him one day, so I phoned the apartment. A woman answered the phone. Sure enough, I was kidding myself and didn't want to acknowledge it. Worse, I let it develop from week to week as we met during my office hours in the cafeteria, letting my romantic aspirations flow out to him and hinting that I hoped he was completing plans for himself and me.

Frank had persuaded his wife to sell their home in Winnipeg, which she was glad to do since both their sons and families now resided in B.C. Frank's cousin Ken said he never saw Frank's wife so pleased; they had purchased a handsome chesterfield and two matching seats to make their new home cosier.

When Frank finally told his wife he wanted a divorce, it shocked her. Understandably; she, too, felt she'd been duped; and now she was without home and a husband. In retrospect, in trying to make sense of it all, I must ponder what part I had in Frank's unkind, hurtful treatment of his wife. My own delirium along with girlish anticipation, had taken me into a sticky situation. When I told my Mother that Frank would be moving into our home she said only, "Well, it'll be nice to have a man around the house."

On December 12, 1972, Frank and his cousin moved Frank's few belongings into my home, including the newly purchased chesterfield and chairs. As Frank's wife was not a young woman and had no means of support, and Frank was still employed, the entire sale of the Winnipeg house would go to her.

And then Victoria beckoned.

CHAPTER EIGHTEEN

Looking Back;
Moving Forward

My parents used to sing a song that I still sing: "There's a long, long trail a-winding into the land of my dreams...." There is a wide comparison between the romance depicted in the song and the deeper romance of the winding trail of my own life, where it has wound its way through the vagaries I encountered, some of my own doing, others, I believe, decreed by my Creator.

If a life were a train, then mine, I'm afraid, would cause insufferable waits where railway and road intersect; the long stretch of passenger cars rattling awkwardly past the barricaded crossing; bells clanging, lights flashing, sparks obscuring the wheels, the train's whistle and rush of wind announcing its passing – noisily, rhythmically – car after car, like a slow motion replay of scenes from a life – my life – that sequence of events that began at my birth, sixty-one years before Frank and I moved to Victoria, BC.

"What prepared you for the new work in Victoria? What influenced your feminist views?" someone asked. Peering inside the train's cars, at the 'passengers' whose lives intersected with mine, who accompanied and influenced my life with its vast experiences, provides, I think, at least a partial answer.

There's Grandmother Spencer Wells, that brave woman who crossed the Atlantic on the last sailing vessel, she newly married and pregnant with a daughter she'd give birth to and bury at sea. Grandfather Spencer Wells may have been referred to all his life as The Major, but Grandmother was not beneath his command. The Major liked to play poker and one evening used the family home as collateral; and lost. Though his friends insisted he didn't have to pay up, he stuck to his bargain; after all, he was an English gentleman, a man of his word. Following the loss of their home, Grandma had their properties put into her name. Records indicate that they eventually owned six pieces of land, likely acquired when The Major worked for the Land Titles' office, a job Grandmother assumed when the Major died in 1910; and she did it well!

There's Rosalie Mathie, my mother; that long-suffering soul, who, because of her nine-year-long illness, wasn't able fulfill her great potential beyond applying her skills as a seamstress. If they had nothing else, her daughters were always well and fashionably dressed; and that – a lot, given her circumstances – instilled in each one a sense of pride. And thus, in the area of attire, she followed her father's advice, "if a thing's worth doing, it's worth doing well", rather than her husband's opposite creed: if a thing's broken, don't mend it.

There sit the women of McAuley and Rocanville, those who exhibited "snobbery"; they influenced me to do the opposite: to model and educate women in "the sisterhood". It is only when women of all backgrounds treat one another as equals that their demands to be treated as equals with men will be realized!

There's Doris Masters, who, against her mother's and sister's wishes, remained a good and true friend in a time when most others in Rocanville shunned me.

There's Miss Roberta Porter, who took in her two orphaned nieces as well as a third, non-related young girl. She was truly "a single mother". And a non-judgemental woman. When, after leaving Bill for the first time, I visited her, she listened carefully, and then said, "You've had enough, Jean." Time and again, wherever she lived, McAuley or Winnipeg, we visited, she always building up my self-confidence in times when my personal life was in shambles. It was Miss Porter who instilled in me (and all her students) a deep appreciation for music and passion for singing, the very thing that got me through the years of our family's poverty and life's difficulties that included working for five dollars a month.

There are the two women from Balcarres, for whom I worked as 'the hired help'; one was a minister's wife, and the other sang in the same church choir as I. On Sunday I was soprano soloist in church, but from Monday on I was scullery maid or worse; I was 'the help'. From the time I walked out on Mrs. Hart, the minister's wife who treated her terrier with more respect than me, her employee – and following that, worked for Mrs. Harring, who "let me go" before our contract ended, even knowing I had no other work – the seeds of feminism were sown. Those women taught me the importance of respecting all women, from housewife to CEO. And of the importance of "sisterhood", something my friend Alice, a single mom, understood so well; it was she who gave me shelter when I left Mrs. Hart's employ with such unexpected abruptness.

Working for Mr. & Mrs. Jackson, a farmer and his invalid wife who paid me less than their hired man though my work

Miss Roberta Porter, a tower of strength and beauty, visiting her home in 1967.

began earlier in the day and ended well after supper – this was the ground in which the seed of my feminism germinated.

And then there was Mr. Forrest, who attempted to take from me what he believed was his due as my employer; and this, knowing I needed the work....

In Calgary, my occupation changed from housework to the office. Without question it was a step up from the never-ending chores in housekeeping; and if the office manager was competent and fair, one's lifestyle improved. When I worked at No. 2, Wireless and Air Gunnery Commonwealth Training school, one's work classification determined one's pay. You could improve your status and pay by writing the required test. It was fair, considering the times.

In Vancouver I had the good fortune of meeting Eileen Sufrin, a woman of rare calibre and competence. Before anyone believed it was possible, Eileen Tallman Sufrin organized working women. Her rare combination of sympathy, courage and belief that women's rights are everyone's responsibility are a reminder of the words in the song, "Bread and Roses: For the rising of the women means the rising of the race...."

Eileen's life-long friendship and mentorship enriched my life with a sense of purpose and direction. Our meeting marked the beginning of my association with the trade union movement and when I began that work on December 10, 1946, it was with only a tiny inkling of the passion and zeal it would engender from that day forward. Now I was a member of the Office & Professional Workers Union, where, another decade hence, some recognition was given to women's working conditions and pay. Women's voices were heard and the rumble for reform was becoming a roar. A march on Ottawa was threatened; and the Prime Minister, with a promise of action, begged Laura Sabia, the organizer to call it off. The Royal Commission on the Status of Women was commissioned. The Canadian Labour Congress asked to be part of the Commission since it represented two thirds of all working women in Canada. The request was declined. The CLC did write and present a brief and the BC Federation of Labour honoured me by allowing me to represent the brief. The brief is now an historical document. My involvement with that influenced and taught me so much.

There's my friend, Sally, who, in 1951, entrusted me with her secret, her decision to have an abortion. Accompanying her prepared me for future battles to establish better medical treatment than was available, namely, by 'back room butchers'.

There's another friend, Freda, a single mother who, one mid-morning summer day in the '50s, sat at her kitchen table, sobbing. Two weeks earlier, a water main had burst and there was water damage to her rental suite. She'd hired movers, confident she'd find another place to live; now, the moving van was on its way to move her things. She'd looked at many places, but nobody wanted to rent to a single mother with two kids. Freda was heartbroken when she picked up the ringing phone and heard, "This is Jean, Freda; and I felt I had to phone because I haven't seen you in ages. How are you?" I listened to her story, then advised her to, "Go dry your eyes and wash your face. When the moving van arrives, get all your stuff piled in and come to my place. I have room in my basement for your furniture and you and the kids can stay here until you find a place." It was another lesson in the society's bias against single mothers and the need for reform. (Freda remembered this. In April 2005, she wrote me a letter about "the day that I was touched by the hand of God in my life". She recalled staying for ten days before finding other accommodation. "That was a long time ago. God bless you, dear Jean – I will always remember your thoughtfulness, your kindness to me and my kids – and they will remember, too. My grateful thanks.")

Equally inspiring were the stories countless women shared

with me of being unfairly treated at work, too afraid to complain lest they jeopardize an income their families depended on for survival. As one woman negotiator said about employers, "Where others have a heart, those guys have a dollar sign." And then there are the office place dynamics I encountered, including the blatant sexual misconduct that I experienced and witnessed between colleagues as well as employer and employee, the employee, fearful of losing her job, remaining silent. How could I not continue to fight for workplace reform?

There's my first husband, of course. It took five separations to leave him for good and twenty years to be rid of him legally, by divorce. Like so many women, I was a victim of the flawed Marriage Act. Laws were written by men of education, and women, in their opinion, were not to be considered as equal to men. The Law said if you are a woman seeking a divorce, you must find the domicile of the man. I had no idea where Bill was. Secondly, the only cause for divorce was adultery and you had to prove adultery. Pragmatically speaking, that meant 90 per cent of people hired investigators who set up a phoney scene in a phoney hotel (price: $150). "What was the man wearing?" the judge would ask. "He wore a singlet my lord." "And what did the woman wear?" "She wore a pink slip," answered the so-called investigator. And with that, a divorce was granted!

Then there was the matter of money to pay lawyer fees and court costs. If, as in my case, you didn't have the money to pay a lawyer, you did nothing; or you searched for a lawyer who would defer his fees or, by some miracle, were found by one.

Throughout my life there have been little miracles. At work, I met people from many walks of life, among them a lawyer who asked me why I hadn't gotten a divorce. "I have no money for a divorce," I replied. "Well, then," he said, "let's see what we can do to fix that."

Locating Bill was another matter; he was a drifter and, last

I knew, he was still in Calgary where Mother had spotted him on a train. My lawyer friend told me not to worry about that, and instructed, "Write it up for me on the weekend; just generally say what happened." And so I did; and adultery had nothing to do with it!

That Monday Bill appeared, out of nowhere! I don't know where he'd been but I told the lawyer to go see Bill and he was able to charge him and finally, in 1951, I was divorced from Bill Mohart. But not until I read his obituary in the Vancouver Sun was I finally rid of the man.

Of course, my experience with Bill Mohart influenced my fight for changes to divorce laws as well as my involvement with the Transition House movement.

And the train that is my life grew longer, gathered speed, and moved towards another destination: Victoria!

SUMMER 1973

I was working at CJOR, a Vancouver radio station, feeling somewhat resentful because I was doing the work of a Girl Friday. I had been hired to share the interview work but found that each day I looked at what was coming in and set up the program only to see my co-worker do the interviewing – even on subjects I knew more about. Then, out of the blue, I received a phone call from Dr. Mason Gaffney.

Dr. Gaffney, a well known American economist, had just been hired by Bob Williams, then Minister of Forests. The provincial government was setting up an economic think tank in Victoria, the first think tank in BC, and Gaffney was calling to ask me if I would care to work with him on that in Victoria? "Well," I said, "anyone's who's had their name in Fotheringham's column three days in a row and running, is somebody important; I know who you are." But why me? I asked him. "Because Bob Williams recommended you." Bob and I knew each other well; we'd both been involved in the East Hastings NDP office and knew one another through our involvement with the Credit Union as well. Dr. Gaffney asked if he could come for a visit, and we set a date to meet in my home on 13th Avenue.

If I had any trepidation about accepting the position that was being offered, it might have been that I had never attended university. Dr. Gaffney was renowned in the field of taxation and economic policies relating to natural products, and I knew before I met him that the Barrett government expected wide interest and participation by all interested parties in this significant venue. Was I up to the job? When I mentioned that my formal education was from high school, with no university, Gaffney reassured me by saying, "I don't put all that credence in formal education...though it has its value, it is not a necessity." As for my age (then sixty), he responded with, "I believe people can and should do things as long as they are able." After a brief chat, he departed, each of us looking forward to working together.

Vancouver had been my home base for almost thirty years when I accepted the job offer in Victoria. A day later, I received a letter from New Democratic constituency asking me to be their nominee in the next election. (How ironic! I was an active member of the NDP, influenced by women like Dorothy Gretchen Steeves, Mildred Fahrni, Laura Jamieson, Grace MacInnis and others. I'd done every 'joe job' in a campaign always run by the boys in the back room. A few years earlier, I'd asked to run, was given a hearing, but stone-walled.) I declined reluctantly, and kept my eyes turned westward.

I was to begin my new job as administrator for the newly established Institute on September 1; and now I had to start a lot of planning! I gave notice at the radio station, surprised when my co-worker and manager showed genuine disappointment. I clarified that if promises had been kept, I might have reconsidered; however, now that this other interesting opportunity had come up, I had accepted. Frank said that he'd move to Victoria with me and would try to keep his business going there; he was still employed by the International Order of Foresters, selling fraternal insurance. (Unfortunately, when we moved, he was not assigned a territory, which, of course, is a necessity in order to build a clientele. That was very disappointing to him.)

I asked my son and his wife if they'd care to move into my home and Pat said "Mother can live with me". That was a relief; I knew Mother would be 'at home' with Pat.

In August, Frank and I went to Victoria to look for accommodation, both of us aware of all the forward-looking aspects of our new environment, including the bonus of a family connection: Frank's sister Sheila and her husband Lorne lived there (they had been very good to Frank when he was trying to mend his life after drinking nearly destroyed it) as well as Frank's niece, Pat Carfra, who became famous as "The Lullaby Lady." Both she and her husband Jim gave us such a warm welcome that to this day warms my heart. (Although there is a forty year age difference between us, Pat and I are soul mates and we enjoy each others company to the nth degree. I have a deep affection for her; she is as close as any one can be when not a blood relation; as dear to my heart as a daughter.)

Because Frank and I were pressed for time when we looked for a place to live in Victoria, we settled for the most available accommodation: the "Dingley Dell" apartment. It was a fine choice until the autumn temperatures dropped and the radiator in our bedroom clanked irritatingly and beginning at 4 a.m. "Oh dear, I guess I forgot to tell you that would happen," the landlord said when I mentioned it to her.

CHAPTER NINETEEN

Victoria 1973 – 1980

Victoria; a most fulfilling experience, both in my daily business work, where, for the first time in my life, I earned a five figure salary; and in my living with a husband, something I had never had. In Victoria, I had this wonderful home, where I could entertain and grow things; it was never equalled. I was active in every realm: political; spiritual; social; work; and at home. It was a very rounded lifestyle.

THE INSTITUTE FOR ECONOMIC POLICY ANALYSIS

The Institute for Economic Policy Analysis was created by the government in power (NDP) and was located on University of Victoria campus, a moot point as it was not a part of the University's faculty; however we had a pleasant relationship. I had known Dr. Walter Young, a highly regarded faculty member, for several years before he became president of the Institute Board of Directors, so we worked together well, planning and carrying out many large, important conferences.

As Dr. Gaffney's administrative assistant, I was very busy, and glad to be given a job where I could do some managing. In a previous job I'd said to my boss I didn't have enough work to do, so could I perhaps do some writing? "No," he answered abruptly. The writing job had been delegated to an editor friend and that arrangement was unalterable.

Now, a typical morning went something like this: I'd arrive at 9, look at upcoming dates for conferences and get to work on the planning. We had a Gestetner and a copier and worked hard; no days were lazy or off days, there was always work to be done. We always had a fine typist, sometimes two if necessary, as it was when we were running off results from conferences. It was very important that speeches were accurate, and when these were forwarded to speakers for correction, speeches sometimes had to be redone.

A huge bonus of working on the garden-like University campus was the creative ambience. Every Thursday afternoon, I'd walk down the tree-lined Avenue to the Hall and listen to a free concert of piano, voice or violin. I remember when the well-known American composer and pianist William Bolcolm and his wife Nancy performed at the auditorium. I'd heard them on CBC, and though he was known for composing modern music, on this day the concert featured old Victorian songs such as "Take me Out to the Ballgame" and "Daisy, Daisy". As I listened, I wished with all my heart that I could be doing what Nancy was: singing.

The University library was handy, too; and I spent many noon hours there. I read avidly and I was always hooked on autobiographies and biographies.

Happy times in the garden of our Wascana Street home, Victoria, Summer 1974.

After a few months, when Dr. Gaffney came in and asked, "How are you this morning, Jean?" I answered, "Tired!" I *was* tired. The noisy heating system at the Dingley Dell apartment had taken its toll; and it was time to move. And so we did; in January 1974 we moved to a lovely heritage house on Wascana Street (a nice old Prairie reminder). It was a fine old house; and happier times were never had than when Frank and I lived there.

November 17, 1974

Dear Edna: I have been meaning to get a letter away to you for ever so long, but each day takes its toll of time and my good intentions are all I have, and they don't show. Well, now we have shorter days and the rains have started in earnest, so perhaps I'll try to fit a letter into the fast-moving pattern of hours that seem to fly by me each day. Today is Sunday, and it began a little less hurried than most days, but very early the old hurry-up routine took over. I'd bought some real good soup bones yesterday, so started a great potful that will last us for several days. I do it that way because I'm usually very tired by the time I arrive home and a bowl of hot, home-made soup is still the best thing to rev me up. My office is more than five miles from home....

Now it's 8 o'clock and I'm going to get this letter done so I can sit back a little later and enjoy Masterpiece Theatre and perhaps even get a little reading done. So that's today. Did I bore you?

I've just bought myself this brand new electric typewriter. It's great — not of course as ritzy as the $1000.00 model I use at work, but I found it just too hard to use a standard model at home after using an electric one at the office....

Yes, Edna; I, too, was very sorry you weren't home when we arrived in McAuley, but I don't blame you in the least for taking advantage of your daughter's offer of a trip. Please don't say we may not see each other for another ten years though, for that means we'll just croak at each other and creep along with our canes! Well, not exactly… especially if we're anything like my Mother. She's a wonder – 90 and still takes a good walk every day; and last weekend when Frank and I visited Pat, Mother was chasing me round the coffee table when I was sassing her and having a bit of fun.

I'm sure you can understand how badly I felt at seeing McAuley disintegrating. It seems to have gone back even more since the last time I visited you. When we couldn't find anyone home at your place, I drove slowly over past the church and stopped at Mcaree's machine shop. There were four men standing watching a fellow welding. I said, "I am Jean Mathie. Does the name "Mathie" mean anything to any of you?" One said he faintly remembered hearing it. He was Byers, and of course I remembered that name. I stopped at Mary Wilson's house (is it still hers?) and left a brief note and signed it but have never heard anything from her. So there just wasn't anyone from my old school days at all to talk to, and we drove on to Rocanville where Frank and I were allowed to walk through the lovely (well, it was truly lovely once) old house he lived in; but that, too, was terribly disappointing …and I sort of wish we hadn't seen it…they've put layers of horrible paint on the beautiful oak staircase, and put paper on walls and then painted over it. In fact, the entire house is in a sad state.

And that brings me to asking you, dear Edna, aren't you going to try to see this beautiful part of Canada? Here on the table beside me is a bouquet of white and russet chrysanthemums and we still have four kinds of roses blooming. We love Victoria so much that we want to remain here. And I'm actually surprised that I feel that way, as I found Vancouver a good place to live. Let me know if you make a trip out this way. I'll find a comfy bed for you anytime. Much love, Jean.

WORK, WORK, WORK!

During its time, The Institute for Economic Policy Analysis held eight conferences: some in Victoria and a few in Vancouver. Topics included Forestry, Mining, Water, Electrification, and another big one, Natural Gas – anything to do with the economy of the province. When a conference was held in Victoria and we had to billet people around town, we were very busy.

I loved working there and was very involved in the Forestry conference, an aspect of life I was familiar with from working with the International Woodworkers. Very different things were happening in the woods now, with new machines; and every new machine obliterated jobs. Even people who were not a part of the political regime were still very, very interested in what was going on, and many wanted to meet Dr. Gaffney.

COMMUNITY INVOLVEMENT

Most of the work I've done on a voluntary basis was done because I wanted to and liked doing it. Perhaps I've never put high enough value on my services; if I'd been more business-minded, I could have done better and made more money. But if I can believe the cause is just and it deserves the best that I can do, I do it; and am still doing it today, in 2005, with my singing and piano accompaniment.

One of my main activities in Victoria was belonging to the Unitarian Church; I became involved there immediately.

They were struggling; had bought a piece of property that had been a former fisherman's hall. I love being part of something that is growing, and it was. One of the nicest people I met there was Dr. Keenlyside, formerly with the United Nations. On another occasion I invited my great friend Dr. Leonard Marsh and his wife Betty, to present a morning service on the music of Schubert, with Dr. Marsh's opening comment being, "you know, everything Schubert wrote was beautiful." What I liked so much about the Unitarian church was its wide, eclectic spectrum of people, and how art and religion are thoroughly entwined. I recall one lecture by an artist who mentioned the work of Pizarro, an artist who, I was so pleased to learn, always put working-people in his art.

I also, of course, connected with the NDP party in Victoria and visited the Legislation Building whenever I could. Because I love people, I have no problem making contact, and becoming involved with the NDP in Victoria felt like I was having "old home week" with a lot of old friends and coworkers. I loved the Victoria group; they had a nice little office downtown and gladly welcomed me. I wasn't getting used to anything new, I was simply renewing old acquaintances; and we were involved thoroughly with all goings on. Frank was very active too; he did a lot of canvassing in the big apartments, as we were down by Gorge Road; so we were both up to our ears in political activity. It was a lively time, politically speaking, as the NDP were the elected provincial government at that time. A special highlight for me was when the great Canadian, John Kenneth Galbraith, who'd worked for President Kennedy, was a guest speaker. He came to Victoria because he was in very friendly territory; and I listened to him with great interest, proud to meet him. It was exciting to be part of government that was doing such wonderful new things, things that hadn't been tried before.

SWAG & Other Women's Organizations

The Status of Women Action Group (SWAG) was a gung-ho, international organization that kept up with working women's interests globally. The very active organization targeted every topic relevant to women. Meetings were held regularly with good attendance; moreover, they were actively engaged in following their agenda. Many people came to us for advice; and we offered them a comfortable, safe place to sit and chat over a cup of tea or coffee. We also held conferences on the campus of University of Victoria.

One of the most effective projects was "Prime Time: Changing Gears in Middle Years", with realistic programs on women's health, continuing education, and so forth. Involvement in promotion doesn't always bring 100 per cent results, however Prime Time was the answer to questions long in the minds of women without a plan for action ("I'd like to go back to school, but..."). After one of our

Taking a break from my volunteer work with the Victoria Business & Professional Women's organization.

conferences, I received a call. "Jean!" said the woman on the phone, in a jubilant tone. "I just have to tell you what this has meant to me." A non-wage earner for the past twenty years, her outlook on life was bleak after her marriage broke up. Now, after using her newly acquired job-hunting skills, she'd looked for, applied and found work! "I haven't been so happy for a long time," she said. "I feel like a different person and I'm so grateful for getting my life back on track."

Just as active, but with a different venue, was the Victoria Business and Professional Women's Club; it sizzled with action. Long established, with a program for working women, the group dug their teeth into a heavy list of resolutions of current topics of interest, both provincially and internationally.

The Victoria Local Council of Women looked at women's issues with provincial and national links from another point of view. From the Local Council I gravitated into the Provincial and National body, serving as president, as secretary and as National secretary. My invitation to join this organization came from a prim, five-foot-two Salvation Army lass, then president. Her capabilities were endless, but what I most remember is her surprising confession that, as a child, she'd dreamt of becoming a ballerina. I loved her candour!

OCTOBER 26, 1976

Dear Edna:

Before I do another thing today I'm going to write (?), well...type...a letter to you. I've been thinking of you a lot lately...but let other duties divert me.... Oh sure, there are lots of things to do, some that have to be done, but let's just have a little visit. Frank and I, together with (brother) Don and his wife, went to England and Scotland last summer for a month. It was a great trip...and as for Scotland – well, I can now understand the tug at the heart that pioneers must have felt after leaving such a softly mountainous country that Scotland is, especially when living on the flat prairie. We were glad to get back home, though, because we have such a good standard of living, so many creature comforts. We're spoiled, in fact.

You may have wondered how I can be taking time to write a letter at home in the morning. Well, Edna, my job finished September 30th and so I'm now much freer than ever before, in fact, more so than in my entire lifetime. Frank was 65 a year ago and thought he was retired, but a law firm in Victoria asked him if he'd like to do a research type of work for them and he is enjoying it. ...I can take a lot of this new kind of living. I'm very much involved with women's activities, being President of the Victoria Business & Professional Women's Club, and help with the Women's Transition House (a place where women who have been badly treated can find shelter while their problems are sorted out and, if possible, solved). Am also on the Board of the Rape Relief Centre, and I do the music at the Unitarian church, which is a non-creedal type of philosophy. And like Frank, I find Victoria a good place to live. ...I've become quite interested in family history in the last couple of years, and one thing I'd like to do a little research on is my Dad's experience while he was operating the 'tin' store and how he came to suffer the foreclosure that Davidson used...which, if you remember at all, really caused the hardships our family endured for many years afterwards. Are there any records anywhere around McAuley? Is the store still closed, and who was the last operator? These are things I'd delve into if I had some time back there. I may even make a trip back to Brandon shortly after the New Year to see my Uncle Lew Mathie. He worked at the Brandon Sun until just three years ago and has a lot of Manitoba history tucked away in his mind.

I hope to hear from you, and to hear that you and yours are well. …I have been rather tired since my job folded mainly because my boss, although a very nice person, demanded an awful lot of work, and I am not the type to slacken. In fact, I've got to learn how to say "No" to a few of the demands made upon me.

We'll be going to sister Pat's for Christmas. Mother is still well, with only her memory giving her problems at times. Give our fond regards to Reg, and hope to see you in '77. Always, with much love, Jean.

VICTORIA TRANSITION SOCIETY AND TRANSITION HOUSE

It was through Norman Levi, the Minister of Human Resources, who had been involved in the John Howard Society, that funding was secured to establish the Victoria Transition Society and its shelter – a beautiful old house on Trutch Street that had been deeded to the city of Victoria. I was absolutely delighted that battered women in Victoria now had a place to go.

I had heard about the Transition Society through SWAG. "There's a meeting I have to go to tonight," I told Frank excitedly, and dashed off in the middle of the meal! Frank understood my social activism and didn't protest.

The first meeting was thrilling. How wonderful it must be to be assured that there is somewhere where there are people who are trained to take care of the situation you're in, I thought, still remembering that morning when I had walked down a lane so no one would see my face, swollen from crying all night long. I felt so forlorn! To me, the Transition Society and Transition House were seeing a dream come true – and I was part of the change!

The Society elected a president (Judy Brown) and held monthly meetings, with various committees responsible for staffing, reporting and writing reports to the government, and house repairs, for which I volunteered. We had a lot to do to make the house suitable because women who came for shelter needed a room of their own. I remember suggesting to the Board that we ask the carpenters' union to do work on the kitchen, walkway and yard; this surprised the Board and the union, but they did it and it was a great help. I enjoyed doing these things.

It was difficult at first because the new staff, two women, were inexperienced; but, because they also wanted to see it work, it worked; and we all worked together.

I didn't share my story about Bill Mohart with the group in Victoria. I had never talked to anyone about it; it was out of mind because I didn't want to remember it. There are remarkable things about our brain and mind (two different matters, I think); and I believe that the experience had been sleeping there because my life had to go on. And did go on. (It was only when we moved to Chilliwack and I attended a conference on domestic violence where two women from Vancouver lectured, that I finally shared my own story. When the presenters finished their talk, they invited "anyone here who's had any experience like this to share it." Out of the blue, I got up and began to speak; I told them my story. Even reading my own writing, now, in 2005, I have to get up and walk away from it; I have to go outside; it's still painful.)

MARCH 7, 1977

Dear Edna:

Oh, dear! I'm feeling awfully sorry and embarrassed. I forgot your birthday! My only excuse is that I was so engrossed with a big banquet that I had to preside over that I neglected everything else. You see, Edna, this year I am President of the Victoria Business & Professional Women's club and every year there is a big celebration in

February called International Night. We held it in the lovely old Empress Hotel's Crystal Ballroom. There were 150 people there, and it took months of planning, with the final week being just one thing after another. But that's really not a good excuse for having let slip remembering your birthday, so I guess when my birthday comes around I'll have to put through that phone-call and play "Ramona".

Perhaps the reason I remembered it this morning is because Frank's divorce Decree came through, and we are feeling like a couple of teenage lovers again. Silly, isn't it? So, before he left for his law office job, I thought it would be appropriate to play a wonderful old Mart Kenny record that has all the great old songs that were popular when we were necking and running to McAuley and just plain crazy kids. One of the songs on the record is "Ramona" and it was then it hit me: I'd forgotten February 16th!

Thanks for the nice letter you wrote with your Christmas card. I really appreciated it. If there's one thing that irks me, it's to get a once-a-year-card from someone with nothing on it but 'Love, _____ '. I don't love anyone who does that. And I also want to explain, Edna that I didn't intend you to think that I would move back to McAuley to live. However, I would like to spend some time this summer down that way. My brother Don keeps telling me to forget about the prairie, that you can't have climate there, meaning the kind of climate we enjoy here. What I'd like to find out for myself is whether climate means so much that you decide everything about where you'll live just on that premise alone. Living in B.C., and particularly in Victoria, is the most expensive part of Canada, and though I've earned good money in this part of the country I would like to live where it doesn't cost quite so much. Money and possessions just don't mean everything to me. To have some good music, and access to lots of good reading, some light, some heavy, and a few friends to have a good talk with now and then – well, I think that's what I am hoping for. I've made friends here especially in the feminist movement that I truly like and enjoy seeing, and I have to admit that the climate leaves nothing but pleasure most of the time (though we sure need a lot more moisture this year). And the trees, shrubs and flowers...right now I've bouquets of forsythia and daffodils all through the house...and today as I sit here typing to you it's become sunny in the last hour and is warm and lovely outside. But is weather, or climate, everything?

Did I tell you that the provincial government killed the Economic Policy Institute that I was working at? So I am "unemployed". For nearly 50 years I've been slugging away at Monday-Friday, 9-5 pm office work; and do you know, I don't mind not doing that one bit. I have some activities in addition to the one I mentioned earlier...there hasn't been a dull moment since I quit the office routine. In fact, I think this is a good way to live, and I could go on like this for quite a while.

We had a good Christmas. Frank and I went into Cloverdale from Pat's and Allen's farm home at 10:30 Christmas Day and picked Mother up from the very nice Senior citizen's home where she lives. She was bright as could be, and that night I said to her, "Come on, Mom, we've always had a dance at Christmas time", and to my surprise she got up and to the tune of a polka, we did a very delicate little dance, for a few minutes. Pat's son took a picture of it. Next month, April 16th, Mother will be 93.... Love always, Jean

ANOTHER WEDDING!

By the time Frank and I had been together a couple of years he had shown keen interest in many things: good reading, good music, fine dining, family gatherings with his own relatives, a visit to England and Scotland that he found absolutely wonderful and, of course, a visit back to Rocanville in a handsome new Chrysler, his favourite make of car.

Frank was anxious for me to marry him, but I was not anxious to remarry. I had enough difficult marriage experiences and knew that being married was a part of Canadian law; and I liked the informal relationship we had, living together amicably. Looking back, I think I felt pressured by my two sisters and his, who, whenever we met, it seemed, would say, "Really Jean, when are you going to marry Frank?" And Frank would agree with them. So, three and a half years after moving to Victoria, I thought it would be okay to seal the bargain and asked Frank if he would still like me to consider. "Very much," he answered; and we began planning a quiet wedding.

MAY 31, 1977

Dear Jean: It sure is nice to get news about your family. Your Mother must have been happy to have you all together again, as one never knows if it could happen again. Makes me think of the last Christmas we spent with my Mother. She wanted so much to live till Christmas, and then she lasted till March.

June 1st. I don't hear too much about my husband, but apparently people around McAuley were quite concerned about him. He shouldn't be driving a car at all as he is going to kill someone and himself. I did fear for my life in more ways than one at the last. He isn't my concern any more but I can't help but worry and think. I will never go back as long as he is around, not even to visit. No one has told him exactly where I am but I suppose he knows I am in the city. It is very kind of you to offer your help and I certainly appreciate it, but hope I can look after myself for a while yet. I could stay with my family but I don't want to do that....

I hope you and Frank will be very happy and...have many years ahead of you....

Love, Edna   PS Thanks for sending me your wedding announcement.

APRIL 26, 1977

Date: My parents had married on June 19th and we decided to marry on that date as well. Mother, however, became ill, and the wedding took place with only Frank's family present.

Location: Frank's sister Sheila and husband Lorne offered us the use of their Beach Avenue apartment; their lovely living room overlooked the ocean, and was next door to Oak Hotel where we could take photos on the beautiful grounds.

Ring: We were walking up Grandall Street one day and passed a jewellery store in which I saw an unusual ring that looked like four gold ingots with three little amethysts. Frank and I went inside and talked to the jeweller about it and when we told him our early courtship story and how we'd gone forty years without seeing each other and now were about to be married, he was so impressed he gave us a discount!

Wedding Apparel: I shopped for a really nice dress and, after trying on some expensive models ($250), I found one for $39.95 at Miss Prith's. The ankle-length dress was of lovely pink voile with a floral pattern and a pink silk lining and had a lovely almost Elizabethan bodice and sleeves. It was very graceful and I wore it for years afterward; it's so pretty I can't bear to throw it out. Frank wore a nice grey trouser and a jacket I selected from Straith's Imported British Goods, a wonderful shop in Victoria.

Flowers: I carried a bouquet of garden flowers and Frank wore a carnation boutonniere.

Attendants: Pat Carfra's daughter was my little bridesmaid, and as we got ready for the wedding, she said,

"Oh, I hope someone catches the bouquet!" and I said "well, there aren't many people out there who could catch it because it has to be someone who wants to get married; and if they're already married, they can't." "Oh, well," she responded, matter-of-factly. "Aunt Peggy's baby in her tummy could, she could just call out, 'I'm here!'"

Music. Sheila had no piano, so I suggested that we use the song we'd whistled to one another on the boardwalk, the first lines of "Blue Heaven". Frank whistled his line to me from where he stood, and I responded with mine as I walked towards him. That was our only music.

Ceremony: A female Unitarian minister married us and we wrote our own vows – Frank wrote his in ink onto his palm in case he forgot the words; and I recited mine from memory. Readings included Kahlil Gibran's poem, "Let there be spaces in your togetherness..." and the passage about love from I Corinthians 13. I had decided to change my name, as I had no reason to want to hold onto the name Mohart; Frank was happy that I chose to become Mrs. Jean Scott.

Reception: Sheila had a lovely cake made and lunch was catered by the Oak Hotel next door. I don't think there were

Frank & me, after we were married, April 26, 1977.

338

any alcoholic drinks.

Our Big Day was a lovely affair, but then it was time to get changed into my new slack-suit and catch a ferry to see my family. As we left, we walked out to the car with our guests and discovered that two of the fellows at the wedding had tied cans under the rear fender and written 'AT LAST' on the rear window with shaving cream. Frank didn't like a lot of clatter and noise about things, but as we approached intersections, the noise was simply terrible and pedestrians on the sidewalk or waiting for the green light at intersections turned to stare and ask, "what's coming?" Someone had phoned ahead to the ferry to say we were on our way and we drove frantically to get there on time. As we approached with this awful clatter, people stood on board waving and yelling! While we sailed from Schwarz Bay to Tswassen, some very nice fellows disengaged the cans.

We went directly to Pat's where there was a big family party the next day; then, after visiting for the weekend, we returned to Victoria.

I loved the house we were living in since January 1974. It was a fine old house on Wascana Street; and happier times were never had than when Frank and I lived there. Here we enjoyed dinner parties for friends and our blessed new (to me) relatives. One memorable dinner party was a birthday celebration I hosted for Frank's 62th birthday. It was a very special occasion; both Frank's father and grandfather had died at 62, and Frank, I think, assumed it would be the same for him. I baked all his favourite desserts: trifle, lemon meringue pie and chocolate cake.

My big piano sat in a special room where the Business & Professional Women's club that I belonged to rehearsed songs like my parody to "There'll always be an England"; my words were "There'll always be a woman; and women must be free; if just means as much to you; as Justice means to me...."

Our front yard with its little fountain smelled of the

abundant peaches that grew there, along with flowers, fruits and vegetables. In one photo, Frank holds fresh produce; and the caption beneath reads, "this is Frank taking a leek in the garden."

We knew it wouldn't last forever, but the four and one half years in that house were like heaven. After the newly elected government decided to do away with the Institute (even though it had been established 'in perpetuity'), it was time to find a home that Frank and I could manage in retirement. We found an unusual smaller home on Saul Street where we took much pleasure in renovating – both house and remarkable yard which lay 75 feet lower than the house's foundation. A river had run through here in the past; and the soil was fertile, resulting in corn higher than 'an elephant's ear', tomatoes by the bushel, and plums so bountiful that the branches broke under their weight. Not only that, we could look out our living room window and see as far away as Sooke. Life was so good!

Me and Frank and another bountiful harvest from our garden.

HEART ATTACK

On March 27, 1978 I returned from a Business & Professional Women's Club meeting to find the lights on in the house. This was unusual. "Hey, what's going on?" I called as I ran up the steps. "Are you having a party?" Inside, I was greeted by Bob, our neighbour, who had come over at Frank's request, and by Frank, who walked towards me saying, "Jean; I'm not feeling well. I have pains in my arms and across my chest."

"Oh, you just did too much," I replied, thinking of the hard renovating work we'd been doing on this old house. But then I asked, "Are you sure you have pain running down your arms?" When he answered "Yes", I immediately called an ambulance. After I explained his symptoms, the Royal Jubilee Hospital ambulance was dispatched. I followed behind, and don't you know it, got lost! When I arrived, I was told that, "Yes, Frank's had a heart attack." There was a blockage of one artery in the lower aorta.

Frank stayed in the hospital for several weeks, and even though we got him ready for hospital in less than ten minutes, and I thought he was resting in the chair while I packed his bag, he had managed to smuggle in cigarettes. When he was found smoking in the men's hospital washroom, the furious doctor called me. If Frank repeated the offence, he would be kicked out of the hospital. I went in to see Frank and found him with a terribly flushed face after being bawled out by the doctor – he felt very guilty.

When we had moved from the lovely old heritage house it seemed we were going to enjoy retirement in Victoria. But after the heart attack, Frank's health was never back to what we loosely describe as 'normal'; from then on his heart was a concern; and his left lung seemed to collect fluid. As time went on his heart apparently enlarged somewhat and, of course, there was deterioration from the cardiac arrest. Frank's energy and mood changed; as would our future.

January 12, 1979

MATHIE, *Rosalie Annie Spencer Wells, born April 16, 1884, only daughter of the late Major Arthur Charles and Annie Alice Spencer Wells. Rosalie was born just outside Brandon, in a small district then called Rosedale.... Her father was present at the driving of the spike when the CPR was completed as far as Yale, British Columbia. Her mother was instrumental in bringing a traveling library to rural areas in Manitoba. In 1907, Rosalie married Gordon Mathie; all five children were born in Brandon. In 1940, Mr. & Mrs. Mathie moved to British Columbia. Rosalie Spencer Wells Mathie will be lovingly and gratefully remembered by her children and grandchildren, and by everyone who knew her for many outstanding, splendid characteristics, and particularly for a rare gift: that of an unfailing and beautiful sensitivity to others, which was reflected in every aspect of her life.*

FEBRUARY 13, 1979 VICTORIA TIMES

"Twenty outstanding women in the community were honoured by the Victoria council of women..." reads the caption above a news photo in which I appear as president of Victoria Council of Women. In my scrapbook of that time, is the statement I made on "Women & Employment":

"There are many reasons why we, as members of an organization dedicated to "the highest good of the family and the state", should give constant support to all women who are employed in a workplace that still gives women only 62% wages as compared to the male worker in the same job. Every time you are served by a female, imagine her opening her pay envelope while the male working with her opens his; say to yourself, "How is it possible that this state of affairs still exists, when I know that she is one of a great majority who is a home supporter, perhaps a single mother, who wants to improve her earning ability and

hopes to give her children a proper education, not to mention a better enjoyment of life for herself?"

Governments do move but they move with greater force and speed when prodded. We prod them with our Briefs, but if we are instilled with a deep desire to effect real change for your working sisters who are being short-changed because of their womanhood, we will keep this struggle in the forefront of our endeavours; we will make it a litany in our daily thinking, and a labour of love — that will truly bring what is only right and fair to reality."

SWAG

While I was with SWAG, we were given a non-refundable grant, just a few thousand dollars, but enough to procure an office and fund public awareness ads about our existence. It was timely. I recall hearing from a young female doctor who was anxious for women to be involved in such an organization. She shared how tired she was of Pharmaceutical sales reps who stopped by her office regularly to promote new sedatives, like Ativan — targeted for 'anxious' women. "Just give your patients a couple of these..." they'd say.

When SWAG sent out questionnaires we were astounded to receive an almost one hundred per cent reply to questions such as, "Do you feel that your husband is cheating on you?" Another eighty-five per cent of respondents replied 'yes' to the question: "Have you been on a sedative drug?" This was not a huge surprise for me as I'd had a personal experience when I entered the hospital for my first hip operation in October 1979. When Frank and I arrived at my designated room, we were stopped at the door. A young woman, assisted by a male physician, was leading her heavily sedated mother to her bed. The Mother was in a terrible state. "Do you want to be sent to the Mental Institute?" the doctor asked her threateningly when she protested. "Mom, don't listen to him," the daughter consoled her mother after he'd left. That evening the young woman came to my bed and we talked. I told her how surprised I was at how the doctor spoke to her mother. "I'll tell you what I did with him," the daughter replied angrily. "I saw him this afternoon and I told him 'Look; you have got my mother into this state; and you are jolly well going to take care of her till she's cured!'" And these were exactly the kind of women out there that SWAG wanted to hear from and help.

JUNE 6, 1980

Dear Friend Edna:

I haven't heard from you for a long time, and so I am fearful that you haven't been well. Perhaps I am being pessimistic; but if such is the case (my looking on the bleak side) just drop me a quick note and reassure me that you are OK.

My second total hip replacement took place April 29, 1980 and by now I am back to feeling better although my blood count is away down, so I feel weak at times – too weak to do much of anything; but I'm faithfully taking iron pills and next Thursday the doctor says if I'm not improving he will prescribe 'drastic' treatment, whatever that means. I am so relieved to have the surgery over, because it is not pleasant, but it is a wonderful thing that it can be done and that's the way I must look at it.

We are planning to be in Regina July 4th, when the Regina Normal School graduates of 1929-1930 are holding a reunion. That's Frank's year, and…I sure wish I knew whether you'd be anywhere in the vicinity at that time, and I'd make an effort to see you.

Now that Frank's son has moved from Winnipeg there's nothing to take us down that far, especially when it's more traveling by car for me. We expect to fly to Regina. The car causes me to feel some vibration yet. I hope, however, that in four weeks' time I'll have less discomfort than I have at present. I've lost 14 pounds, but that was really a blessing, since I have put on far too much weight while my arthritis was bad and I couldn't exercise. Now I'll have to make sure I do plenty of walking, etc. and try to keep this nice new figure.

I do hope you can drop me a line, dear Edna. I love to hear from you.

LEAVING VICTORIA

Both Frank and I spent our formative years in small prairie towns. Our favourite reminiscences always held a scattering of quips, jokes, or quotes from the halcyon days of our youth in Rocanville or, for me, from my McAuley days. Thus, it was as easy as falling off a log to say to Frank, "You know, dear; I think I'd like to be back on the Mainland"; to which Frank responded, "Me, too." My family – my son and his family, and my sisters and brother and wife – were finding the cost and time of travel difficult, particularly when small children were tired and hungry while waiting for the next ferry sailing.

How long the idea of moving simmered before we finally said "Let's move" is imponderable, for we loved Victoria and all it meant to us, yet we were unable to shake the need for a less-than-city-size community. Once the words were spoken, there was no turning back; we would leave Victoria.

(When writing about the Victoria era, I was surprised at how rounded that time of my life had been. "What were your expectations?" I was asked. "Expectations?" I responded. "I don't live on expectations; even now I live accepting things." That's a lesson you learn when you survive living through the Great Depression on the prairie; you take every day as it comes – some of it's wonderful, some of it explosive...when it's bad you accept and you maintain your equilibrium thru it. The only valuable

thing was learning to cope, which I still am doing, especially now that I have certain limitations. Recently, the banker with whom I discuss my finances advised, "Jean, I think you can lock this one in for three years for more interest." Without in any way being soulful – I am not morbid – I replied, "When you are 93, you don't try to lock something in for three years.")

CHAPTER TWENTY

Chilliwack 1980 –

The aspect of a quieter life in a semi-rural community was appealing; particularly after hip surgery, and the word "retirement" was the lodestar. Never having learned to say "no" caught the unsuspecting, and there is evidence to support the statement that retirement can mean working harder than ever before....

In the early 1970s, when we lived in Vancouver, Frank and I had taken a drive one day through the serene countryside of the Fraser Valley. We had no destination in mind, but just prior to noon we reached Chilliwack and stopped for lunch. As we drove through the quiet streets, we admired the profusion of flowering shrubs that seemed to adorn every yard, boulevard or street.

"Do you like living in Chilliwack?" we asked the young woman who served us a home-style restaurant meal. "I love it!" she said enthusiastically. "I wouldn't want to live anywhere else. Here," she explained, "I can walk from my home, a mile out of town, on a vehicle-free road that passes by farms. From which," she added, "the very products are served here!"

What she couldn't have known was the impact of that conversation and the effect it had years later: We moved to Chilliwack in the spring of 1980.

DECEMBER 3, 1980

Dearest Friend Edna:

I never like to send a Christmas card – especially to a dear friend like you – without adding something, so let's have one of those little trips down Memory Lane now that this *wonderful time of the year is here again. I'm getting your card off early because you seem to go tripping around the country and might not be home later on. I think it's great the way you get around to see your children and grandchildren, and of course the main reason Frank and I are here is so that we can enjoy family visits more than we ever could in Victoria. We will be going to his elder son's and wife's home on Christmas Day and my good sister Pat and husband Allen will be back too, and now my son and family can be out from Vancouver in $1\frac{1}{2}$ hours. I still miss Victoria, and had worked so hard on renovating and redecorating that little house, and loved it so much that if I didn't like what we live in now, and where we are.... But Chilliwack is a very impressive part of this province; and certainly a double-wide mobile home is a fine way to live. I've never in my life moved into a brand new place, with such a spacious living room, and a great kitchen, in which I thoroughly enjoy cooking. Maybe you'll drop by...so easy to locate.*

Well Edna, December never comes but you start thinking of past Christmases, and...with you that means McAuley, in its heyday, when it was a dandy place to live, and one didn't have to be entertained by exotic things like television. The Christmas Tree concert was so exciting and that one year when Gladys Baird was only in about Grade I it was too exciting for her, and just as the entire school got on the platform in the IOOF hall...and the platform was full up right to the front with the youngest kids, poor Gladys' stomach threw up right then and there, all over the stage and anyone close enough to be in the way! I'll never forget it. What a scramble to get it all wiped up, and oh, I can still remember the smell!

I loved the terrific pleasure I got when our teacher marched us upstairs to the upper hallway, and Miss

Porter conducted us in the Opening and the Closing chorus, while Miss Isbister played the piano...and oh, those drills we girls did....

The only disappointing thing about that first Christmas concert in McAuley was that I expected something terrific from Santa, and what did I get? A tam-o-shanter and scarf set of brushed wool in a sort of greeny-blue shade with a broad band of yellow and brown. It was a nice set, but the thing that absolutely ruined my appreciation for it was that Mrs. Shopland had an identical set, and she'd just had all her teeth out that winter and looked positively horrible. Furthermore, I knew that my Mother and Dad had simply picked it out at our store, and that Santa had nothing at all to do with it – and even tho' I had learned that there was no mythical Santa I still hoped I'd get something more exotic than a brushed wool tam and scarf, and as I recall it, I hardly wore that outfit for fear I'd get the life teased out of me and be called "Mrs. Shopland" by the two worst teasers in our school, namely Floyd Pateman and Ken McAuley!!

For years and years I took great care of the nicest gift you ever gave me, one of the nicest I ever got from anybody. It was Christmas 1926, I believe, when I opened a little parcel and found a little blue china lady, so dainty, so very pretty, with a top that lifted off just at the middle of the full skirt; and for many years I used it for the very few bits of jewellery I had. In all the moves I had to make it survived until about twenty years ago, when the poor little lady got smashed beyond fixing, and she'd already had her head glued on more than once. Remember?

So, that's my letter to you this Christmas, and with it, Frank and I (who are happier than we've ever been) send to you and yours, and to Joan and anyone else who was part of those never-to-be-forgotten great days in little old McAuley, our best wishes. Love, Ever Jean.

MARCH 1981

Dear Edna:

I'm glad you get a kick out of my little stories of 'way back when'. I've been trying to rewrite one about the Orange Hall in McAuley but when one likes to write it's hard to be satisfied.... Anyway, you're my No. 2 fan (Frank's my No. 1 fan) so I'll type it out and you can sound off when you write back just like Miss Porter...tell me where it needs improvement. Naturally, I'll avoid any reference to 'bringing the cows home on horseback' because that would be stealing your lines.

Yes, Edna, we do love our new home. And now hear this: I awoke this morning for the first time in years and felt no pain my left hip. The right one is pretty good, only hurts

Edna and me 'way back when'. How I cherish these old photos!

when I've tired it too much; but the left one, which was operated on April 30, 1980, has taken much longer to get well. Since I didn't have any soreness or pain I jumped into my old wool slacks, tossed on a sweater and went for a walk – at 7:40 a.m. I still take a cane when I'm walking outside, but I can tell you it was simply heavenly to have that walk...the air is full of the perfume of thousands of blossoms, I guess it's the cherry trees... We had the most wonderful weather in March right up to the last week and then it began to be rainy...but it's still lovely. Right here we can't have gardens, so all I have is wooden pots of daffodils and lovely, plump red tulips. Well, come and see for yourself.

APRIL 26, 1981

Dear Jean,

...so glad that you are feeling so much better. It will just take more time for the pain to all leave your hips. You better be careful and not get too rambunctious, like going for early morning walks. Aren't you afraid of getting mugged? I have a friend here who went for a walk and a man came up to her and put his arms around her. She got away from him but shortly after that experience a man drove his car close to the curb and exposed himself. By the news that happens quite often now. They even have special pants made for that purpose. There are all kinds of queers running around.

Jean you have no idea how much I enjoy your letters and stories. Your memory is so good...I can't even remember when you lived in the Orange Hall...I remember when you lived in the restaurant, and you playing "Let Me call you Sweetheart" for Artie Grist. Then when you were living in the cottage. It was used for a bank by the credit *union…but now Jim Ross lives in your cottage…. Keep your stories coming. Hope this finds you both well. Love, Edna.*

May 18, 1981

My dear Friend Edna:

Sorry I haven't got another story ready for you at the moment….

When your letter came at 9:30 two weeks ago today, Frank and I were all packed up and ready to be driven into Vancouver by his son Glenn, where we got a plane to Toronto. For a couple of years Frank has been picking up the threads of his "roots"…

Can you imagine how exciting it was to hear McAuley mentioned on the CBC National News? Oh, my! I was so glad to hear it, because the last time I saw it, it nearly broke my heart. You see, Edna, I have such a real soft spot in my heart for McAuley. Those wonderful happy childhood memories…your Mother's amazing tolerance of our antics, and her never-ending willingness to watch us eat and eat and eat. Gosh! And say, Edna, does anyone ever say anymore, "Please read the table" like she always asked you to do? Sometimes I see the little, soft brush and pan that you had for that job in an antique shop and I'm tempted to buy it just for sentiment's sake. One thing I'll never buy for sentiment's sake is the old chamber-pot and commode pail. I'm glad to be finished with those items, thank you….

Gee, how I laughed when you said in your letter you wondered if the Orange Hall was where Houle Thompson had his bootlegging joint. No, Edna, if you can picture in your mind…it was…quite close to Collyer's.

We used to borrow a cup of sugar and they used to borrow a cup of flour, and so on, every day. I distinctly remember Isobel being sent over for "Two teaspoons of baking powder". ...I still like to hear all the McAuley news you can give me.

Now, dear girl...one of these days you are going to need a rest...and you can come to Scott's Rest Home! Much love, as ever, Jean.

OCTOBER 13 1981

A photo in The Chilliwack Progress of me, as president of Upper Fraser Valley Transition Society, cutting the ribbon to kick off a ten kilometre hike-a-thon to raise money for Chilliwack's Ann Davis Transition house. The 70 walkers raised about $5400.

OCTOBER 25, 1981

I receive a certificate of "recognition for 25 years of initial and continuing contributions to the Memorial Society of BC".

JUNE 12, 1982

This is the 'sad' letter to Edna after her son, Murray, died.

Dearest friend:

Ever since we received your letter telling us about your son's death we have been trying to think of some way to express sympathy. After several attempts, I went outside and looked at the flowers in our small garden. That's when I remembered the little flower to say what I am unable to say: the Bleeding Hearts sprig of little blossoms.

I remember being with you when he was born. My heart goes out to you now, and of course the family as well. As well as we are able, we are with you while you grasp to deal with the terrible extra pain because his body could not be found for two weeks. For your sake, we are relieved to know that the government searchers were able to close the dam at Fort Qu'apple and locate his body.

We just hope that you and your family will now feel a measure of ease and comfort. I can only share your sorrow in this way, and I know that you understand that. Our prayers for your lessening of grief, and as always for these many years – much love, Jean & Frank.

MARCH 5-6, 1982

After promoting the idea and helping plan the event, I co-chaired Chilliwack's International Women's Day celebrations (March 5-6). Rosemary Brown, MLA, was keynote speaker; the theme was "Celebrate – Why?" I led the rousing singing of feminist songs; and the following day, local businesswomen showcased their activities in the cause, etc. The Chilliwack Progress reported on the event on March 17th.

APRIL 18, 1982

I received the Soroptomist Women-Helping-Women award in Saskatoon.

SEPTEMBER 27, 1983

Dear Edna: ...First I must apologize for leaving as we did on the Sunday afternoon, and I'm afraid it was because of me and the pain in my left hip. In addition to the hundreds of miles of driving to get there I think the drive to and from McAuley and Moosomin every day caused a vibration...very tired...by...Sunday...plumb tuckered out. But...so glad we went...good to see you again. I have two regrets: that we never found a quiet spot or convenient time to just have a visit and chat over things. The second thing that was disappointing was that I experienced the very first occasion in my (long) life when I asked if they would like me to sing at the church service and was told "it probably wouldn't fit in with the service"! Because I started my singing career in McAuley I thought how nice it would be to sing there again, and so it was hard to believe that for the first time in my life I was rejected. Oh well, there has to be a first time for everything....

OCTOBER 20, 1983

The District of Chilliwack Chamber of Commerce conveyed a "Certificate of appreciation" for "your services in making the Citizen Dinner 1983 a success". I had sung "O Canada" at the event.

FEBRUARY 23, 1984

Dear Jean,

...Thanks for your nice cat birthday card. I think I received four cards with cats on so I guess I am known to be a lover of cats....

By what you said on your Christmas card you didn't receive my letter telling you about Joan's death (Edna & I played with Joan during our McAuley childhood; Edna and she remained life-long friends). She passed away quite suddenly – apparently of a heart attack. She had only been home about a week after being at Kelowna, Calgary and Vancouver. I sure miss her...hope you receive this. Love, Edna

My Dear Friend Edna:

Apologies for not having communicated sooner. The Chilliwack Museum and Historic Society has literally eaten up so much time and energy that I've not been able to do other things. However, the time has come to take a break (after the end of this week when our Canada Day celebrations will be over) and I want to get the word off to you that on July 7th, Frank and I are taking the plane to Regina...hope to rent a car in Regina...and if there's a chance...will phone you in Winnipeg to see if you have been home long enough to pick up your mail.... If we do connect...that'll be great. If not...there's a guest room in our home.... As ever—with love, Jean

AUGUST 15, 1984

My dear friend Edna:

Yes, I know...that was a too-short visit...ever since Frank's heart attack of 4 years ago he gets up very early (they told us in hospital, that "You'll have a change in sleeping pattern") and he has to have an after-lunch sleep. On the day we met...Frank had been up since 6 am....

Well, anyway, we drove to McAuley...had an ice-cream cone at Jamieson's Mr. Scoop, not the 5¢ kind that we once bought from Allan Jamieson at the Barbershop & Poolroom, but a 65¢ one. And let me tell you, there's a real feeling of your age when you look at the people sitting on the picnic bench...and you don't know a darn one! Oh yes, Sid Norbury sat there with the...very young ball team...no use speaking to any of them because not one of them would ever have heard of the Mathies, and anyway none of them were interested in anything except eating and getting on their way. I remembered the uniforms worn when you and I stood and yelled our heads off in the 1920s; marvelled now at the new, tight-fitting white uniforms with orange trim.

...I asked if anyone there had ever heard the name Mathie. Sid was the only one. He remembered us from last year's celebrations. When I pointed a few feet away and said, "That's where Mr. Margeren's horses disappeared down the fire well and he sent me running for help," the guys looked at me and asked a few questions, and when I said that happened in 1924 one of them said, "That's the year I was born" and laughed, and Edna, he had grey hair, so when the grey-haired ones are telling us that they weren't even born when we were silly and flapperish, well then you know you're a wee bit 'over the hill'; wouldn't you say? One thing I must add for fear you think I'm being pessimistic: I never had it so good, and I think Frank and I are about as lucky as any one could be, to have good health and a fine home and the ability to enjoy life, both of us now over 70!

I left Frank talking to the fellows and slowly strolled down the little street where my girlish footsteps had walked, run and stumbled so many times with such extremes of feeling many years before.

Because I am trying to write about my family's fortunes – or misfortunes, as the case certainly was – I took a picture of the little granary-sized building that was my Dad's last stand – or last hope – in McAuley.... I went around the Municipal Hall, and oh the memories...remember the Saturday night when you invited me to spend the night at Wilbert's with you; but we were in one of our very flirtatious moods and Harold Collins and Lyle Patterson were able to persuade us to sit with them on the

Municipal hall steps? When your Mother and Wilbert were ready to pack up groceries, etc., and drive out to the farm they started driving around (in the buggy) looking for us. What a couple of smart-alecks we were! We let them drive around and around, calling our names, too. Finally we did drag ourselves away from the boys and let your Mother know where we were. That poor woman couldn't understand why we wouldn't have heard her long before we let her know where we were, and she said, "But we drove around and around, where on earth were you two?" and we just played dumb! Oh, gee, makes you wonder about your younger years, and if kids of today ought to be judged harshly. We all go through those periods, I think.

So then I sauntered up the land, sorry that the Manse is gone. Wards lived in it when we moved to McAuley and Muriel became a friend. When I sat behind her in Sunday school I wished with all my heart that I could have a flowered moiré silk hair ribbon at least 4 inches wide and held with a gold barrette holding my braids just like hers. And that brings up another story I must tell you, about the church deciding that the manse could have a veranda built at its front. While the men were constructing it, Mrs. Charlie Miller walked by, asked what they were doing and who gave them authority to build anything, and without further ado, she ordered them to cease – right away! She said (apparently) that the Ladies Aid hadn't ok'd that and therefore it must not be done. I talked to Muriel about that, years later. Remember, she was the oldest of the family and there were six children – the two younger were just babies and Mrs. Ward took in two school teachers to help augment the meagre pittance a minister got in those days. Muriel said her mother was terribly embarrassed and angry over that incident....

I also looked at the former Jamieson home. When I first saw the inside of that house the Conquergood family had moved in from their farm… I do recall being so excited to go Beatrice's birthday party there in 1921, and it was the only time in my life where we had a taffy-pull at a party. I took her an embroidered handkerchief that mother found in her big trunk that we kept on the landing of the second floor of the big house we then lived in. I enjoyed the Conquergood family…. Their Mother Molly was a lovely person. I remember she…was in bed almost whenever I visited. Mr. Conquergood (George) used to ask me to sing, and then he would sing a pretty little song about "When the springtime comes, the robin singeth his song merrily…" The next thing I remember about that house is you and I visiting Mrs. Jamieson and her letting us play her records over and over. Do you remember "When the rest of the world is sleeping, I'm alone, thinking of you?" And the song "Memories". And I recall Cliff and Cora, newly married, saying Goodnight to us and walking upstairs tougher. I envied their married status!

It still seems strange to see Mr. Chipperfields' house with any other color than yellow. (From there I walked)…up the lane…Bill Carefoot (was) pumping at the old well, and carrying a pail of water at a time over to his parched garden…as I walked, a car slowly drew up beside me and the woman next the driver said, "I'll bet you're doing a lot of reminiscing". I didn't know her but I said, "I sure am", and I told her how frightened I was of Charlie Levin the Halloween when he said he was going to be out there with a black-snake whip in case anyone thought they were going to push his backhouse over. That Halloween was cold, wintry, and there was ice on the road between Bell's house and Chipperfield's and I can still feel the pangs of fear I had that night. I guess I was too sensitive and couldn't bear the thought of a black-snake whip curling round my calves.

Well…I suppose you have heard from Ruth (whom you said phones you often!) that Marian Bell (I forget the name she now has) was the person in the car that slowly caught up to me. She said "You probably don't remember me", but I assured her that I did, and we had a nice chat about McAuley things, and…walked up to Bill Carefoot and he said, "I think I'd have trouble remembering you (meaning me) because my memory is playing such tricks these days". I truly felt sorry for him…so many people…finding themselves somewhat 'lost' without their marriage partner of many years.

Edna, dear girl, will you please get word to Marian (Bell) through Ruth what our address is… I assured them that we are in the telephone directory as Scott-Frank & Jean, and the other day the new directory arrived with just Scott, Frank! I could wring their necks. After all the years that the Women's groups I've worked with bugged the telephone company to allow the wife's name as well as husband's, and we were listed that way last year, now they've gone back to the old listing. No doubt because we moved….

I've got to finish this long drawn out scribble because there are several things awaiting my attention. I do want to say again how wonderful it was to see you again…. Please remember me to any of the McAuley people you may be seeing and do drop me a line whenever your schedule of visitors or telephone callers or friends or whatever allow it. Now, with, as always, MUCH LOVE, Jean

OCTOBER 10, 1984

Dear Jean:

...You have a remarkable memory to remember those silly things we did about sixty years ago. It really makes me feel ancient... I had forgotten about sitting on those steps with Lyle and Harold, but you brought it all back to me. I can remember being scared of my mother.... Do you remember Charlie Fraser and Dave Duncan? One night they went to Brandon (I think they went for a bath) and we were feeling so downcast. Mrs. Adam did the cake walk to cheer us up. She is now in a nursing home in Trail and has lost her memory. Jim still writes to me. He is remarkable for his age....

What do you and Frank do for relaxation? Do you watch television?... Hope you both are keeping well. Love, Edna.

It would be easy to speculate that if we had remained in Victoria and close to his fond relatives, Frank could have been happier, however, the decision to move was mutual. But there was a change in our relationship at home. After being the target of some insidious remarks I was hurt enough to cry out, "How can you be so mean!" At one point, in 1984, I took two weeks away and went to visit my Aunt and her daughter in Edmonton. When I returned, Frank and I had a candid talk. I said, "I don't love you anymore." "Well," he said coolly, "what can you do about that?" Another time we were driving home, the mood between us unpleasant, and I said it was enough to make me separate from him. Frank laughed and said, "You can't afford to. You have nothing." I replied that I had fended for myself before and could again if need be.

By now, my long years of paid employment were over and through the benevolence of the government I received the regulatory pensions: OAP and CPP. Our OPEW Local 15 had pushed for pensions for female workers, but by the time I left the IWA, only male staff was pensioned. The house I still owned on 13th Avenue in Vancouver was, in essence, my "pension plan"; I only needed to sell it. That was a decision I didn't want to make, but there was no choice when no buyer could be found for the mobile home we bought on moving to Chilliwack.

I moved back into Vancouver to work on the house. Frank was to find a realtor to list the mobile home, but that year interest rates went sky high and mobile homes were a drag on the market. To help finance necessary renovations of the house, I took in a university student boarder. Frank left the Chilliwack home empty and joined me in Vancouver. The boarder loved my cooking, appreciated the new shower next to his room, plus the fact that I did his washing – so many blue jeans; he changed them every day! The young man was friendly and offered to help Frank out, but Frank just said "No". At mealtimes, Frank ignored him, so the young fellow and I made conversation.

When the Vancouver house sold and we resettled in Chilliwack, in a home I bought with the proceeds of the sale, we had to find a doctor for Frank and were accepted by a fine young physician who gave Frank extraordinary care to the end of his life.

JANUARY 27, 1985

Dear Jean: Sorry to hear about Frank's illness, but it's nice to know that he has made such good progress. He will have to take it easy for some time yet.... Hope this finds Frank much improved and you in good health. Love, Edna

MARCH 20, 1985

The Chilliwack Progress reports: "Museum to get $500,000". Funds had been raised to upgrade the City Hall to current building code standards, after which it would become the new home of the Chilliwack museum, now located at Evergreen Hall.

Society membership reaches 1000 through the prodigious efforts of long-time members and committees. In the newspaper article, I state, "I think that great credit is due to the council members for having taken this step.... We have been lobbying the council pretty well for a year."

In the 1985 Museum Society's AGM president's report, I write: "as past president I'll keep nagging and I hope, doing something. As one Board member once said to me, 'You may never have a road named after you, Jean, because you won't be able to claim residency for at least 25 years!', but I warn you: I intend to be around (and be heard from) for some time yet! (It is 2005 as I write this; 25 years after moving to Chilliwack! I fulfilled my "intent to be around".)

APRIL 3, 1985

Dear Edna:

I hate to apologize at this late date for not getting a birthday card in the mail – same excuse.... President of the Museum & Historical Society, singing here and there and the day's work seems to eat up my time. In March I caught a bug for about a week. It sure takes the starch out of you. Frank caught it too, but miraculously didn't get as sick as I was. For that we are thankful, because last year he was very, very ill and it took him months....

I am taking a day off and just staying home (I have to go into the town of Chilliwack almost every day on Museum business). We held our regularly monthly Board meeting last night and I think I have earned a day to myself. And the weather is telling me, too, that there will never be a better time to stay indoors and get my correspondence up to date.... Today I got up very early – don't know why – 5:30 am; it was a most beautiful morning and I thought to myself "Oh, I'll go for a lovely walk". Well, by 6:30 it was cloudy, then it got darker and began to rain. Just after the noon hour we had such gusts of wind I wondered if the roof would start to peel off. Now it is quiet again, but still a 'moody' day.... Your last letter reeled off so many trips you were planning that I said, "I wonder if Edna gets time to read her mail when she gets home before she takes off

'ANNIVERSARY' CELEBRATION — Chilliwack Museum and Historical Society held a celebration March 26 to mark the first anniversary of having reached its goal of 1,000 plus members. Above, society president Jean Scott put down her gavel and picked up a knife to make the first cut in the celebration cake.
— Photo by Michelle Mallette

Newspaper clipping from the Chilliwack Progress, March 30, 1985.

again!" Good for you…it's great…I often say rather sadly that I wish my Mother could have enjoyed the kind of good life we live. Mind you, her life in her latter years was a great deal better than those awfully hard days in McAuley and Rocanville, and I made sure when she lived with me that she got to the musical concerts she enjoyed, and every time I had a party at my home where she lived she stayed up till the very end, protesting when I would ask if she wanted to say Goodnight to guests, with "Oh, now, Jean, I'm enjoying every minute."

We own this beautiful Motorhome (taken in trade for the mobile home) and we are talking of driving it when the good weather comes. Whether we'll ever take it over the mountains is something I rather doubt. I know Frank would like to do that, but I am a little hesitant to plan such a long drive. At our age I would rather fly than rent a car, so I don't know when we may come that way again; it would be nice for you to come out this way.…

Frank and me in our Garden of Eden in Chilliwack, 1985.

I went to Ottawa January 24 and did my secretarial duties at the Executive meeting of the National Council of Women then spent the evening of January 30 with a former Rocanville friend; and I have to say again, Edna dear, that I am always hungry for news of McAuley. That's hard to explain, I know, because I have lived in many places since my 1920-1927 days there. There can be only one explanation and it's the age-old one: that our youth is a time we cannot forget, and strangely enough, most of what I remember is good, and that too is very odd, because it wasn't all good. I guess growing older takes the rough edges off our memories and lets us think kindly of the past.

...and come and see what it's like to live in Sardis – the Garden of Eden....

JUNE 18, 1986

A headline in The Chilliwack Progress reads: "Scott Named Co-ordinator". The article goes on to say, "The National Council of Women of Canada, representing over 1500 women's organizations and 750,000 women from all parts of Canada, recently held its 93rd annual meeting in Halifax, where Jean Scott of Chilliwack was named National Status of Women co-ordinator...the council, acts as a catalyst for its federated associations by advocating for the improvement of social, economic, environmental and political conditions for women, the family, and society as a whole. The resolutions debated at its conference form the basis of its annual brief to the federal cabinet."

JULY 8, 1986

Upper Valley Times reports: "Women's Council Seeks Members." As provincial secretary for the Canada Council of

Women I was attempting to revive the group in Chilliwack, together with an ad hoc committee of five other women. The council is set up as an umbrella organization to draw not only women who are active in community organizations and club life, but in all walks of life. "That is its strength," I say. "It's speaking for people who already have the broad interests of the community at heart."

July 25, 1986

My dear friend Edna:

…Your letter arrived while we were still in Britain. We got back on May 13th and I had to attend to the necessary housekeeping duties and hop on a plane for Halifax, where I took all the minutes at the National Council of Women's annual conference. That was not only a tiring thing to do, but when I got home (and got used to BC time once again) I had all those Minutes to transcribe in the rough first, then re-type them in a neat and clean final draft. That took me over a month and I didn't allow myself the luxury of attending to any of my heart's desires. I was really tired to the point of being dull and stupid, but I got the job finished; and for the last time, since I have declined to let my name stand for the Secretary's position any more.

We've had our usual crops of strawberries, black currants, tayberries, and raspberries to make into jelly and jam and we decided to take a long 'circle' trip over the Yellowhead highway to see my dear Aunt Marie Hill and her daughter who lives with her in Edmonton; then down to Calgary (where I lived from 1940-46), saw friends and on to Kimberly, BC to visit a couple of days with my very dear sister Betty and a wonderful drive home, both Frank and I taking turns driving. What a country we live in!

Sure, England and Scotland and Germany are wonderful to see; but there is nothing like this part of the world for us, and our comfortable home means more to us than anything else we can think of...when are you going to pay us a visit?

I picked up the Archie history book...I will never forget those very happy days in McAuley, when you and I...thought life was 'just a bowl of cherries'. I read again how you roared at me that I was combing my hair with Rock's Moustache comb; and Mrs. Adams' crazy antics that made us laugh at ourselves....

We had expected to see at least a few visitors from McAuley and Rocanville because of Expo, but I guess they are just like you...on tour and haven't time...wish we were close enough for a visit and a chat.... I will never live long enough to forget my McAuley days and our wonderful, silly times together.

Nov 11, 1986

Ever since Frank's heart attack in Victoria, his energy level was down. Our nice home in Sardis had a wonderful lot and Frank thought if he'd just sit down and lean over, he could plant strawberries. But it was exactly the wrong thing to do because he was giving his heart less room to move. I had to take him to the hospital again and this became a matter of course in Chilliwack, on more occasions than I can remember.

It happened again on November 11.

I was supposed to be at the celebration of armistice at the cenotaph, but when I woke up that morning and saw Frank wasn't in bed I knew something unusual had happened – I always got up first. When I looked into his ensuite washroom and saw a cup of coffee sitting there, I quickly went into the hallway where I met him walking towards me, his hand on his throat as he tried, but couldn't make a sound come out. Finally, I thought, what's doing?

When Frank found a pen and wrote something down that was utter gibberish, I phoned Spencer. "Something has happened to Frank; and I don't know what to do," I told my son. "Well, Mother have you phoned the hospital?" he asked. I phoned immediately and when Dr. Quinn answered, told him, "I think Frank has had a slight stroke; he can't speak." Dr. Quinn didn't mince words. "Madam, your husband has had a TIA," he said. "Get him in as fast as you can. Do you drive?" "Yes." "Well then you just get him in here as soon as you can!"

It was a transient ischemic aphasia; and Frank recovered by the end of the day. Don and wife came out immediately from Vancouver and we got Frank home by noon. The doctor had instructed us "to keep him talking, don't let him sleep"; and by evening, Frank was able to put two words together, he could say 'the' and very hesitatingly add, 'paper'. Within a few days he could put a few words together; but for the next year, when he'd resumed his little walk after supper, he said the walk upset his nervous system; and his knees were very shaky. To me, it seemed that Frank's whole nervous system had such a jolt that he never returned to his normal pace of doing things again.

DECEMBER 1, 1986

Dear Friend Edna

I was so pleased to get a letter from you.... Time and distance have taken us a long way from our former days, haven't they?

And I don't know whether I'll ever want to visit McAuley again. It must look very different, and the Main Street can't bear any resemblance to the way it was in my younger days; but we all know that everything changes, and if that's progress then we shouldn't complain.... When I lived there...the old garage was next to the tin store...In the Mathie's happier and less poverty-stricken days we had a model T Ford. To fill the gas tank the front seat had to be removed and the tank opened. I can remember helping to lift my youngest sister Betty down and have her stand beside me while the gas was poured into the tank, and she always turned white as a sheet (not a modern, flowered one – the good old-fashioned plain white kind). Betty...was just a very little girl and she would get so sick...I'll never forget my terrible fear when...I had to go for the milk in the morning and at night...the Chicago papers used to come to McAuley and there were the most gruesome stories (which of course I read) and I could imagine being caught, dragged off and murdered in some utterly ghastly fashion nightly. Isn't it a wonder I survived?

December 3, Wednesday

...the Provincial Council of Women met yesterday in Vancouver and since I'm secretary and Frank likes to mosey around in Antiquarian bookstores, etc., (while I'm busy jotting down all the immortal words of my fellow members), we used that day as a time to do a bit of shopping in that large Mall called Oakridge. Of course, with Christmas so close everything was a glorious sight to see. I bought a silver teapot...and when you have that long-deferred visit with us you and I will crook our little finger just so, and sip tea and reminisce about days when we (the Mathies) were lucky to have a cracked old brown Betty, and it had a rubber spout where the original one had broken off! Better hurry up and make that date to visit, Edna....

I guess there's never a year that I don't recall Christmas and Rutherglen School in McAuley when I sang two solos: "The Bluebird" and "I've Been And Had The Measles."

DECEMBER 11, 1986

My Dear Friend Edna:

You would have every right to think I had died...not so – not yet, anyway. I guess I won't know the meaning of retirement until I get a few of my local responsibilities off my shoulders.... Time after time I have thought of you and said to myself (not loudly enough, I guess) must write to Edna. As president of Chilliwack Museum & Historical Society I have almost a full-time job...been very interesting...but I think I'll step down next year....

When we got back home last July our yard and garden had not got the care they needed, so we were busy...the fruit season...upon us. I always preserve quite a bit...spent more time these past few months on tomatoes than ever ...and oh, my! ...frozen tomatoes, canned tomatoes, and tomatoes in pickles, green tomato mincemeat; it's delicious...last of the green ones...on the kitchen window....

...When we drove back west we stopped again in McAuley and went into the Drop-in Centre...only one I knew was Sid Norbury and he looked really peaked as compared with him in 1983. I went next door and rapped on Wilson's door and spoke very briefly to Mrs. John and called a 'hello" to John, but he looks so old now and didn't seem to want to talk. So, all in all, it wasn't a very enlivening experience. I...took pictures of the "tin" store because when I get off the busy track...going to write about that era of my life....

It wouldn't be Christmas if I didn't mention...fun we had ...how generous your Mother...eating two Christmas dinners...after the second one at your home we lay together on the big old brown davenport and groaned...ready to burst...your...Mother...laughing at us...the same year that I saw the first "chesterfield"...that came to McAuley. Patterson's got it and I sat in the chesterfield chair and just before the train arrived (which of course we had to meet!) Lyle came walking through the house part of the station...singing "Baby Face...you've got the cutest little baby face..." I tell you I was almost swooning when he passed by where I sat because I thought he might be singing it to me. You know, Edna, once in a long while I have some reason to go through my old music, perhaps because I play the piano and sing with 'seniors', and I never see "How do you do, Mister; how do you do?" without the entire tune going through my head.... When I think back of the REAL fun we had I feel a bit sorry for the present day youth because they can't possibly get the same kick out of things in this fast moving modern technological world. I guess that's enough deep thinking for this letter.

...I should tell you that this page was stuck in the typewriter from last Wednesday until this morning, Monday, Dec 16th because I've been really knocked out by a nasty flu bug, and worse still, I passed it to Frank and now he's coughing and hurting. Oh dear...a real hearty wish for...good times and that your health stays good.

JANUARY 26, 1987

The Ann Davis Transition House awards me again with a Certificate of Appreciation for my volunteer efforts.

1987 AGM report for Provincial council of Women (by Jean Scott, Convenor, Women & Employment)

"Before we go any further re women and their work, let us remember that ALL women work, whether outside the home or in the home. …Like many other matters too long kept from public scrutiny, we are hearing and reading that sexual harassment is causing women who experience it to lay complaints, and in some cases to lay a charge. We don't have to look far afield, it's too close to us to ignore, and it's a disgusting, sordid occurrence we'd all like to see phased out. That will take courage by the aggrieved, and it needs assistance, both from individuals and groups.

Similar to the findings of those operating Transition Houses for battered women, we are reading that sexual harassment occurs in any area where women work; and is just as apt to happen in professionally oriented workplaces as anywhere. Close to home, a university researched their campus, recommending that "sexual harassment officer" be appointed to draw up policy (to curb) and that an office be opened to deal with the large number of complaints….

MARCH 1987

The Chilliwack Museum opens in its new location; and I sing "O Canada" at the opening ceremonies. The Society bestows an honorary lifetime membership on me.

MARCH 1987

The Ann Davis House Commemorative Celebration on or near Int'l Woman's Day in Chilliwack. Fund raiser and consciousness raising event always with a feminist theme, the evening including singing, a guest speaker, a skit (in 1987, I wrote: "If Men Didn't have the vote but wanted it"; in 1988, "The Fight for Personhood"; in 1990, "Canadian Women

1890-1990) and a ceremony commemorating local 'ordinary women', each selected woman presented with a rose and a loaf of home-baked bread. The song title "Bread & Roses" became synonymous with the annual event.

APRIL 7-9, 1987

Canadian Daughters League: Provincial Convention, Chilliwack. Opening speech:

"Most of us have the pleasantest memories of receiving a greeting from our Grandmother. Well, the National council of women is indeed the grandmother of women's organizations in Canada. Founded in 1893, in five year's time we will celebrate our 100th birthday. And next year, 1988, will be the one 100th anniversary of the founding of the International council of Women.

Our esteemed founder, Lady Aberdeen, said "We should go forward grasping that magic a wand of love, determined not merely to tolerate one another's opinions, but to understand one another and to UNDERSTAND THE VALUE THAT UNDERLIES ONE'S WORK".

...From the first ever Brief to the government and right to this day, Council continues to prove that we do understand the value that underlies each person's and each organization's work. Council at every level is still highly regarded and continues to deal with matters of utmost importance to the individual, the family and the nation; that's our oft-repeated purpose....

As I said, being of Grandmother's age means more than you're apt to realize. There is the wisdom from having coped with life in all its facets, the satisfaction of measures of achievement and the priceless experience gained over time. It is from that kind of well-earned reputation for good works that I, as recording Secretary and on behalf of our Provincial Council, extend our good wishes to a younger relative in the family of women's organizations....

JUNE 21, 1987

Dear Jean,

...Ever since you phoned I have been waiting to hear from you. I understood you to say that you would be in Regina on the 19th of May and that you might drive to Winnipeg from there. Maybe I was in a state of shock and didn't hear you right. I did want to be home if you decided to come.... I tried to find the last letter that I had received from you and the only one I could find was dated Dec 1986.... I will be waiting to hear from you to see what happened, also give me your telephone no: with the postal strike it's hard to say how long it will take a letter to get through. Still waiting. Love to you both, Edna.

JUNE 29, 1987

My Dear Friend Edna:

There was a very good reason why we didn't make it to Saskatchewan and on to see you in Manitoba. Frank's health deteriorated about three weeks prior to when I – and he – planned to be in Regina for the National Council of Women convention, May 16-21. For about 10 days he seemed to get less and less energetic, didn't sleep well and didn't eat. I finally said he must see our doctor and he willingly said OK It was high blood pressure. There is a remarkable drug used these days, but Frank doesn't take any foreign substance very well, and he didn't take to this one. However, after seeing the doctor again and getting the dose reduced it worked; that is until he again (about 3 weeks later) seemed to go downhill. Back to the doc again and this time it was diagnosed...he also suffers from emphysema. It is not advanced, and can be controlled; but he still hasn't regained anything like his former energy, and it pains me to see him with his chest heaving, trying to draw a deep breath when he exerts himself, such as when I was transplanting tomato plants and he wanted to help me. He has always enjoyed a small garden; but we know, of course, Edna, that we are not indestructible, and that we are now aged 77 and I am 75 (he will be 77 in November).

It's a very sobering thought, to see someone lose interest, energy and what we take for granted as "simple good health"; and so I had to phone Regina and cancel my reservation – a real disappointment; but one does what one has to do, doesn't one?

So Frank, being the thoughtful type, has read everything he can on blood pressure and emphysema and…when he got the medication under control…it does exactly what it's supposed to do. Except for the energy that he hopes to regain.

But it has meant a lot of extra work for me, and although some of that is good, it also eats up the time, and of course my energy. I really enjoy the outdoor exercise, even though I still have a lot of soreness in my left hip.

It's about 8 o'clock in the morning and today we have some cloud. I love to walk outside, just in my nightie and housecoat. I always tell Frank, "I'm going to take a walk around the farm" and then saunter from back around to the eastern side of the house…right now the Sweet Williams are showing off, with the tall hollyhocks behind them now about 5 1/2 feet high, and the border is a riot of colour with the vivid blue lobelia and the different coloured pansies. Clinging to the white stucco wall of the house is a great trail of TAYBERRY vines. The Tayberry…is a cross between a raspberry, a loganberry, and a blackberry (and perhaps also a boysenberry) and is delicious. After I finish your letter I'll go out and pick another bowlful, and that's about the 8th this season!

One of my deepest pleasures is still being about to sing, and yesterday I sang the O Canada at the opening celebration for Canada Day at the Lion's Club celebrations at the local Exhibition Grounds. I sang a very good and very demanding solo last Sunday in church and was soloist at a wedding two weeks ago; and with a man with a fine tenor voice I will sing a duet on Sunday morning. Do you know Edna, I don't think I've sung with a tenor since (young) Dr. Goodwin and I sang "Seek ye the Lord while He may be Found" in the former now long ago United church in McAuley. And, dear Edna, that's a long, long time ago.

My dear sister Pat and husband Allen live an hour's drive from us, so we meet half-way at the Eaton's Mall in Abbotsford about once a week and have lunch and visit. Pat and Allen will be married 50 years this October; she was only 19 then…and I played The Wedding March.…

Frank and I are still thinking we may travel to Saskatchewan and Manitoba this year; but this time we'll fly and maybe rent a car when we get there.…

Do you ever see or run into any of the school friends we had? I was so disappointed in 1983 when the torrid, humid heat was so oppressive and my hip so sore from the long car trip…the only visiting I managed to have was in the rink at meal times…I think Ken McAuley thought I was being hard on him when I told him what a tease he (and Floyd Pateman) were to me. "Oh, I wasn't really that bad, was I?" he asked, and I said, "You two were the bane of my existence." Floyd teased me all the time, about everything, and one day he said "Mathie's boots are for kicking snake's eyes out." Those were hard times…I was wearing a pair of boots that laced up and the toes were pointed; they were my Grandmother's. I hated them, but I also was awfully mad at Floyd for making me feel so acutely embarrassed.

One of the things that make Frank's and my living together work is our mutual teenage background and our pleasure in recalling those far off kid years. Even yet, sixty years later, I'll be doing something and suddenly relate it to something of those many years past. Will I ever forget you and I picking dandelion weeds the year we lived in the 'little' house? We even got our hoped-for wine to the stage when it was sitting in the tiny pantry after cooking the leaves and making the syrup. I sat down at the piano and started to play and sing and then pretended I was happily drunk. We all laughed, you and Mother and me, too. But the next morning our lovely dishpan full of brew was missing. When I asked Mother what had happened she said, "I threw it out." I was astounded and asked why on earth she would do that, wasting all that good sugar and our efforts. "I am not going to have any of my children become fond of liquor," she said with some firmness; and it was only several years later that she told me that one of her Father's weaknesses was that he drank a bit too much. "I always thought that my Mother nagged him a bit too much," Mom added. She said that having been a British Army officer in India probably caused him to be fond of a drink, and just a few years ago Uncle Lew (who died two years ago) defended my Grandfather by saying that anyone who'd served in India liked his drink. I have so often wished I'd known my Grandfather, for Aunt Marie and others have told me what an interesting and very likeable person he was.

Now, Edna, I must cease this and get my hair 'done', as I'm singing in Vancouver at the memorial service for a

*truly wonderful woman I used to know. Vivian Dowding
persevered in giving knowledge about birth control even
when she was hounded for it, and Catholic priests
reported her to doctors. All she ever did was offer
information about contraceptives, or 'Planned
parenthood' as it is known, but it took rare courage in
those days, and I'm proud to sing at the service for her. It
will no doubt be a great service. And I still miss my
Vancouver friends, so I am looking forward to it.*

JULY 3, 1987

Dear Edna

*…Frank's health has improved…so after much discussion
we are planning to leave here on July 29th (by bus!) and
may be in Winnipeg about August 4 or 5. I refuse to drive
across the mountains and over those long miles of flat
prairie any more, and I have finally persuaded Frank that
buses are comfortable vehicles these days. He has never
traveled by bus.*

*If you are at home around that time we will try to have a
visit. I would love to see you, and this time to have a little
more time with you. Hoping we'll meet, and with love,
Jean.*

45285 S Sumas Road, Sardis, BC

Wednesday Aug. 5, 1987

My Dear friend Edna:

*Well, Look who's here! Back home before we really got
started on our 'eastern crusade'. So I am dashing off this
note to you in haste in case you are staying close to home,*

hoping to hear a jingling of the telephone saying we've arrived in Winnipeg. Tough luck, but I think we have to say it could have been worse.

Here's the story: Frank got a good report from the doctor Tuesday morning, had all his now numerous medicines for heart, blood pressure and off we went Wednesday morning on the bus. We stayed in Revelstoke that night after a great day of scenery worth unmentionable grandeur and went on to Calgary on Thursday, still enjoying every minute, arriving in Regina Friday evening to be met by his sister Marjorie. On Saturday and Sunday his blood pressure went 'way up again and no medication or rest would bring it down and by Monday morning he was worried and uncomfortable to the point that I asked if we shouldn't go home and both he and Marjorie agree...so at 9 pm Monday, we were back in BC...and it's so beautiful here; but I really am very disappointed not to have fulfilled our plans.

Frank is much better already, so we are wondering if the altitude affected his condition.

Anyway, Edna...have a good summer....

NOVEMBER 1987

My dear friend Edna:

I know it's a long time...I do value our keeping in touch, especially when you take the trouble to send Frank and me such a lengthy description of your "travelogue". ...We almost felt tired, too, after I read it all aloud.... We haven't been able to get any holiday this past summer or fall...Frank's health...isn't good enough.... When you said you were near McAuley but didn't stop in I was a bit disappointed but since then I've thought, why still keep *thinking about McAuley, when it really is so far back in the past and I wouldn't know anyone there now, I suppose. But just when I get to that point something happens and another vivid memory pops up. This time it was a song...Frank...went to Vancouver Public Library and in the Old music department upstairs asked for "The Bluebird" (not the Bluebird of Happiness, but "the Bluebird", circa 1920!) By golly! It was there...I've been enjoying singing it ever since.*

Thursday Nov 19! Here I am again, another instalment. I was going to ask you if you remember when Isobel McLeod got married. Mr. Chalmers was the minister. Everybody in the entire town crowded into that little church that afternoon. You and I were over on the left side, squeezed into the front seat. We had never seen a "formal" wedding, but we certainly knew this was AN EVENT. It was The social affair of the year – in fact McAuley had never seen anything like it, and I guess Mr. Chalmers knew it was the greatest wedding he'd ever perform there. Anyway, he got very excited and stood in front of the pulpit before the wedding party got started down the aisle and he called out, "Who gives this bride away. Who gives this bride away?" and that wasn't the only boo-boo. After starting the ceremony he walked away from the bride and groom and sat down on the chair Ed Jamieson always used at Sunday school. Isobel leaned over and whispered loudly, "Mr. Chalmers, the ring, the ring!" He got up, walked back in front of them and finished the ceremony.

The memories I have of those days are very fond ones, and one of the fondest is revived every time I go from the main floor of our home to the lower floor. On the wall facing the stairs is a picture of Frank and me, ages 16 and 17...I have the coat Mother made from blue material ordered from Eaton's, she made my hat, too, and I am wearing the pink silk scarf that the Sunday school gave me as a "Farewell" gift when the Mathies moved from McAuley to Rocanville. How I loved that scarf! I wore it and washed it and oh, so carefully ironed it out. It was real crepe de chine – something non-existent now. In that same picture Frank is wearing SPATS and when we mentioned than in the presence of some young folks here they asked, "What are spats?" so goes the world, Edna, what was something of great importance to us once is not even known today. I used to think what an amazing series of eras my Mother had seen in her lifetime, having been brought into Brandon on an ox-cart, then traveled by horse, then car, then air-plane; but now I have to realize that in my own lifetime the changes I've seen – and you and all our generation – are too fantastic to believe. Wonder what our kids are going to see in their lifetimes?

Well, Edna, here it is Tuesday morning, Nov. 24th, and come hell or high water I'm going to get this letter in the mail. I got a nasty cold a few days ago and it sort of knocked me out, but as usual I'm pretty tough and will pick up today and get doing a few things – like writing up some Mathie history to go with a few good pictures...speaking of people's homes, I was truly saddened when you told me that your Mother's home had been demolished. Oh, what good times we had under that roof! Can you believe now that your Mother would be so kind as to get that huge black beauty of a kitchen range going at night so that we could eat "cheese dreams"? ...what gluttons! Yet she...let us eat her out of house and home and just laughed at us. Kids miss so much real, good fun these days...and they could never, possibly, know what it was like to smooch through a "Moonlight Waltz" with a Rusty Cowan or a Dick Sedgwick! Incidentally, I was eating in the Quonset hut at Rocanville's sports ground (1971) and mentioned Dick Sedgwick and the man across from me said he was that man! Fortunately, my grey hair and the span of years didn't cause any ripple of jealousy from his wife, who sat beside him.

I absolutely LOVE that picture of the Grist orchestra in the Archie & District book. Oh, the great dances we enjoyed to their music, and when we moved to Rocanville the music didn't sound nearly as good, nor did anyone announce the dances like Cecil Grist always did: "Take y'r partners for the Waltz Velita" or "Get your partner for a Quadrille", and then watch to see who'd get swung right off her feet and spun around with her feet level with her shoulders. I was watching a quadrille one night when Miss Isbister (Mrs. John Wilson) lost her pants, (not panties – pants were a lot larger than today's briefs) and what did she do but scoop them up while she gasped "Oooo" and dashed up behind the curtained part of the stage and I hope found a good big safety pin to keep them up for the remainder of the evening.

I must quit – have a list longer than my arm of THINGS TO DO. I'm president of the local Transition House for women who've been abused physically, mentally or psychologically; and am also active with the local Academy of Music and lately have had to conduct the choir I'm in because the regular one had surgery for a hip replacement; and now Christmas is coming and I don't give 'boughten' presents any more, but I do make the best darn Christmas cake and other fancy goodies, so must get busy. Keep writing; I really love to hear from you, as does Frank.

March 1988

The Chilliwack Progress cites the following remarks I made in my opening comments as President at the annual Ann Davis Commemorative Celebration: "I wish all the women in Canada who are seeking the shelter of transition houses could be in such a safe place."

April 28, 1988

My dear friend Edna:

Now how do you like my new typewriter? Pretty snazzy isn't it. 'Way back around 1924 you and I would've said it was "the cat's panamas" and if anyone had said one word against that we'd have countered with "So's your double-breasted Aunt Het!!!!!!" Gee, we thought we were so smart, and life was great and we literally had the world by the tail.

Your lovely birthday card to me came...and you asked if we were still planning to visit your part of the country late May...we've revised our plans...Frank got an invitation to attend the hundredth anniversary of the establishing of the Finish colony outside Rocanville July 1-3 and he has written (and paid the $50) for us both to attend...we are going to drive...think we can do it...will spell each other off every hour or so...can take it in easy spells and enjoy it. We'll have our LeBaron car checked carefully...when the Finnish festivities are over, we'll begin our eastward trek...seeing you sometime in the week of July 4th. Does that coincide with anything...?

Frank's health is so much better...he really wants to nosey around his old stomping grounds again, and we felt cheated last summer at having to fly back home before we ever got farther than Regina...maybe we'll have time to do some fond reminiscing this year...see some of the pictures you must have. And please tell Ruth Bell Anderson that I thank her for her remembering me. Now, dear Edna, do take care of yourself.... I just wish you could be here right now, our yard is looking lovelier every day...it's the best place in the world to live. If we only had a cow, what cream we'd have!

AUGUST 25, 1988

The Kiwanis Golden K club awarded me with a Certificate of Appreciation.

Last letters to Edna

Dearest Edna: Glad to be home again. We made it without any more car trouble. Our all too brief visit in your 14th floor apartment gave me lots to think about on the long drive home. When we began chumming together we had good times playing the gramophone (sometimes to your mom's distraction), and no one would believe us now when we tell them that there was nothing nicer than a walk to the cemetery on Sunday afternoon. You liked the tombstone that had an open gate with the words "gates ajar". My favourite was one with a little lamb and the inscription, "budded on earth to bloom in heaven".

Your family really keep you on the move, too; and what a great celebration on your 80th birthday. Considering the ups and downs I think we're doing well; and I hope you'll be able to cope with the difficulty you're experiencing with your heart.

Edna, do you think we'll ever get the same kick out of small pleasures we did 'way back then? Remember when those two guys were boarding at your mom's while they were temporarily hired by the CPR – Dave and Charley.

Weren't they just the handsomest ever! And didn't we swoon every time we sat down at the dinner table together. We were absolutely lost when they took the train to Brandon for a weekend, just so they could have a bath! Your mom's lovely china wash basin wasn't quite good enough. Look at how we live now: bath as often as you want, nice homes, cars, food and clothing and even this new computer. I wonder, does it actually improve the quality of life? Better sign off, I'm getting a bit too philosophical.

AUGUST 1990

Elected President of the Chilliwack Academy of Music.

FALL, 1990

My dearest, longest-ever friend: How very thoughtful of your daughter to let me know that you are in the hospital where she lives. At least you are close to her and not that far from your other family members. I won't expect you to

Woman of the Year; one of many honours bestowed on me in Chilliwack.

write until you feel stronger. I hope you like the flowers that we've ordered, because no one knows and appreciates flowers like you do. Best wishes for your health, dear Edna. Is there a 'phone in your room at the hospital? Please get better. I just can't get along without you and your wonderful gift of friendship.

Two weeks after being admitted to hospital, Edna died of heart failure; her daughter Pat phoned me with the sad news. Since Edna's death, I correspond with Edna's daughters.

OCTOBER 8, 1988

An article by journalist Lois Dickinson appeared in Chilliwack's "Weekend Extra". She wrote that "Jean Scott has crammed more service to Chilliwack into her eight years residence than many people do in a lifetime. She tramped the streets of Ottawa one icy winter day to obtain funding for the city hall museum project. She sang for all who rejoiced that our history would be displayed in the grand old building, and she sang for all who feel a particular love of country.... At thanksgiving Jean would remind us that in the midst of Thanksgiving, there are those who suffer. She speaks sadly of the stories she has heard, and she asks that we be more aware."

GOVERNOR GENERAL'S PERSONS CASE AWARD
OCTOBER 16, 1990

I am not much different from anyone else when some moment causes deep longing for one's Mother, along with the excruciating ache if only she could be here right now. If Mother was proud of me – and I think she was – she was careful not to say it in so many words. It's likely that her parent's English 'stiff upper lip' extended even when the occasion was a joyful event. Mother was the epitome of what Paul wrote in his letter to the Corinthians, "Love does not behave itself unseemly...is not easily puffed up", and gently warned me: "Jean, that means you don't let any praise go to your heart and you do not indulge in self-praise or flattery."

I stand in Rideau Hall, Ottawa, my two sisters Pat and Betty, Pat's husband Allen and Frank seated behind we six nominees about to receive the large medal on which "The Famous Five", women who won personhood for Canadian women, are exquisitely carved. Mary Collins, Minister for the Status of Women, had carefully rehearsed each of us: When your name is called, you will rise, take five steps forward, curtsy or incline your head toward Their Excellencies, then stand while your citation is read. When the Governor General is handed your Medal and steps toward you, you will stand perfectly still while official photographs are being taken. He will take the medal and hang it around your neck and perhaps (he did) give you a handshake.

Hey Mom, can you believe it? That precocious, fractious, jazz-singing and playing daughter of yours is standing here mute and dignified (and a little unbelieving that this is really happening), wistfully thinking how wonderful it would have been if you could

Receiving the Governor General's Persons Case Award from Governor General, Ray Hnatyshyn, October 16, 1990.

have been here. Just want you to know, like you always said when I departed from home 'Remember, Jean; always be a lady.' Just want you to know that I am.

The smartly dressed young woman over in the front corner of this elegant room goes on to read the citation: "Jean Scott first became aware of women's issues during the depression, when she noted that hired women worked harder and longer than hired men, but made less money. She came to believe that the fight for equality had to be a continuing battle and that all women should be encouraged to join the fight...."

Let this be a healing moment to forget all hard knocks, disappointments, screwed up plans; this is the nicest thing that could happen....

"...According to her nominators, Jean is totally committed to promoting full personhood for all women. It is her lifeblood, a 24-hour a day campaign...."

"Jean Scott was nominated by the Ann Davis Transition House."

The citation is finished. I can't believe it.

"Very deserving, very deserving," whispers His Excellency.

We – the entire assemblage – partake of refreshments in the reception room. My hand is shaken so often it's hot. One of my specially invited guests was Senator Pat Carney. When she was a columnist for the Vancouver Sun, she frequently came to the IWA to interview then Regional President Jack Moore; and she once wrote a column about me when I was making news for the Memorial Society.

My family and I were whisked into another room where portraits of elderly bearded men in ceremonial dress watched as we posed for photos, keepsakes for ourselves and our heirs, to point to later, and say, "That was the night that...."

The Award Led To Many Speaking Engagements:

October 31, 1990: Guest speaker, Rocanville; address Welwyn & Rocanville Women.

November 1990: The BC Federation of Labour hosts its 35th annual convention; part of the program includes honouring my achievements.

December, 1990: The Chilliwack Rotary Club invites me to speak at their meeting; at the conclusion of my address, I receive a standing ovation. That same month the local Royal Canadian Legion honours me by requesting I speak to its members.

March, 1991: I speak at the Victoria Business & Professional Women's Club's 70th annual meeting.

April – September, 1991: I am a speaker at the Kiwanis club, Chilliwack Community Services, at Agassiz-Harrison Community Services' AGM; and local church women groups.

THE FIGHT GOES ON!

Chilliwack's Transition Society was registered and in action in 1979. I joined in the work soon after moving to Chilliwack, as a member and then President of the Society. It was hard going for a few years. We were all groping, learning, not always getting it straight, putting in long hours, hearing my neighbour calling out, with some humour, "Doesn't that woman ever stay home!" After winning the Person's Case Award, I continued to work in the community and received public recognition for my efforts.

March 1992 I am mentioned in Chilliwack Times in the article "Celebrating Women's Day"; and again in the Chilliwack Progress for my involvement in fund-raising for the Academy of Music.

April 27, 1992 Awarded a Certificate of Appreciation from Ann Davis Transition House for 217.5 Board hours.

1993

I help organize the 7th annual Ann Davis Transition House Commemorative Dinner, and am cited in the local paper's report of the event, saying, "many go unnoticed, such as the lady who has knitted more than 400 pairs of socks for the disabled children's hospital; and she has never even asked to be reimbursed for the cost of the wool."

HERITAGE SINGERS

Music has always played a huge role in my life and in Chilliwack I participated in the church choir as well as sang solos. In March 1994, together with the Director of the Museum, an ad was placed in the local papers where we invited anyone interested in singing some of the fine old songs that seemed doomed to obscurity, to join a choir. The response was very pleasing. One of Chilliwack's remarkable women, Ethel Stevenson, agreed to be accompanist, with Teng McKay serving as backup. And now, I formed the Heritage Singers, a mainly seniors group. We needed no further advertising and were soon in great demand at public events as well as local hospitals and rest homes, the age-group where our songs revived memories of younger days. In 1995, the Heritage Singers performed thirty-four times.

Our group also participated in a gathering of musicians from the Fraser Valley at the Legion in Abbotsford. When

Leading the Heritage Singers, 1994.

our group went on stage, and I was ready to present the choir, a woman called out, "Where are you from?" over the chatter of the audience. "Chilliwack," I called back, "where we are neither chilly nor wacky, but warm and wise." This was followed by hearty laughter and warm applause. That experience was symbolic of my entire experience of living in Chilliwack – being warmly received and appreciated.

After a couple of years The Heritage Singers had a professional sound engineer, made a few tapes and sold them. However, in 1998 Frank's health and his need of care eventually made it impossible to continue.

JEAN SCOTT TRANSITION HOUSE: ANOTHER HONOUR!

"Shelter named after women's activist" reads a headline in The Chilliwack Progress on October 18, 1995; and "Hope transition house named officially on day after Person's Day, as Jean Scott Transition House." In the report I am quoted as saying, "The comfort to me is in knowing that the Jean Scott Transition House is a place where people go to get healed from hurt. There is nothing more important for me to be

With Mary Woo Sims, the chief commissioner of the B.C. Human Rights Council in November 1997. What an amazing woman!

associated with than that." The House is funded by The Ministry of Women's Equality and by private donations.

On October 25, 1995, I attended and delivered a speech at the first Annual General Meeting of Jean Scott Transition House and received an honorary lifetime membership in the Hope Transition Society.

FRANK SCOTT: THE LAST YEARS

Saturday evening, February 12 1994. Frank's 'puffer' that he uses for his emphysema, isn't easing his breathing. With a worried look, he agrees that I should take him to Emergency. He had been using the puffer for several years; and by now the Emergency staff on duty recognized us. On this night his condition worsened more quickly than usual, and he was booked into a bed for further care. When I visited him the following Monday – on Valentine's Day – he had bad news. "The doctor told me this morning, 'You have an anal cancer and there's nothing we can do about it.'"

"Just like that?" I asked. "Yes", he said, noticeably upset.

A further assessment by another physician provided the possibility of treatment by fulguration. Frank's heart and lung condition made general anaesthetic impossible, so surgical treatments were carried out under spinal anaesthetic. With oxygen at home on a 24-hour basis, we eliminated our frantic visits to the emergency ward.

The cancer treatments began, with sometimes months intervening, however Frank was never robust and each treatment weakened him further. "Should he be subjected to further treatment?" I questioned the doctors. The ruthless progress of the cancer created additional problems: weight loss and bowel incontinence. Losing strength, yet wanting to remain mobile, he had many falls. After a time he became bed-ridden. He stopped observing regular clean habits; and that was difficult. Only when the Health support worker refused to give in to his wishes, did he submit to being bathed.

"Jean, why don't you put him into a care-home?" close friends advised, with the best of intentions. I couldn't. In spite of everything, I knew how Frank dreaded that, how unhappy he'd be and difficult to deal with. An unusual (high abdominal) colostomy was performed and it brought some relief; but nothing relieved Frank's now continual dependence on medication, the only thing to provide a small measure of control. He experimented and adjusted his own medication; following a serious reaction, he was hospitalized until his condition was corrected. That gave me a long-overdue break.

Frank spent his last two weeks in a care facility. After nearly seven years of caring for him, I was exhausted. Frank wasn't pleased about the move, but what choice was there? As the ambulance attendants carried him out the door, past the garden where we had spelled in small white stones, he looked at the words, and sadly whispered: "Goodbye Scott-land".

Soon after, while discussing Frank's condition with our doctor, I concluded my appointment with the question, "and what about me?" "What about you?" he asked. "I have a lump in my right breast," I told him. The doctor ordered an immediate mammogram. "I'm not saying it's cancer," he told me, "but it might be."

It was August 20, 2000.

Frank's life ended much as it had began: arguing against the status quo, finding it easier to criticize than praise, yet appreciative of music and literature, particularly poetry. Edward Fitzgerald's Rubaiyat Of Omar Khyyam was his credo; he quoted this, to the end:

The moving finger writes, and, having writ moves:
not all thye Piety nor Wit
Shall lure it back to cancel half a Line
Nor all Thy tears wash out a word of it. ......
Oh Thou, who Man of basest Earth did'st make,
And who with Eden did'st devise the Snake;
For all the Sin wherewith the Face of Man
Is blackened, Man's Forgiveness give – and take!

In 2001, I traveled to Rocanville to scatter Frank's ashes next to his mother's grave. I imagine Frank's final 'homecoming'; how, when he arrived at the "Pearly Gates", the Angel Gabriel laid aside his horn and brought to his lips a clarinet, Frank's favourite instrument, the one he played in those earlier, happier years, along with the Sunday School orchestra.

The Sunday School Orchestra that Frank and I participated
in back in Rocanville, Frank is on the far right with his clarinet
and I am third from right.

LIVING ALONE

Living alone after a spouse dies takes getting used to. However, following Frank's funeral, my own health was of immediate concern.

When the doctor delivered the news that my breast lump was indeed malignant, he told me I had two options: radiation and/or chemotherapy; or, he said, "You can have surgery. I'll leave it entirely for you to decide." I considered radiation and chemo; and I was in a pretty unsettled state of mind, having just finished taking care of Frank; and I thought, well, I've been thru surgery – an appendectomy, had my tonsils out and all my reproductive organs removed – and I know what it involves.…"Surgery," I told the doctor; and he, obviously relieved, said, "I'm so glad to hear you say that; if you were my Mother that's what I'd have wanted to her to say.""Well," I replied, "And I wish I knew your mother because she has an awfully nice son." He thanked me and said the nurse would be in touch regarding the arrangements.

Well, this is just one more thing, I told myself as I left. And you just take it as it comes.

Rainbow Estates; with souvenir of Rocanville in the front yard.

Frank died on 20th of August; on the 12th of September, 2000, I had a mastectomy. After the surgery, the doctor visited me. "I've spoken to Spencer and Sonya," he told me, "and when I told them you were okay and that I think I got it all, Spencer responded with 'You know Mom; she's a tough old broad.'" (Aside from losing the feeling on my right side of my chest, the surgery was, indeed, successful. Tamoxofin was prescribed afterwards, but after enduring its side effects, I decided to discontinue it. I know at my age I don't need to take it anymore.)

On October 31, I was in Victoria to speak to the Memorial Society; in a photo taken of me there, I sit with my leg up on the chair – Nicky, my cat, had scratched my leg and I didn't know that it was turning into something more serious. When I came home, I felt indescribably miserable. Someone came for a donation for the NDP and I recall speaking to that person, thinking I'm doing this, but I don't feel right. I felt stranger and stranger. By now my leg was red and swollen. When Art, the minister at Carman United Church happened to phone, I spoke to him in a quavering voice. "I'm sorry," I said, "Art, I'm sorry; I'm feeling terribly ill…" I didn't know that I had gone into shock; shivering no matter what I did, not even an electric blanket helped. So wasn't it lucky that my step daughter-in-law, Joyce Scott, walked in and found me lying on the floor!

Spencer came right over and drove me to the doctor. Yes, I answered; I was nauseated. Yes, to chills; and yes, yes, yes – to all his questions. The doctor nodded and recorded my answers. "Spencer," I said, "show him my leg." It was swollen from toes to the knee, scarlet coloured and rock-hard. Spencer pulled up my slacks, the doctor took one look at the bulging blood-red veins that ran right up to my knee, as if blood couldn't get through, and, to use the old cliché, leapt into action. He picked up the phone, and said in a calm but urgent tone, "Medicine bed, medicine bed." Then he turned to me and said, "Get to the hospital immediately." Apparently, he thought I was forming a clot and was worried it would travel to the heart.

In the hospital they put me on a high dose of diuretics; and it worked! Over and over, I passed black water. Black! I had been that close to dying! (Not the first close call I'd had in a hospital setting. During my recovery from my left hip replacement, my roommate asked me, "Did you know you nearly died?" "That's too bad," I said, "I wouldn't have known anything about it." Apparently, I'd nearly bled to death. When Frank said, "Can't you give her another transfusion?" he was told, "We've already given her three, and that's all we can give her…" But there again, I came through it, though it took three months to build the blood back up again.)

SPRING 2002 UCFV HONORARY DEGREE

There can be no doubt that the award the University College of the Fraser Valley bestowed on me was a highlight of my life. I have always regretted not receiving a higher education and now, at the age of 90, I was to receive a university degree! How did this happen?

Early in 2002, I received a telephone call from someone at UCFV advising me that I had been nominated to receive of an Honorary Doctorate of Law degree at the June convocation. I wasn't certain what that entailed; however, a few months earlier, Anne Russell, in UCFV's Communications Department, called me on a business matter and came to my home. During that visit we talked of my career in feminist interests. When she left my home, she took with her whatever she wanted to know about my passionate aspirations for 'the betterment of women'.

"Would you have lunch with President Bassford?" the voice on the other line asked. Of course I would! I couldn't have known how genuinely personable he would be, someone whose company was enjoyable. As we ate lunch, I told him that all my working life I had hoped to be able to go to university; but making a living didn't allow for it. "Well," he said cheerily, "now you're getting in – from the top, aren't you?" What a great riposte!

There's another anecdote in connection with this beautiful bombshell of life-time happenings: my good-looking sister, who really knows fashion, was concerned that I should look 'right'; and I agreed, but wasn't having any luck in finding just the right thing. Time was short when I ventured into a high class dress shop with stepdaughter-in-law Joyce Scott, who is no ordinary person to shop with – since that's her background. With her and the sales person assuring me that this was "just what you have to wear!" I bought an English imported outfit for an astonishing amount of money; but I could assure my sister that I had *The Dress*.

On the day of receiving the honorary degree, my sister and other family members were seated in the front row of the auditorium. Fine; and ha! I and others to be on the platform are shown into a dressing room, gowned from neck to floor in

One of my proudest moments: Receiving an Honorary Doctorate from the University College of the Fraser Valley in 2002. I'd always regretted not going to university and here I am finally getting a degree at the age of 90!

a voluminous black gown, with not one tiny bit of anything beneath it showing; and then the splendid satin and velvet hood is placed on my shoulders. There was no possibility that I could show off that ultra-fashionable three-piece; no chance to give a quick little kick, flinging the black gown open to my knees, or use any trick to let my sister have a peek. As if to make a mockery of all this, my sister had to leave early because the air conditioning overhead was too chilly for her comfort!

As I recall that day, there is but one thing to say: every moment was better than anything I'd ever known. Son Spencer arrived at 10a.m. to drive to the President's House, where an outdoor lunch would be served. As we waited for others to arrive, Spencer and I entertained at their grand piano, singing our favourite songs that the other guests obviously enjoyed.

Later, when the young, buoyant graduates streamed in, led by President Skip Bassford, our part of the parade marched in to the ever-great sounds of Elgar's "Land of Hope and Glory". I was certain that I was the only person in that entire crowded hall singing, at the top of my lungs, though it couldn't be heard by anyone except me, due to the noise around me.

When my turn comes and I turn toward the assemblage and hear the President introduce me as "Doctor Jean Scott", I am alone in my mind for a split second, wanting to say what I said in Rideau Hall: *Look Mom; it's me, wishing I could have foretold that something you wanted for me and each of us, has happened.*

My speech is brief, spontaneous, well received, and concludes with Robbie Burns'"Mary of Argyle". To the grads, geared to a future of their own, I offered the thought that 'goodness' and all it means, makes life worth living.

MOVING AGAIN!

In late winter 2003, I moved to Langley, BC. The 'experiment' in Assisted Living failed; as a staff member there said, "she was too young for that place!" I returned to Chilliwack in Spring 2004, where I live now, on the third floor of an apartment complex which I share with likely the last male in my life – my beloved cat, Nicki. I've never lived this high up, this close, one might even say, to heaven! Sitting on the deck, in the shade of a tall evergreen, my potted plants at my feet, Nicki purring on my lap, I could not be more grateful for all that remains in my life – music, books, ongoing opportunities for service, church friends, family, and always, foremost, my son Spencer and daughter-in-law Sonya, along with my dear grandchildren.

I was born in a small bedroom at the back of a grocery story, by a north-facing window. Nowadays, I have a nightly ritual. After bidding Nikki, who curls up on the headboard, Good Night, I turn down the covers and then, in the warm comfort of my bed under the window, surrounded by family photos, I pray the words from "Thoughts On Solitude", by Thomas Merton:

> *My Lord God, I have no idea where I am*
>
> *going. I do not see the road ahead of me. I*
>
> *cannot know for certain where it will end.*
>
> *Nor do I really know myself, and the fact*
>
> *that I think that I am following your will*
>
> *does not mean that I am actually doing*
>
> *so. But I believe that the desire to please*
>
> *you does in fact please you. And I hope I*
>
> *have that desire in all that I am doing.*

I hope that I will never do anything apart from that desire. And I know that if I do this you will lead me by the right road though I may know nothing about it. Therefore will I trust you always though I may seem to be lost and in the shadow of death. I will not fear, for you are ever with me, and you will never leave me to face my perils alone.

CHAPTER TWENTY ONE
Final Thoughts

"As the ancients say, 'Don't try to be perfect, it annoys the gods.' Well, if that's the case, I'll be right up there on Olympus or wherever they exist."

Life teaches us many lessons, and I believe it's important to share what we've learned with others. People sometimes ask, "How did you do it, Jean?" I think the following letter that I wrote to a friend faced with difficult life challenges answers how I got through.

Dear Penny: "I am entirely sympathetic to what you are going through; and it's not a superficial remark because I speak from experiences of some time ago that still make me aware of how heartache can sear the soul, leaving you feeling that your world had collapsed and wondering how you could ever put it together again. Time and again, I have reassured myself with a trite but positive reminder that life is not static, and that all things pass. I can remember shaking my head while I'd think that, sometimes saying it aloud as if to convince myself that it COULD mean something.

Perhaps it was fortunate for me that there were demands on my time and energies and talents; and now I look back on these episodes in my life and realize that I recovered – and better than I once believed was possible. It would have been easy to be self-pitying (because there was no doubt I wasn't getting fair treatment) or letting bitterness govern some of my reasoning. Both of those would have been costly, and I didn't think I could afford such luxuries. Besides, other persons dear to me were affected, too, so there was always the thought that no one else need or should be put to any unnecessary pain.

None of what I'm saying is intended to be preachy or self-praise; but I have to tell you that it did please me a little when, years after one difficult experience, a woman who wasn't exactly my best friend said, in her usual cool manner, that she was surprised how I seemed to take an upset and keep pace with life.

I know you'll be looking for that same 'open door' I've groped for more than once when the space I was in became difficult, unkind, and unreasonable and minus the beauty we all need every day of our lives. Just be your own good self. Perhaps my life has been coloured by something my Mother said back about 1922 when our family was in the worst of situations, forced out of home and Dad's business, and Mother then beginning her long illness.... A friend called out as Mother and I walked near her home, "Sorry to hear of your troubles, Mrs. Mathie". I wanted to cry out, "For goodness sake, why do you have to remind my Mother of that right now?" but to my utter astonishment, my Mother said, with composure, "Thank you, Mrs. McAuley, life is sweet." And as the Yorkshire dialect would put it, "It's better than nout."

Me and Spencer entertaining at my 90th birthday celebration.

ABOUT THE AUTHOR

Jean Scott was born April 21, 1912, and was 93-and-a-half years old when this book went to press. Jean has been a social activist longer than most people have been alive. She has devoted her life to causes that promote social justice, women's equality, and the rights of the common person. She also has a strong commitment to community service.

She received the Governor General's Persons Case Award, recognizing outstanding contribution to promoting women's equality, in 1990, and an honorary doctorate from the University College of the Fraser Valley in 2002.

Growing up poor and coming of age in the Great Depression taught Jean many valuable life skills. Jean started her working life young in her father's store on the Canadian prairies. She also worked as a domestic servant, and as a secretary, before finding her true calling working in the union movement, and later playing a key role in the early years of the Memorial Society.

Since "retiring" to Chilliwack in 1980, she has continued to be very actively involved in issues related to women's rights and social justice, and also in general community affairs.

And of course, she has been a devoted mother to Spencer for almost seven decades, a mother-in-law to Sonja, and a grandmother to Greg and Melanie. She remains a devoted sister as well, and takes a strong interest in her entire extended family.

Throughout her life Jean has always had a deep love of music. That love has continued into her 90s and you can find her most Sundays singing to "the old folks", who are actually much younger than her, at Chilliwack's hospital.

She jokingly notes that now that she's in her 90s she's turned into a "nice old lady with a cat", but Jean is seldom found in a rocking chair. Since turning her attention to finishing this book, she has had to cut back on a full schedule of meetings, potlucks, classes, volunteer sessions, and other activities, but she remains actively engaged with her community.